D0401899

ONE IN
THINE HAND

ONE IN THINE HAND

Gerald N. Lund

Deseret Book Company
Salt Lake City, Utah

©1982 Deseret Book Company
©1987 Gerald N. Lund
All rights reserved
Printed in the United States of America

No part of this book may be reproduced in any
form or by any means without permission in writing
from the publisher, Deseret Book Company,
P.O. Box 30178, Salt Lake City, Utah 84130.
Deseret Book is a registered trademark of
Deseret Book Company.

First printing in paperbound edition, September 1987
Second printing in paperbound edition, July 1988
Third printing in paperbound edition, July 1989

Library of Congress Cataloging-in-Publication Data

Lund, Gerald N.
    One in thine hand.

    I. Title.
PS3562.U48505   813'.54   81-19418
ISBN 0-87747-894-5 (hardbound ed.)   AACR2
ISBN 0-87579-125-5 (paperbound ed.)

To Lynn,
my traveling companion
to Israel
and other destinations,
including the
eternal ones

One

Heathrow Airport was like the streets of downtown Saigon at rush hour, masses of bodies jostling back and forth, people milling around aimlessly, always seeming to stop where they could most effectively snarl the traffic flow. And judging from the lines in front of the Trans-World Airlines ticket counter, the majority of this swarm of tourists had not heard there might be other airlines competing with TWA to transport people out of London.

Brad Kennison ignored the crush of people and focused a burning glare in the center of the ample back of the lady ahead of him. She was pawing through her purse in search of her ticket, a bag easily large enough to carry half the files of the National Archives. The scowl darkened his even, tanned features and pulled his mouth, usually quick with an easy smile, into a tight line. He brushed his hand impatiently across his dark brown hair, then massaged the back of his neck.

When they had opened this new ticket window, Brad had jumped quickly and bettered his place in the line by six positions. Now he was still waiting, thanks to this woman, and the man in front of her who had required the frustrated clerk to recite every possible flight time to every possible city in Europe. The man in the line next to him finished and moved away as Brad's gray eyes smouldered. Originally that man had been four places behind him.

Suddenly the lady with the huge purse gave a squeal of delight. "I knew it was in there," she said triumphantly.

"Thank heavens!" Brad muttered, more loudly than he had intended.

The lady glanced back at him quickly, flustered and embarrassed.

Hey, come on Kennison, he chided himself. *The plane doesn't leave for two hours yet. Why so uptight?*

He shrugged off the question, as though absent-mindedly brushing away a fly. He had been home from Viet Nam for nearly four months now, and some time ago had come to terms with the fact that he was impatient, easily frustrated, and even irritable at times. He stared out the airport windows, shimmering and wavy in the early August sunshine, peeved as much at himself as at the delay. Maybe in Israel the restlessness that gnawed at him could be put aside.

Finally the lady in front moved hurriedly away, clutching her ticket in her hand. Brad pushed his camera bag across the polished tiles with his foot and stepped up to the counter. The ticket agent was a pert blonde with a dazzling smile. The smile warmed noticeably as she gave him a quick appraising look. After the bumbling, flustered lady, this tall, striking young American would be a welcome reprieve.

"Good morning," she said brightly, taking his ticket. "Tel Aviv, sir?" Her English accent warped the syllables in a delightful way, but he didn't take notice.

Brad nodded. He watched her process the ticket for a moment, then asked, "Is this going to be a crowded flight?"

She laughed. "Not as much as TWA would like. It's only about half full. Everybody seems to be going to America, not to the Middle East."

"Good," he said, ignoring her cordiality. "I would prefer to be alone. Can you seat me where no one else will be by me?"

2

The smile slowly faded. "I'm sorry, Mr. Kennison. But it's open seating for passengers boarding the flight here in London. This flight originated in New York, and many passengers are continuing on to Greece and Israel. We don't know which seats will be occupied."

The dark scowl returned. On the flight across the Atlantic, Brad had been stuck next to a couple from New York on their way to Italy. Sunglasses, Bermuda shorts, nonstop talk, and a furtive cigarette whenever the flight attendant wasn't around to remind them they were sitting in nonsmoking seats—they hadn't done much for his mood. In fact, they had pretty well destroyed the deep excitement and anticipation he had felt when he first boarded the plane in Salt Lake City. And he resented that loss, for planning this trip had provided the first real satisfaction he had found in the four months since his return from Viet Nam.

"Can't you do something?" he demanded.

"No, sir. I'm sorry." The clerk handed him his ticket and boarding pass, avoiding his eyes. "Gate fifty-six. They'll board at two P.M."

Brad snatched the ticket, his frustration mounting. He yanked up his camera bag and spun away.

As he did so, the ticket agent murmured under her breath, "Mister, just give them a look like that and you'll have the whole row to yourself."

He whirled around and glared at her. She jerked up, obviously startled, and then instantly her face flamed scarlet. But she stood her ground and stared back at him.

Gradually Brad felt his face relax into a grin. "Was it really that bad?" he asked.

Her relief at his sudden change was so evident that his smile broadened even more, crinkling the lines around the corner of his eyes.

"You were pretty grim," she admitted. "I'm sorry. I shouldn't have said what I did. That was rude of me."

A flash of the old Brad Kennison flicked across his eyes, and he pulled a wry face at her. "To give a man his just due is not rudeness," he said. "My mind was some-where else. It is *my* rudeness that needs an apology."

That restored her smile completely. "It's all right. Have a good flight."

"Thank you." Brad shouldered his camera bag and turned away again.

"Mr. Kennison?"

He turned back in surprise. "Yes?"

"There should be plenty of room on the plane. If you would like to sit alone, you could set your camera bag on the seat next to you until takeoff. It shouldn't be a prob-lem."

"Thank you very much," he said, smiling in genuine gratitude. "I'll do that."

And then, as he strode down the concourse toward the departure gates, he did something he hadn't done for over a year. He began to whistle softly.

* * * * * *

By the time his flight was announced—forty-five min-utes late—the cheerful mood had evaporated, and frustra-tion, like an old familiar jacket he had temporarily dis-placed, had embraced him again. He fought it at first, then finally surrendered, rationalizing that a good part of it was just fatigue. It was now nearly twenty hours since he had left Salt Lake City and almost thirty since he had had any sleep. His body had switched over to quarter speed. His eyes were bleary and burned from the cigarette smoke that had turned the air of the boarding area a thick blue-gray. His dark hair, thick but cut fairly short, now had a slightly tousled look. Black stubble was taking over his lower face, hiding the square set of his jaw. Normally he had an air of alertness and friendliness that quickly put people at ease. Now he just looked tired and rumpled. As he waited he had slouched into a chair between a cigar-smoking Frenchman and a large black man in an Arab headdress, and anyone seeing him now would have underestimated his height, which was slightly over six feet.

4

In spite of his deep weariness, his mind kept alternating back and forth between the prospects of being in the Holy Land and the faint sense of guilt he felt at leaving. *But why should I feel guilty at being different?* he demanded of that part of his mind that kept nagging at him. *You can't expect to spend two years teaching the gospel sixty and seventy hours a week, be home only six weeks, and then be drafted for another two years into the army, and not come home different.* The last thirteen months of duty had been in Viet Nam. He had left as a nineteen-year-old kid who rarely thought of anything more serious than whether to go waterskiing at Flaming Gorge or Lake Powell. He had come back with a great longing to embark on life, to do something with himself. And he couldn't help it if Karen and he were not meant for each other as they had first thought. There had been no promises, no dateless waiting on her part, and she had sensed it was over almost as quickly as he had. And why enroll in school when he had no idea what area to pursue?

The loudspeaker blurted out its usual unintelligible blast of noise, and the people around him began to stir themselves into action. Brad pushed aside the thoughts that dogged him and stood up. He stretched wearily, but the smoky-gray eyes were bright with anticipation. The next time he stepped off the plane—. He nodded almost happily as he moved toward the boarding area and into line. Maybe in Jerusalem.

* * * * * *

Brad moved inside the huge cabin of the Boeing 747, handed the flight attendant his boarding pass, and smiled briefly in response to her greeting. Moving quickly to an empty row, he eased into the window seat, and, feeling only slightly guilty, set his bag squarely in the middle of the aisle seat. He was exhausted, and if he could guard the two adjoining seats, there would be room to stretch out.

Someone had left a New York *Times* in the seat pocket in front of him. It was dated August 8, 1973, which made it almost two days old now, but he glanced through it idly while the rest of the passengers boarded. It didn't do much for his mood either. Watergate still dominated the headlines, as it had since April. John Dean's testimony threatened to take the guilt right into the Oval Office, though President Nixon still flatly denied any knowledge of the growing scandal. The Arab oil embargo was in full swing, and three people had been hospitalized after a fight erupted in a New Jersey gas station when someone broke into the long line. Elizabeth Taylor and Richard Burton were rumored to be near separation because, as she had said, "Maybe we loved each other too much."

Brad crammed the paper back into the pocket with a sigh. It was the stuff of which American news was made, but since his return from Viet Nam he had little patience for it. He had come to love America with a passion that surprised him, and it didn't help at all to watch what was happening to it.

A moment later the big doors swung shut and were sealed, and the flight attendants launched into their "welcome-aboard-and-we'd-like-to-introduce-you-to-the-safety-features-of-this-aircraft" routine. Brad was grateful he had followed the counsel of the smiling ticket agent. The row was his unchallenged. Relieved, he reclaimed his camera bag and slid it under the seat in front of him, tightened his seat belt slightly, and leaned back, closing his eyes.

When the flight attendant announced that the captain had turned off the "fasten seat belts" sign and they were free to move about the cabin, Brad yawned wearily and pulled up the arm rest between the seats, suddenly anxious for sleep.

But before a minute had passed, a deep voice at his side startled him. "Excuse me, do you mind if I sit here?"

Two

The look on Brad's face should have stopped anything up to and including an M-60 tank, but it went totally unnoticed by the young man who was already hoisting a small, incredibly battered case into the overhead bin. Brad stared at him, unable to believe that anyone could have misread the "No Trespassing" signs he left hanging like daggers in the air.

The intruder was obviously an Arab. Brad had had numerous Arabic students in his classes at the University of Utah—Iranians, Saudis, Jordanians—and this young man was definitely one of them. He had dark, olive-brown skin, jet black hair with a slight wave to it, and eyes so deeply brown as to be almost black. He was short, probably two or three inches shorter than Brad, but lean and muscular, like a marathon runner. Tight Levis and a red pullover shirt emphasized his slim figure. His face was darkly handsome and was split by a broad smile and brilliant white teeth.

Brad groaned inwardly at the sudden evaporation of his solitude. He decided it was worth one last attempt, so he gave the young man an icy look that should have frozen him rigid to the spot. It didn't. The intruder tossed his windbreaker into the center seat, slid into the aisle seat, and stuck out his hand.

"Hi! My name is Ali Mohammed Gamal Abdel Khalidi." He grinned broadly. "If that seems a little heavy, just call me Ali. Not Alley, like most Americans say, but *Ah-lee.*" He pronounced each syllable slowly and distinctly.

Dazed by the verbal barrage, Brad took the proferred hand and dutifully repeated, "Ah-lee."

If Ali noticed the lack of enthusiasm in Brad's voice, he kept it well hidden. "Good!" he bubbled, pumping Brad's hand vigorously. "And you're . . . ?"

"Oh. Brad. Brad Kennison."

"Great! I'm glad to meet you, Brad." Ali leaned back, his dark eyes suddenly sober. "I guess I shouldn't be so sensitive."

Sensitive! Brad thought. *Surely you jest.* But he managed a polite look.

"About my name, I mean. But I get so tired of having it mispronounced and made fun of. I've been called everything from Ali Babba to Alley Cat, including Alley Oop, Tin Pan Alley, and Little Nasser."

"Little Nasser?" Brad repeated. He had lost a turn somewhere. "What has that got to do with Ali?"

"Nothing. It was from my other names. Gamal Abdel. Those were the names of President Nasser, Gamal Abdel Nasser. You know, the late president of Egypt."

"Yes, I know," Brad inserted hastily, before his seatmate decided he needed a semester's course in contemporary Egyptian personalities.

"You're American," Ali continued. It was not a question, and so there was no point in pausing for an answer. "You almost sound like a Californian, too. Are you from California?"

Brad smiled in spite of himself. He had spoken less than a dozen words. Could this conversational volcano be a linguistic expert as well? "I was on a—" He caught himself, realizing that the word "mission" would require substantial explanation. "I lived there for two years," he amended.

"Aha!" Ali said triumphantly. "I knew it. What part? Southern California, I'll bet."

"Yes. Anaheim."

Ali's speech was pure American, and Brad could detect no trace of accent. At first glance Ali had seemed younger, maybe nineteen or twenty, but now as Brad studied him, he could see that the leanness of his face made him look younger than he was. Brad reassessed and put his age at close to his own twenty-four years. In spite of himself, Brad's curiosity got the best of him, and he forgot his determination to play freeze-out.

"You asked if I was from California *too*. Are you from there?"

"Most recently from Westwood." Ali reached for his windbreaker, holding it up so Brad could see the UCLA stenciled on it. "Just finished my degree there. Before UCLA I lived in Long Beach for thirteen years. I'm Arab, you know."

"I wondered," Brad said, unable to repress a smile.

Ali laughed. "I guess that was kind of dumb," he admitted. "If I had introduced myself as Gerhard Schwartz, I might have had you going for a while, right?"

Maybe this was going to be all right after all, Brad thought, as he nodded with a smile. Ali's face radiated an uninhibited, unrestrained love of life, and there were even little crinkles around the corners of his eyes from what Brad guessed was a near perpetual smile. Even now the smile started with the mouth, quickly spread across his face, and finally erupted in those nearly jet black eyes. Brad felt his irritation slipping away in spite of his tiredness. It would be very easy to like this young Arab.

"My father owned a chain of men's clothing stores in the south harbor area," Ali said. "Hey, did you ever hear of Frank's Stores for Men?"

"No," Brad admitted. "But I didn't get down around Long Beach at all." He started to ask a question, hesitated, and then decided *he* was being too sensitive. Why not follow Ali's own example of openness? "*Frank's* Stores for Men?" Brad asked. "Is your father's name Frank?"

Again that infectious laugh burst forth. "No way,

man. His name was Fawzi. But he was shrewd enough to sense that 'Fawzi's Stores for Men' lacked a little something in Long Beach. So he Americanized his name to Frank." Ali rolled his eyes upward in mock horror. "Business is business. Anyway he sold out in 1965 and we went back to Palestine."

It was like an ant trying to follow a hummingbird. While Ali flitted from flower to flower, Brad was crawling through the dense conversational grass, trying to keep up. *"Back* to Palestine?"

"Oh, yes. My father's family had owned land near Bethlehem for eight or nine generations. When Israel was made a nation in 1948, my father and mother and my older brother had to flee during the so-called War of Independence. An Israeli kibbutz ended up with my family's land, and my family ended up in a refugee camp near Jericho. That's where I was born."

Ali flashed his white teeth again in a broad grin. "Hey! How does it feel to be sitting next to a real live Palestinian refugee?"

"You hardly fit the typical image," Brad admitted with a wry smile.

Ali's hoot of laughter startled the very English-looking lady in the row in front of them, and she peered severely at them over the top of her seat. Ali just beamed at her, as totally impervious to her withering look as he had been to Brad's initial coolness.

"How did you happen to come to America?" Brad asked.

"My father had a brother in Long Beach. He had moved to America in 1939. Conditions in the refugee camp were terrible. So my father worked at any and every job he could find until he saved enough money, with some help from Uncle Akhmud, to bring us all to the States. That was in 1952, when I was two years old. At first my father worked in the fields alongside the Mexicans as an itinerant worker. He saved every penny and finally bought a small tailoring shop in Long Beach, which he eventually parlayed into a very respectable men's store, and then two men's stores, and finally five. He was the hardest-working man I've ever known. A good man. A good father." Ali's mood became suddenly somber, and his eyes clouded.

"Was?" Brad asked.

"Yes. He was killed five years ago." Ali paused for a long moment, and then seemed to shrug off the mood. "But anyway, in 1964 my father decided it was time to return to our homeland. That was a terrible shock to my brother and me. America was our home. I couldn't even remember Palestine. We spoke Arabic in our home, of course, but English was my language. I even dreamed in English."

"You do speak perfect American," Brad nodded.

"I know. I *was* American. I was on the football team. I dated American girls. I loved hot dogs and hot rods. Then suddenly I was told I had to move eight thousand miles away to a new country, a new culture, a new everything. It was pretty traumatic for a sixteen-year-old. But in our culture, family ties are everything, and the father's word is law. My father was adamant. Even mother fought him. But he wouldn't budge. He said he had betrayed his ancestors by leaving their homeland. Now he had enough money to return." Ali's dark eyes were grave. "And so we returned."

"Wow! That must have been some adjustment."

"Like you can't imagine," Ali said fervently. "I came home from my Arabic school with black eyes for nearly three months. Every kid in the school had to take on the 'rich American pig' who claimed to be an Arab, but didn't know how to act like one. My mother bawled, and my older brother and I ran away three different times. But my father always hauled us back and we stayed."

Ali closed his eyes and leaned his head back, a tiny smile on his lips. "I can look back now on those times and laugh, but then it was pretty serious." He fell silent, lost in the memory of those days.

Finally Brad, who had completely forgotten his original desire to be alone on this flight, broke the silence. "So is that why you decided to go back to the United States?"

"No, not then. Actually two things happened that deeply influenced me."

"Oh?"

"Yes. First I found myself starting to fall in love with the land and the people. I didn't want to. I fought it like mad. I was convinced I was an American, even though my father had never let us become citizens. But Palestine is a fascinating place. Americans read a lot about how the Jews have an almost mystical love for the land, but nobody ever says anything about the Arabs and their attachment to the land. It is there, as powerful for my people as for the Jews. I began to sense what my father felt for his homeland. I began to feel it was *my* homeland."

Brad nodded. That was one of the reasons he had decided to come to Israel. He had even heard Mormons talk about the subtle but powerful draw of the Holy Land and how it affected them. He hoped he could find at least some of that for himself. "And the other thing?"

"The other was June 5, 1967."

Brad looked blank.

"The Six Day War."

"Oh, yes."

The light mood had fled now, and Ali's dark eyes were grave. "Suddenly our family were refugees again. It was a tremendous shock to all of us. One day we were Jordanians. A few days later we were part of the territories known as the West Bank, which was occupied by the state of Israel. Fortunately this time my father didn't flee too far. When the fighting was over we came back, and after several months of wrangling with the Israelis, he got his little tourist shop and our home in Bethlehem back. In the long run, it turned out to be a blessing, because the

12

business has really boomed with the increased tourism. Our family eventually bought two more shops in the Old City of Jerusalem."

"Then how did the war change your mind about being there?"

"That's when I became an Arab," Ali said. "On the first day of the war, the Israelis smashed through the Sinai and devastated the Egyptian air force in four hours. I was humiliated. Along with the other guys at the school, I ran down to the *souks*—the markets of Old Jerusalem—and bought weapons. I got an old, rusty British Enfield rifle, twenty rounds of ammunition, and three hand grenades—two of which turned out to be duds—for fifteen dollars. Remember, by this time I'm still not quite eighteen."

His voice dropped almost to a whisper. "It was Wednesday, June 7, the third day of the war. At nine o'clock the Israelis launched their attack on the Old City of Jerusalem. About twenty of us were hidden just inside St. Stephen's gate on the east side. I was up on the wall when they rounded the corner and started up toward us. I could see the paratroopers coming up quickly behind the tanks and half-tracks. I knew we didn't stand a chance, and suddenly I was crying. Not because I was scared, though heaven knows I was that, too. No, I was crying because my people—," his voice rose in sudden intensity, "*my people*, the Arabs, stood helpless in front of the Israeli army. I ran down the steps, firing blindly and hurling the grenades at them as they punched through the gate. One of my friends—one of those I'd had to fight in school a few months before—pulled me back, and we hid in the Old City until it was over."

Ali shook his head with the shame of it, his lips tight with bitterness. "They took the Old City, a soldier's nightmare of twisting, narrow streets and limited access, a perfect place for guerrilla fighters to defend—they took the whole thing *in less than three hours!* And I cried because it was my people who surrendered, my people who ran. And suddenly I realized that never again could I be an American. I was Arab. It was as though somebody had thrown away the old me and given me a new body, a new mind, a new heart. And I wanted desperately to get even, to somehow take away the shame of my people. It was a bitter, bitter thing." His voice trailed off, and he stared at the ceiling of the plane.

"I don't understand," Brad said softly, hesitant to break into Ali's thoughts. "If you found yourself, found your identity, why did you go back to the United States?"

"Ah, well, that came a little later." He grinned at Brad, the sober mood lifting. "You must remember that we Arabs invented the art of dragging out a story forever. You know the legend about the woman who saved her life by telling stories for a thousand and one nights?"

Brad chuckled as he nodded.

"Fear not, I shall attempt to finish in only half that time." Ali paused, searching for the right words, then plunged in. "I was so full of shame, so full of bitterness, so moved with a passionate desire to do something for my people. When three of my friends told me they were going to slip across the border into Syria and join a PLO training camp, I decided to join them. I thought maybe hate would be sufficiently strong medicine to wash the taste of shame out of my mouth."

As he spoke, his voice was low, and Brad could sense the tension in his lean body. "Well, I should have guessed what was coming. I wasn't training for the redemption of my people. I was training for terrorism. They taught us how to use every conceivable weapon, how to make and use explosives, and how to kill with our bare hands. I kept telling myself that this was the answer, that this was how I could erase the shame, how I could best help the Arabic peoples. But I knew it was all a lie. My real problem, I am happy to admit, is that I am not a terrorist at heart. In spite of all my hate, in spite of all their propaganda, it wasn't me, and I knew it. I had just about decided to sneak away from the camp at the first opportunity, when word came of my father's death."

It was as though Ali had somehow been suspended in time. He was staring at Brad without seeing him. Finally he continued, his voice very soft, yet firm. "He and my younger sister had gone to Hebron to buy pottery and glass vases for the shops. Their car broke down, and they had to leave it with a mechanic, so they caught a bus back to Bethlehem. Someone had planted a package of explosives near the back, just two or three seats from where my father and sister sat. They and eleven others were killed instantly."

Ali took a deep breath and gradually came back to the present. He shrugged his shoulders, his face showing pain. "I suddenly had a new perspective of the effects of terrorism. Yasser Arafat and the PLO claimed credit for the deed, though, of course, everyone at the camp deplored the fact that—," his voice became softly mocking, " 'innocent people sometimes have to die in the cause.' But it provided the perfect excuse for leaving the camp without fear of retaliation."

Ali fell silent as the flight attendant approached with a tray of drinks. Brad took a Seven-Up, but Ali just shook his head. When she was gone, he brightened visibly. "It's not really that grim. My older brother took over the family business, and I decided that if my people were going to be saved, it had to be through service, not slaughter. UCLA accepted my application, and I returned to the United States. I have just completed my master's degree in educational administration, and now I'm going back home to try again. For my people." He paused, then added softly, "And for my father."

"That is absolutely fascinating," Brad said, suddenly ashamed that he had tried to discourage Ali from sitting next to him. "So what now? You're going back home to teach? To be a school administrator?"

"Both," Ali said, the smile completely conquering his face again. "My family is putting up the money, and we're going to start our own private school—a combination elementary, secondary, and vocational school. It may not be as direct or dramatic as a bomb or a knife, but I think it beats the PLO all to pieces."

"That is great," Brad said with genuine envy in his voice. "That is really great."

Suddenly Ali hit his forehead with the heel of his hand. "Ah!" he said in disgust. "You stupid one!"

"What's the matter?"

"What my mother says is true. She says that I talk more than six Bedouins at a sheep auction. Here I've been rattling on for half an hour, and you've hardly said a word. What a stupid one I am. You know my whole family's history, and I don't know anything about you but your name."

Brad smiled. "Don't apologize. I've enjoyed every minute of it."

"You're very kind," Ali replied, "and a good listener. I really had no intention of going into all that."

"I'm glad you did. It really is an incredible story."

"Not really." Ali laughed, dropping his voice into a deep southern drawl. "I'm just your typical run-of-the-mill Palestinian refugee turned all-around American boy, turned screaming Arab terrorist, turned UCLA graduate student, turned Christian, turned schoolteacher."

"Turned Christian?" Brad asked in surprise.

Ali shook his finger at him. "Oh no, you don't. You get your thirty seconds of conversation before I launch into my next half hour. So you're Brad Kennison from California. Are you going on to Israel, or are you getting off in Athens?"

"No, I'm going to Israel."

"Great! Have you been there before?"

"No, this will be my first time."

"You'll love it. Business or pleasure?"

16

Brad hesitated. How did you answer that question—both? neither?

"I'm sorry," Ali apologized, noting Brad's hesitancy. "You'd think I'd got my degree in law or something. I didn't mean to pry."

"Oh no," Brad said quickly. "It's not that at all. It's just that I'm not sure exactly why I am going there. I guess in a way I hope to do what you did—to find the real me, to work out some things, to leave some things behind."

"I certainly understand that," the young Arab responded. "So how long do you plan to stay?"

Again Brad hesitated, his gray eyes darkening slightly as he considered the discontent of the last four months. "Well, dumb as it sounds, I'm not sure of that either. I may even look into the Hebrew University in Jerusalem, see if they offer enough classes in English that I could work on a degree." He lifted his hands in a gesture of frustration. "I don't know. It just depends on what happens. Money is a consideration, of course."

Ali nodded. "Isn't it always?"

"If I stay," Brad went on, "I've got to find some kind of work. I saved almost all my service pay during the year I was in Viet Nam—"

"You were in Viet Nam?"

"Yes."

"Combat?"

Brad nodded. "For most of the time."

Ali gave a low whistle. "So you've had a pretty exciting life of your own."

"I'm not sure 'exciting' is the exact word I'd choose," Brad mused. "Anyway, I've got enough money to see me through several months, but if I decide to stay, I need some money coming in. I know it sounds strange to come this far not knowing for sure why you're coming or what you want to do, but—" He brushed absently at his dark hair. *That's what everybody kept telling me at home too,* he thought. *"If you even knew what it was you're looking for, it wouldn't be quite so pointless.*" He sighed, suddenly aware of his deep tiredness.

Ali nodded soberly. "So where will you be staying while you're there?"

Brad shrugged. "I don't know yet. I thought I'd start in Jerusalem and kind of let it happen from there. I'll find a youth hostel or a cheap hotel once I get there."

"No need to worry," Ali beamed. "I know just the place. Khalidi's Inn for Weary American Travelers. It's run by a very respectable Arab-American family in Bethlehem, only six miles from downtown Jerusalem."

"Oh no, I couldn't stay with your family." The words came out more forcefully than Brad had intended. "Thank you," he amended, more softly. "That's very kind, but I wouldn't want to impose."

Ali studied him for a moment, his dark eyes probing Brad's. Finally he smiled and said, "The *Arab* in me says that 'no' is an unacceptable answer. Hospitality is a very sacred obligation in our land, you know. But the *American* in me says, 'Sometimes it's easier to work certain things out when you're alone.' But a dinner at the Khalidis' every now and then. That's a nonnegotiable item. Is that a deal?"

"Deal," Brad agreed, grateful for Ali's understanding.

"Tell you what," the young Arab said, snapping his fingers. "I know a small hotel near the Jaffa Gate. It's in a great location near the western entrance to the Old City. It would even be within walking distance of the university, no more than a couple of miles. It's clean, has excellent food, and is very reasonable. We supply the little tourist shop in the lobby. If I take you there, I think they'll give you a special rate. Our family has done the owner a few favors."

"That sounds great," Brad said. He had worried somewhat about finding a suitable place, and this was an unexpected solution. He sipped his Seven-Up, his face sobering again.

Ali Khalidi studied his seatmate closely. The gray eyes were tired and the otherwise pleasant face was lined with fatigue, but it was hard to tell how much was just traveler's fatigue and how much had been there before the trip had begun. Ali had sensed the quick resentment when he had moved to take this seat, but now he was glad he had. The coolness had thawed quickly, and he felt a genuine warmth and openness beneath Brad's reserve. And there was a quiet strength in this young American that he liked. He nodded to himself and decided to trust his instincts by moving one step further.

"You said you were going to Israel to find some answers. What is it exactly that you're looking for?" It was asked cautiously, as if to say, if you don't want to answer that, it's okay with me.

A look that lay somewhere between frustration and self-anger shadowed Brad's face. "If I even knew that much, I would at least know what direction to start looking. My folks kept asking me the same question. 'What's the matter, son? What is it you want? Why aren't you happy?' And then the girl everybody hopes you'll get serious with starts in. 'Brad,' " he mimicked, " 'what's wrong? You're just not the same anymore.' "

"Is she pretty?" Ali asked gently.

Brad reached for his wallet, turned past the picture of his parents and brothers and sisters to the snapshot of Karen, and passed it to Ali.

Ali's eyebrows lifted in surprise as he gave a low whistle. "Wow! She isn't pretty. She's beautiful!"

"And rich too," Brad added glumly. "Her father's a big executive with Univac Corporation." Suddenly he felt guilty for giving Ali the wrong impression. "Karen wasn't the problem. She is really a super person and not pushy at all. We weren't engaged or anything, and we both know things aren't going to work out for us. I'm the problem. Suddenly I felt as though I was smothering."

"What a way to go!" Ali said fervently as he handed

back the wallet. He touched his forehead with his finger. "You're crazy, boy! We could get ten camels and a Land Rover for that woman at the marketplace. You'd be rich! I'd be rich!"

Brad started to laugh in spite of himself. "Ain't it the truth?" he drawled.

Gradually their laughter subsided to quiet chuckles and finally to sober silence. After a long moment Ali spoke in a low voice. "In all seriousness, I do know a way you can find the answers to what you are seeking."

"Really?" Brad asked skeptically. "What?"

"Does the word 'Mormon' mean anything to you?"

Brad stared at his new companion, completely dumbfounded. He couldn't have been more stunned if Ali had revealed himself as one of the Three Nephites. "What?" he nearly shouted at him.

Brad's reaction startled Ali, and for the first time he seemed thrown off balance. "Do you know anything about the Mormon church?" Ali asked hesitantly, his face serious.

Brad tried to play it straight, but it was more than he could contain. Through a grin that was rapidly threatening to degenerate into outright gales of laughter, he said, "I know enough to know what the next question is. 'Would I like to know more?' Right?"

Ali was perplexed. He hadn't done this very often, but he'd never had a reaction quite like this. And then the light came on. "Are *you* a Mormon?"

The look on Ali's face didn't help Brad's self-control in the least, and his hoot of laughter brought another devastating look from the lady in front of them. "You got it!" Brad finally managed with a nod.

"You're kidding!" Ali said, disbelief still plainly written all over his face.

"Nope. Elder Brad Kennison, Salt Lake City, Utah. Member in good standing for twenty-four years."

His face was a perfect study of bewilderment. "But you said you were from California."

"No, I said I *lived* in California. I was there for *two* years."

"You were there on a *mission*?"

"Right!"

"Can you believe that?" Ali asked of no one in particular, still obviously struggling to believe it himself. "I joined the Church in April, just four months ago. I hope to go on a mission too, but my bishop in Westwood said I could do a great work among my own people in the meantime. So I hurried and finished my degree and here I am on my way home." Then suddenly Ali's impish grin came stealing back. "I have a confession to make."

"Oh?"

"Before I got on the plane, I decided I would pick out the person I thought would make the best Mormon and sit by him so I could eventually talk about the Church. I saw you getting on and decided you were the one. Not bad, huh?"

"Well," Brad said sheepishly, "I also have a confession to make. I wanted to be alone, so I put my camera bag in your seat. I had just barely moved it when you came and sat down. Some Mormon, huh?"

"I know," Ali smiled. "I watched you. At first I thought you might be saving it for someone. Then I saw you glaring at anyone who came close. You about scared me off then. But I finally decided that underneath all of that, there probably lived a very pleasant person. So I took my chances."

"So you set up a typical Mormon ambush?"

"Guilty as charged."

"Well, I must admit I'm glad you did." Brad really meant it. This had turned out delightfully well.

Suddenly Ali's face lit up. "I just had a brilliant idea. Is anyone meeting you when the plane gets to Tel Aviv?"

"No."

"Me neither. I plan to surprise my family. We could take a *cheroot*—a taxi—to Jerusalem together. What do you think?"

21

Brad looked into the shining eyes of his new friend for a long moment. "I think I am very glad that you thought I would make a good Mormon, Ali."

"Me too!" Ali said. "Now, I'll shut up and let us both get some sleep. You look beat, and I am too." With that, he reached up, grabbed pillows for both of them, and promptly closed his eyes and went to sleep.

Three

The Mercedes lurched to a halt, jerking Brad's head up in startled surprise. He looked around wildly, trying to make his mind process the data his eyes were feeding it. Only when they focused on Ali, who had leaned forward and was speaking rapidly in Arabic to the driver, did he remember. He shook his head vigorously, then rubbed his eyes with the heels of his hands. It felt as though the inside of his eyelids had been lined with number two sandpaper, but at least when he finished they stayed open. He peered at his watch in the dark. It was a little after ten-thirty. Ali was out of the taxi and headed for the doors before Brad could respond to his quick "Hold on and I'll check things out."

Stifling a yawn, Brad watched Ali push through the glass doors and enter the brightly lit lobby, then leaned over and rolled down the window. The night air was cooler than he expected, and filled with a hundred odors blended into one mixture that somehow smelled exactly as Brad thought Jerusalem should smell. He breathed deeply, reminding himself that this was Holy Land air, the air that Jesus had breathed, and Abraham and David and Peter. He felt a sudden stirring of excitement in spite of his weariness.

His eyes were curious as he studied the building Ali had entered. Large, bright red letters of translucent plastic announced in Hebrew and English that this was the Jaffa

Hotel. It was a small building, only three stories high, made of square blocks of a white-beige stone. Brad quickly counted the windows and estimated that there couldn't be more than thirty-five or forty rooms. Good. He wasn't after flocks of company.

Through the lobby doors he could see Ali talking to a dark-haired girl behind the main desk. His new friend pointed in Brad's direction, and the girl leaned over the counter and peered out at him. It was tempting to give a little wave, but he resisted and pulled back from the window. The girl shook her head sharply as she turned back to Ali, and kept shaking her head as he spoke. Ali became visibly more agitated, punctuating his sentences with articulate and eloquent gestures, his hands in near constant motion.

Suddenly the girl slammed her hand angrily against the counter and nodded. Ali was instantly all smiles. He turned quickly and came out of the hotel.

"Okay," he said as he opened Brad's door. "It's all set."

Brad made no effort to hide his dubious look. "Are you sure?"

"Sure," Ali beamed. He spoke briefly in Arabic to the driver, who climbed out, moved to the back of the Mercedes, and opened the trunk.

Brad got out of the taxi stiffly and joined them. Ali studiously avoided Brad's questioning gaze as the driver swung his suitcase out and onto the ground.

"Ali!" Brad finally exclaimed.

The Arab's face was full of innocence. "What?"

"That hotel clerk didn't seem overjoyed with the negotiations."

"Who, Miri?"

"You know who I mean. Look, I don't want to cause any trouble."

"Trouble?" Ali said in amazement, as though he'd just heard the word for the first time. "It's no trouble. Miri is the daughter of the owner of the hotel. He's not there right now. I'll speak to him tomorrow afternoon. We'll settle on the rate then."

"You mean—" Brad started. Suddenly he didn't like this situation at all. "If she doesn't feel good about this, then I'll pay the full rate, or if that's too much, I can find somewhere else to stay."

"Whoa!" Ali soothed. "As I told you, the owner is an old friend of my family. We have done him many favors. He has done us many in return. He has told me many times, 'Ali, if you ever need a place for your friends or relatives to stay, you bring them to the Jaffa Hotel and I'll make them a special deal.' "

"Has he told his daughter that?" Brad asked, still unconvinced.

"Miri?" Ali shrugged. "Miri is what we in America used to call a spitfire. She's angry because—" He threw up his hands in exasperation. "Ah! Who knows what makes a woman angry? Pay her no mind."

Brad's protest was becoming noticeably weaker. He was too exhausted to pursue the objection further, and the thoughts of having to find another hotel at this hour were utterly depressing. "She's not going to kick someone out of his room, is she?"

That irrepressible grin flicked momentarily across Ali's face and then was gone. "Just a recently widowed lady with nine children who's pregnant with twins and due to deliver any moment. But in the Middle East you learn to be firm. It's part of the inscrutable Arab image."

"All right, all right," Brad laughed. "I give up."

"Good. Mr. Shadmi will meet us at three o'clock tomorrow afternoon. Everything will be fine." Ali absolutely oozed self-confidence. He pointed up the street. "The Jaffa gate is just around that first corner. Five minutes and you can be in the heart of the Old City. I wish I could be with you tomorrow and show you my homeland." He smiled and shrugged. "But my family—we will be celebrating my return all night and most of tomorrow."

"I'll be fine," Brad replied. "I really appreciate all you've done."

"Including the ambush on the plane?"

"Especially that." Brad shook Ali's hand warmly, then had a sudden thought. "How much is the taxi fare?"

"Don't worry about it. I'll—" Brad's look stopped him short. "Okay, okay. Sorry for even suggesting it." Ali spoke to the driver, who answered without hesitation. Ali turned back to Brad. "It's thirty-five Israeli pounds or about nine dollars. Your share would be four-fifty."

Brad pulled out his wallet and counted out the amount plus a generous tip from the money he had exchanged at the airport. Brad ignored Ali's strenuous protests and handed the money to the beaming driver.

"*Shukran, shukran,*" the driver said, nodding again and again in a little bow.

"That means thank you," Ali explained.

"How do I say 'you're welcome'?"

"*Ahlan wa salan.*"

"*Ahlan wa salan,*" Brad repeated. His pronunciation was atrocious, but it pleased the driver immensely.

"*Shukran,*" he said again, showing his discolored teeth happily. "Wel-come. Wel-come."

Ali reached out and took Brad's hand and shook it again. "Okay, my friend. We'll see you at three o'clock tomorrow."

Brad gripped his hand firmly. "Thanks. For everything. I really mean that."

"You're wel-come," Ali said with a grin, pronouncing welcome in a perfect imitation of the driver. "See you tomorrow."

Brad gave a final wave as the taxi disappeared around the corner, then picked up his luggage and shouldered through the door and into the lobby. He walked to the counter, but no one was in sight. The hotel was small, neat, and quite modern. The walls were of a beautifully grained white marble; the floors gleamed like a mirror. One wall area had been made into a lounge with deep maroon carpeting. Chairs and couches in tastefully selected accent colors were scattered around three coffee tables, also made of marble. A huge panoramic black and white photograph of Jerusalem's Old City filled the entire wall above the lounge. Brad recognized the Dome of the Rock, which dominated the picture.

Behind him a small shop occupied one corner of the lobby. Its windows were filled with olivewood statuary, brass vases, and assorted Arabic-looking dresses. That must be the shop Ali's family supplies, he thought. He turned back to the counter but was still alone. A light was on in the small office behind the desk area, but it also was empty. Here again the feeling of neatness and order prevailed. The keys were placed in their pigeonholes in precisely the same place in each case. A sign stuck to the window of the office announced in neat hand-lettered English:

Holy Land Guide Service

Individuals or Groups

Reasonable Rates—Excellent Service

Licensed Guides

Inquire at Desk

Growing a bit impatient, Brad picked up his suitcase and set it down again firmly, making a sharp click against the tile floor. A moment later the girl appeared from around the corner of the lobby and walked toward him.

Brad looked at her in surprise. He hadn't been able to see her very clearly from the taxi through the reflections of the glass, but his impression had been that of—what? Now that he thought about it, it was clear that he had formed his impressions on the basis of her angry reaction to Ali, and not on any clear visual image. She had been behind the counter, and he had seen her only in profile. But he had not expected this.

She was not a classic beauty in the same sense as

Karen, but here was a woman who would turn men's heads wherever she passed. A white blouse of a soft silky material and a tailored navy blue skirt revealed the lithe, supple figure of a dancer, slim-waisted but full-figured, with long, perfectly sculpted legs. Her skin, a glowing golden tan, was clear and flawless. She wore her jet-black hair cut short around her neck, but left it full and fluffed slightly around her face. The effect was to soften her features, which otherwise could have been a bit too angular. Her eyes were large and round and as dark as Ali's, her nose straight and narrow. Brad guessed that her lips would normally be full and generous, though now they were compressed into a tight line. A delicate gold chain with a tiny diamond pendant hung at her throat.

"You're the American," she said bluntly. There was not the slightest hint of cordiality in the luminous brown eyes.

"Yes." He rejected his initial impulse to try something light and charming. The climate behind the counter was certainly not conducive to witty chitchat.

She pushed a card and pen at him. "Fill this out, please." The last word seemed distasteful to her, as though she had bitten into a worm while eating an apple.

He filled out the card in quick, bold strokes, pausing only to check his passport number. He pushed it back and felt a little satisfaction as he stared back at her, causing her to blush slightly. The tangle of thick black lashes masked what lay in her brown eyes as she lowered her gaze to study the card.

"How long do you plan to stay, Mr. Kennison?" She spoke excellent English, her voice husky and rich, even in its coolness.

"I'm not sure." He decided to try a smile. "Until my money runs out. A couple of months at least."

She intercepted the smile before it cleared the counter and shattered it in midair. "We'll do our best to take as little of your money as possible," she snapped.

28

Brad bit back an angry retort. "Look," he said sharply, "I wasn't aware that Ali—Mr. Khalidi was going to bargain in my behalf. I don't want to create any problems."

"Oh, it's no problem," she said bitterly. "My father is always giving someone a handout." She gave the stubbled face, the disheveled hair, and his rumpled clothes a slow once-over, obvious distaste in her eyes.

"Now wait," Brad said, really angry now. "I don't—"

But she cut him off with a wave of her hand. "I'm sorry," she said. "That wasn't fair. It isn't your fault that my father is more concerned with other things than making this hotel a profitable business."

Brad let his breath out in a slow, inaudible sigh, a technique he had developed in the service to cope with intransigent sergeants or obnoxious lieutenants who tried to goad you into losing your temper so they could really hang you. Finally in control, he quietly said, "For someone on the brink of bankruptcy, you dress quite well."

Her head shot up, and she stared at him, uncertain whether to take it as a compliment or an insult. Once again he held her gaze until she was the one to drop her eyes. "You'll be in room 312," she said, handing him the key. "I'll call someone to help you with your luggage."

"No thanks," Brad retorted. "One hotel employee is all I'm up to tonight." With that he spun away, picked up his bags, and headed for the elevator, aware of the burning glare she was hurling at the back of his neck.

Four

It was almost more than he could muster, but with a groan, Brad rolled out of bed and stumbled into the shower. He turned the cold water—a purely relative term—on full blast and let it pound into his face until he felt some semblance of life start to flow again in his body. He had fully intended to rise about eight A.M. and spend the day seeing Jerusalem. But at precisely 1:48 in the morning he was suddenly wide awake, experiencing a healthy case of jet lag. Not until the sun had flooded his room with light around five o'clock had he finally won the battle and dropped again into a deep sleep. But now it was nearly noon, and if he wanted to see the city at all before Ali came, he would have to hurry.

Brad shaved off the black growth, then stared at himself in the mirror. His gray eyes were still bloodshot, but shaving and some sleep had made a surprising improvement.

He dressed quickly, deciding not to unpack until the issue of the room was settled. Grabbing his camera bag, he went down to the lobby, preparing himself for a possible confrontation. But to his relief the girl was nowhere in sight. A tall, powerfully built man was behind the counter, head bent over a stack of papers. His hair was a wild tousle the color of coal dust. As Brad laid his key on the counter, the man lifted his head, revealing a darkly handsome face and pleasant brown eyes, which reflected an air of quiet self-assurance. He was probably twenty-five to thirty years old, and, judging from what Brad could see, in superb physical shape.

The clerk glanced at Brad's key, then broke into a broad smile. "Ah yes," he said in a deep, booming voice. "You're the American who came in last night."

"Yes," Brad admitted.

"Welcome to Jerusalem." The young man stuck his hand across the counter and took Brad's in a handshake that bordered somewhere between a pair of vice grips and a nutcracker. "Miri told me you came in last night. I'm Nathan Shadmi, Miri's brother." His English was good, but with an accent more pronounced than his sister's.

"Thank you," Brad said, relieved to find some warmth in the welcome. "I'm Brad Kennison."

"Yes," Nathan responded. "I saw your name on the register. I understand you and Ali will be meeting with my father and me at three o'clock today."

"Yes," Brad answered, somewhat wary.

But Nathan was smiling broadly. "I'm sure we can work something out that will be agreeable to you."

Brad's smile matched Nathan's in broadness. "Thank you. That's most kind."

At that moment the small switchboard in the office buzzed. "Excuse me, please," Nathan said. "We'll see you at three."

Brad plunged out into the blistering noonday heat with genuine enthusiasm. It was exciting to finally be in Jerusalem. In fact, he thought, it was exciting just to be excited again. He strode up the street in the direction Ali had pointed him last night.

As he came around the corner the view of the Old City stopped him in midstride. The pictures he had seen of Jerusalem's walls had not been able to convey the feeling of massiveness that overwhelmed him now. He darted across the busy street that ran alongside the wall and entered the great opening that was the Jaffa Gate.

He had gone only about fifty yards inside the gate when a delicious aroma from a tiny, open shop stopped him. His stomach suddenly reminded him that he had last eaten on the plane the night before. Stepping up closer, he watched a young teenaged Arab boy forming a gooey-looking paste into one-inch balls and dropping them into a pan of boiling oil. That was definitely the source of the aroma.

"What you like, sir?" The boy's smile was warm and friendly.

"I don't know," Brad grinned back. "What you got?"

"We got anything you like. You American?"

Brad nodded, used to the identifiability of his species from his travels in Asia.

"Wel-come. You like *felafel?*"

"Is that what those are?"

"Yes."

"What is it?"

"Chick peas, ground up, mixed with spices. Very good. I put it in pita bread with lettuce, cucumbers, tomatoes." He waved to bowls filled with each item as he spoke. "Then I put sauce on it. Green or red sauce. Very good. You want one?"

"Why not?"

Pleased at his sale, the boy moved quickly, taking a round but perfectly flat piece of bread from a tray. With a little flourish for Brad's benefit, he cut off one edge and, to Brad's surprise, opened the bread, which was hollow, forming a pocket. Into the pocket he then stuffed two of the deep fried balls and the other vegetables he had promised. "You want red sauce or green sauce?"

Brad hesitated, looking at both. "I don't know. Which is better?"

"Red sauce, very hot. Green sauce, very good."

Amused at the boy's salesmanship, Brad pointed. "Okay, green it is. What have you got to drink?"

"Fresh-squeezed orange juice or soda pop."

"Make it orange juice."

The *felafel* was as good as it had smelled, and Brad ordered another one, to the great delight of the young proprietor. Feeling much better, he started into the narrow opening of what at first appeared to be another shop, but on closer look was one of the narrow, covered streets that he would quickly learn were typical of the Old City.

Suddenly Brad was thrust through time and space to a completely different world, a teeming, bustling world of sight, and sound, and smell. The narrow, twisting streets were often mere tunnels under buildings that stretched for as much as a full city block. These were the *souks* that Ali had talked about, tiny markets offering the most incredible variety of wares imaginable. Tourist shops filled with olivewood carvings and brass vases elbowed side by side with butcher shops where slabs of raw meat hung in the open, often dotted black with flies. Even Brad, who thought he was used to anything, pulled a face when he saw one counter filled with neat stacks of goat heads. Shops with a dozen or more huge burlap sacks with their tops rolled down into neat collars displayed spices and beans and nuts and seeds, half of which Brad couldn't recognize. An old man with a face that would have made Methuselah look positively youthful sat at an old treadle Singer sewing machine, embroidering an intricate design in red thread upon a black dress.

And the people! Bedouin women, their faces covered with veils on which were sewn hundreds of coins, ducked furtively past men in western business suits and ties. Women with trays of bread or bundles of clothes balanced neatly on their heads jabbered happily to each other as they maneuvered through the limited space. Brad jumped hastily out of the way to avoid a hurtling pushcart loaded with bales of straw pushed by two boys too small to see over their load.

A donkey straining under a load of sacks marked "United Nations Relief Agency" clopped past, winning Brad's sympathy until he saw an Arab porter staggering under the weight of a refrigerator on his back, held in a sling stretched across his forehead and over his shoulders. Black-robed priests with silver and gold crosses jostled with ultra-orthodox Jews in fur hats and long curls of hair dangling from their temples, a response to the Mosiac commandment not to cut the "corner of the beard."

Brad continued on for another hour, walking slowly, savoring the myriad sights and sounds and smells—though some of the latter caused his nose to wrinkle in protest—and loving the fascination of it all. It felt good to be totally immersed in something again. He had felt detached for so long. *Dad was right,* he thought. *This trip is going to be the medicine I'm looking for.* The thought of his parents turned him into the next shop, where he disappointed the eager clerk by purchasing only three postcards and the stamps to send them to America.

Ten minutes later he glanced at his watch, then beckoned to a small boy who had been tailing him, trying to sell him three reed flutes for a dollar. "Do you know the way to the Jaffa Gate?"

The boy nodded his head, his large dark eyes solemn yet hopeful.

"Will you take me there?"

"Five dollars," came the instant reply.

Brad smiled to himself. He had developed a taste for bargaining in the Far East. "Five dollars?" he said, screwing his face into a look of shock. "Too much! Too much!"

"Three dollars." The young face was unmoved by Brad's protestations.

"One dollar."

"Two dollars."

Brad considered that carefully, as though it taxed the limits of his resources. "Two dollars if you give me three flutes *and* take me to the Jaffa Gate."

"Okay," the boy agreed, so quickly that Brad knew he'd just bid too high. He smiled, good-naturedly accepting the boy's triumphant look. He had been taken, but it felt good. He turned and walked swiftly to keep up with the boy, who was trotting up the narrow street, clutching the two dollars happily in his hand.

Brad had not gone into the Old City as far as he had thought, and by the time he arrived back at the hotel, it was still only ten minutes to the hour. The heat was oppressive by now, and he was perspiring freely. The air-conditioned lobby was going to feel great, but as he pushed open the door to the hotel, he stopped short. At that moment a battered Volkswagen rattled around the corner and started down the street toward him. Even at this distance Brad could hear the tortured sounds of the motor. He made an immediate side bet with himself that it would not make it up the slight rise that ran past the hotel. But he was wrong. It lumbered forward and turned into the hotel's short driveway.

A thick layer of dust obscured the car's color, although there was a slight hint of red beneath the accumulated layers. Whatever the color, it was certain that the paint wouldn't have any sun damage at all. One headlight had been gouged out, leaving a rusty, gaping wound. A crack ran diagonally across the entire width of the windshield, though under the dust it was barely discernible.

Brad started to smile, then jumped up in surprise as the door opened and Ali stepped out and waved to him. Brad fought the temptation as he greeted the young Arab, but it was too much for him, and he stared at the car, his nose slightly wrinkled.

Ali noted the expression. "Well," he said, grinning broadly, "what do you think of it?"

"Is this your car?" Brad asked, instantly regretting that his voice had put the whole force of the question on the word *car*.

"No," Ali said, slapping Brad on the back. "It's yours!"

"Ali!"

"What?" His dark eyes were wide and sparkled with delight.

"You can't—I mean, I can't take this!"

"Why not? It will look better once it is washed."

"You can't just give me your car."

"It's not mine. It's my brother's."

"Well, you can't give me your brother's car."

"Actually, it's my brother's old car. It's just been sitting in a shed in Bethlehem for several months. We almost didn't get it started. And I'm not giving it to you. Just lending it to you for the time you're in Israel."

"But—"

"But nothing," Ali interrupted. "Ahkmud says he thinks the fuel pump is nearly gone. I was going to get that fixed too, but I've got to go to Nablus for the next three days and get equipment for our school. I thought you'd rather have it now and get it fixed yourself than wait till I get back."

"Sure," Brad said hastily. "That's no problem." His voice trailed off, as he was suddenly overwhelmed by the generosity of his day-old friend.

"Then it's settled," Ali said. "It was just sitting there gathering dust," he said, wiping his finger across the hood with a grimace, "and you need some wheels."

Brad threw up his hands. "I can't believe you. What can I ever do to pay you back?"

"Ah," Ali said with a smile, "I thought you'd never ask."

"You name it," Brad said. "Anything. Just name it."

"Okay." Ali looked suddenly solemn.

"Well?" Brad prompted.

"*Anything?*" Ali asked, still hesitating.

"Yes."

"All right. Once we negotiate the price of your hotel room with Mr. Shadmi, you get to be the one who tells Miri."

Ali darted away laughing, as Brad howled in protest. "Remember, you said anything," Ali called as he opened the lobby door and motioned Brad inside.

Five

Levi Shadmi was short and stocky with a barrel chest that threatened to split his shirt up and down the back whenever he moved. His close-cropped hair had once been jet black but now was softened by liberal amounts of gray, and was nearly pure white at the temples. His eyes were a sparkling light blue and danced with hidden amusement as though he had just remembered the punchline of an exceptionally fine joke. Nathan stood next to his father, the resemblance between the two unmistakable. Brad liked Levi instantly, as he had Nathan.

"Shalom! Shalom!" Shadmi boomed, motioning them into chairs in the small office behind the hotel desk. "Ali, it is so good to see you home. How was America?"

"Fine. A great experience."

"Wonderful. And you finished your schooling?"

"Yes," Ali replied, the pride evident in his voice.

"Your brother Ahkmud tells me about your idea for the school each time he comes. Are you still planning to go ahead with that?"

"Yes. In fact, I leave for Nablus tonight to begin purchasing supplies."

Shadmi nodded his approval. "Good! Good! It is an important thing that you are doing."

Ali was obviously touched. *"Shukran,* my friend. *Shukran."*

Shadmi turned toward Brad. "And you, Mr. Kennison—"

"Please," he interrupted. "Just Brad."

"Brad, then. Where do you come from in America?"

"Salt Lake City." Then, remembering that many people overseas thought of the United States as either New York or California, he added, "That's in Utah."

"Yes, I know. We have been there. We visited your—how do you say it? The Square of the Temple?"

"Temple Square," Brad answered. "When were you there?"

"Let's see, about six years ago now," Shadmi mused. "We were there just before the Six Day War, in January 1967. We lived in New York for two years on an assignment for the Ministry of Tourism. We decided to see America before we returned to Israel, and stopped in Utah on our way to California."

"A very beautiful building, that temple," Nathan said. "Are you Mormon?"

"Yes."

"So am I," Ali said proudly.

Both father and son looked startled, and stared at the young Arab.

"I joined the Mormon church four months ago. In fact, that's how Brad and I happened to meet on the plane."

"Well, well," Shadmi said. "It is an interesting religion. Ali tells me you plan an extended visit to our country."

"Yes." Brad paused. "Exactly how long I am not yet sure."

"And you need a place to stay?" Shadmi said.

"Yes, but I don't want to be a problem. You have a hotel to run, and I'm sure every room is critical."

"Every room but the one we had reserved for you," Shadmi said with a warm smile. "You will stay here for as long as you wish. It is a pleasure for us to be able to do something for a friend of the Khalidis."

"Brad is a proud American," Ali said, voicing Brad's biggest concern. "He is a proud American but not a rich one. He will not accept charity and yet he cannot afford luxury. What can you work out between you?"

"Two hundred fifty dollars a month for the room, which will include breakfast and dinner here in the hotel." The words were spoken with finality, suggesting no opportunity for debate. "For three hundred you could eat lunch too, but I thought you might be gone during the day."

Brad stared at him and then started to speak, but Ali beat him to it.

"Ah," he said softly. "That is very generous, my friend. Too generous."

"I expected to pay more than that just for a room," Brad replied. "It is far too little. I have saved enough for several months, and I hope to get some work of some kind to help out. I can pay a fair price."

The older man's eyes were thoughtful as he looked back and forth at the two friends. "I have a proposal," he said at length. "Nathan here finishes his leave day after tomorrow and must report back to his unit." He looked at his son with evident pride. "Nathan is a colonel in the army."

A colonel, Brad thought in surprise. In Viet Nam lieutenants under thirty were called "shavetails." He guessed Nathan's age at twenty-six or twenty-seven. With a start he brought himself back to listen to what Nathan's father was saying.

"—and frankly I'm a little nervous about having Miri work here at night alone. We don't expect any problems, but in Israel, terrorists are always a concern. We have a fellow who comes in from eleven to seven in the morning, but I need a desk clerk in the evenings. Would you be interested in that, Brad?"

"That would be great," Brad said eagerly. "However, I can only speak English. Will that be a problem?"

"Ninety percent of our guests either speak or can understand English. And Miri or I will be around a good part of the time if there are special needs."

"Then that sounds great." Brad's face reflected his gratitude. In one fell swoop he had solved three major problems—a place to stay, food, and keeping expenses down.

"Okay, in that case, if you work five evenings a week, Monday through Friday, let's say from five to eleven—and we can be flexible if you want a specific evening for something—we'll make the monthly rent two hundred instead of two-fifty."

"No," Brad protested. "The two-fifty stands, and I work to justify that."

"But I would pay more than that for a clerk—" Shadmi saw the look on Brad's face and stopped. "Okay, the two-fifty stands, but you can eat lunch here anytime you're at the hotel, in addition to all other meals. That's final," he said firmly. "That way we both benefit. You can start tomorrow night."

"Thank you very much."

"You're welcome," Shadmi boomed heartily. "Tomorrow I'll have Miri show you what must be done. In the evening, there is not much that is difficult."

Nathan laughed at Brad's sudden look of dismay. "Did you meet Miri too? I am afraid my sister was upset last night."

"It was nothing," Brad said.

Shadmi sighed. "That's my Miri." He stood up, stuck his head out of the office door, and bellowed, "Miri!"

Brad held his breath, expecting that battering ram of sound to hurl to the floor everything not tied down, but all was silent for a moment. Then he heard the click of heels on the polished marble floor.

Miri was wearing a soft beige dress with dark brown trim and a neck scarf that pleasantly accented the golden tan of her arms and legs. Her head was high, the dark eyes flashing. If her father's call had intimidated her in any way, she was disguising it well. There was no air of open defiance, but she was miles from cowering in abject fear of rebuke.

Then Brad decided that Shadmi's thunderous summons must be his normal substitute for a public address system, for he was not angry with her at all. As she came to stand by him, he put his arm around her waist and gave her a gentle squeeze.

"Brad, this is my daughter Miri. I understand you met last night."

Brad stood up. "Yes, we did," he replied, noting with satisfaction that her cheeks had colored slightly.

"Miri, this is Brad Kennison, from Utah."

She stepped forward and stuck out her hand, her eyes widening slightly. Her impression the previous night had been that of a sloppy, ill-kempt, and ill-mannered American—typical of so many found on the tourist lanes of the world. But now he was well groomed, neatly dressed, and quite pleasant-looking—quite good-looking, she thought begrudgingly. His gray eyes were clear and met her gaze steadily, holding out an obvious flag of truce. His look was friendly, his mouth on the verge of a smile if given the slightest encouragement. She glanced at her father and then decided Mr. Kennison had already received too much encouragement. "How do you do, Mr. Kennison." The huskiness of her voice made it difficult to read, but it certainly wasn't dripping with cordiality.

"Mr. Kennison is going to be staying with us indefinitely, Miri. We have worked out an arrangement."

"I expected that you would," she said with obvious sarcasm. She shot Ali a quick look, which he fielded with a bland smile.

"He will have his room and any and all meals for two hundred and fifty American dollars per month." Her father stopped and looked at her as he heard the sharp intake of her breath. Her eyebrows shot up in a look of shocked surprise, confirming Brad's conclusion that Shadmi had given him a super deal.

"And," Shadmi said firmly, "he will become our evening desk clerk five nights a week. Starting tomorrow night."

That succeeded in getting through her tight self-control. Her eyes flicked instantly from surprise to anger. "Father," Miri said, her mouth a tight line, "you don't even know him!"

"I do now," Shadmi said. "Besides, he's a friend of Ali's."

She dismissed that contemptuously with a toss of her head. "But this morning you said I would be taking the evening shift."

"Yes, that was before. I don't like the idea of your being here alone. Once we get your Uncle Shlomo's business going well, then I won't have to be gone every night. For now, this is a good solution."

"But he's American!" From the way she spit out the word it was clear that ranked him somewhere between boils and bad breath.

For the first time, Shadmi's voice turned sharp. "Miri! That's enough!"

But it wasn't sufficient to stop the explosion. Brad watched almost in awe as she turned on her father and launched into a tirade in their own language. Her body was rigid and poised like a spear in the hands of a javelin thrower. Her head was held high, regally, like a queen, revealing the graceful lines of her neck. As she tossed her head angrily, her hair reflected the overhead lights in quick bursts of brilliance. The dark eyebrows had drawn down almost to a point as her eyes narrowed into angry slits.

But Shadmi must have dealt with this towering temper before, for he stood his ground as the words tumbled out in a wild torrent. Brad caught the word *American* at least three times as she spoke.

Suddenly her father thundered out a blast with such force that it made his earlier summons seem like an asthmatic whisper. It was as though a huge boulder had been dropped directly over the cone of an erupting volcano. One instant there was fire and spewing lava. The next instant there was a complete cutoff. But one could sense the seething force inside threatening to find new vents of escape for the pressure. Miri shot Brad and Ali one quick, withering glance, then turned and stalked out.

Shadmi shook his head and heaved a great sigh. In the awkward silence it sounded like a force-six gale. "I hope you'll forgive my daughter, Brad. In an hour or two she will calm down, and then she will be very embarrassed and come and apologize to you."

Brad managed a tight smile, trying not to let his own anger show. "Look, if you promised your daughter the job of evening clerk, I can find something else."

Nathan, who had remained unperturbed through his sister's outburst and his father's response, laughed out loud, his brown eyes deeply amused. "Promised her! When Father told her about it this morning we had a scene nearly as explosive as what you've just witnessed. She said she had too much to do in the evenings, that she couldn't be here night after night. No, she is just angry that Father has accepted a lesser rate, and from an American at that. It has nothing to do with you personally."

Ali stood up and poked Brad in the ribs. "I'm just glad I've repented of being an American."

Brad shook his head, remembering the contempt in Miri's voice when she used the word. "Somehow I thought Israel and America were allies."

"I think we owe you an explanation for that," Nathan said. "America is Israel's greatest friend. Perhaps too great a friend."

Brad looked puzzled.

"There are some in Israel—an increasing number— who think we depend on America too much. Now the oil crisis comes and suddenly America begins to pressure Israel to accept the unacceptable." Nathan's brow furrowed as he continued. "There are some who think America is too weak to stand for what is right anymore. They fear your country is willing to sell out Israel in order to be comfortable."

It was evident from the somberness of Nathan's tone that Miri was not the only one in the Shadmi family who had those concerns.

"There are many in America who agree with that one hundred percent," Brad said, matching his own tone to that of the younger Shadmi's. "Unfortunately, our leaders do not speak for the people often enough."

"That we know," Nathan agreed. "We have great confidence in America, the people. But in America the government? Miri just hasn't learned to distinguish between those two yet."

"Well," Ali broke in, glancing at his watch, "Ahkmud should be here any minute now to pick me up. C'mon, I'll walk you out." Brad shook hands again with Shadmi and Nathan, thanking them.

As Brad and Ali reached the lobby doors, Nathan called, his face split by a wide smile. "If you'd like, Brad, I'll train you on the desk tomorrow instead of having Miri do it."

Brad gave him a thumbs-up sign. "You're on! Terrorists I can face, but it might be wise to steer clear of her for a while."

Six

By the time he finished breakfast—an interesting combination of cucumbers, tomatoes, cheese, boiled eggs, hard rolls, and bitter, dark hot chocolate—Brad had overcome the effects of a second night of jet lag and was feeling nearly normal. He had awakened at the same time as the night before, but instead of fighting it, he had gotten up and written the postcards to Karen and all of his family. By three-thirty he felt sleepy again and had slept deeply until seven.

Brad took the stairs up from the basement dining room two at a time, actually looking forward to the day. However, his pace slowed abruptly as he came up into the lobby. The girl was at the counter helping a small group of tourists check out. He was hoping that either Mr. Shadmi or Nathan would be around to orient him to his new job and give him some directions on where he wanted to go today. Irritated by her previous manner, Brad walked up boldly.

The expression in her eyes was still impossible to read, but she managed a fleeting smile. "Good morning."

"Hi," Brad responded, encouraged by the lack of open hostilities.

"Mr. Kennison, I want to apologize for yesterday. I was very rude. I'm sorry." The apology was obviously difficult for her. Her cheeks were reddening, and those large brown eyes dropped as he watched her.

"No apology necessary." He paused for a moment, then asked, "Is Nathan around? He was going to teach me about running the desk."

"No, he's gone until this afternoon. He said he'd meet you at four o'clock and show you then."

"Okay." Brad did some quick calculations. He'd just have to do the car first and Nathan later.

Miri looked at him steadily for a long moment. "I could train you now, but then maybe you'd rather face a terrorist." She smiled sweetly.

Brad's mouth dropped open, then snapped shut again, and he felt his face go instantly hot. He shot her a glance, then looked away quickly when he saw the look of triumph that she was making no effort to hide. For a moment he sought for some appropriate response, but finally gave it up. She had him, and it was his own fault. He should have known she was still somewhere around the lobby when Nathan had called to him yesterday. Then he felt his embarrassment start to give way to anger. The comment he had made yesterday was not totally undeserved. His hackles started to rise. Why was this woman needling him?

"Look," he said shortly, "could you tell me where I can find a good automobile mechanic? I need to get Ali's car fixed."

The air of triumph slowly dissolved, and the cool reserve slipped back into place. She thought a moment, tapping a pen gently on the counter. "Minor repairs or major?"

"Fairly minor. Ali thinks it's a fuel pump."

"There is a garage not too far from here, near the Damascus Gate. Do you know where that is?"

Brad nodded. He hadn't the slightest idea, but it would have taken the combined fortunes of Howard Hughes and the Rockefellers to make him admit it.

"Go east from the gate one block to Saladin Street. Turn left. The garage is three blocks north on Saladin

Street. It is on the right-hand side of the street. It's not very big, so you will have to watch for the sign. It is called Mohammed's Garage."

"Mohammed?" Brad asked dubiously.

"Yes. Is something wrong?"

"Well, no. Do you happen to know a Jewish mechanic?" The instant it was out he regretted it. What in the world had prompted him to say that?

Miri's eyebrows had lifted slightly, and her eyes started to smoulder. "You would rather not have an Arab mechanic?" she asked.

"No, it's not that. I'd just rather—never mind, Mohammed's is fine."

But Miri wasn't about to let him stop. "You would just rather what?"

His anger, now as much at himself as at this cool, raspy woman, threw him off balance. "I don't know. It's just that—well, you know how the Arabs are," he finished lamely.

He had been mistaken about her eyes. They weren't smouldering at all. They were like two dark brown chunks of antarctic rock. "Oh, really?" she murmured. "I'm an Arab." With that she spun away and went into the office, slamming the door behind her.

* * * * * *

Brad set the guidebook aside, giving it up as a lost cause. He glanced at the wall clock. It was ten minutes to eleven, and his first shift as evening clerk at the Jaffa Hotel was nearly over.

It had been a busy evening, and Nathan had stayed around helping him as needed until almost nine-thirty. Brad hadn't seen Miri since his return from Mohammed's Garage, and had hurried through the lobby while she was on the telephone. Even now the very thought of Mohammed's Garage made him wince. What in the world had ever made him say such a stupid thing? He had undergone a critical self-analysis since his morning blunder, and each time he concluded that his statement about Arabs did not reflect his true feelings. He thought of Ali and shook his head. She must think you're really something, he thought. You let an Arab find you an incredible deal on a hotel. You let him find you a job the first day after you arrive in a strange city. And you let him give you a car without being asked. Then you come off the wall with, "Oh, you know how Arabs are."

Brad shook his head, angry at himself that he should care what she thought. She was rude, impertinent, and had deliberately goaded him. He was so flustered by her, he had lost his balance for a moment. He felt a little better knowing he could honestly say those were not his true feelings, but he still felt so stupid to have said it. And to have said it to an Arab was even worse. Just how dense could one person be?

And speaking of being stupid, why had he assumed the Shadmis were Jewish? He groaned inwardly, torn between self-condemnation and irritation at Miri Shadmi. Suddenly Brad's head jerked up. *Hey, wait a minute. Answer your own question. Why did you think the Shadmis were Jewish?*

He let his mind run swiftly over the past two days. Ali had never said anything about their nationality one way or the other that Brad could remember. But when Miri had launched into her tirade yesteday in the office, he had assumed she was speaking Hebrew. He shook his head. His ear wasn't trained enough to distinguish between Hebrew and Arabic. He frowned, then nearly leaped off his chair. Nathan was a colonel in the Israeli army! Now maybe he didn't know much about Hebrew, but he knew enough to know that Arabs didn't become colonels in the Israeli army. Things began to click. *Levi* Shadmi. An Old Testament name. A Jewish name, not Moslem. So was Nathan. Another thought flashed back. When Ali had introduced Brad to Mr. Shadmi, the greeting had been, "*Shalom, shalom.*" A linguistic expert he was not, but he knew at least one word of Hebrew. His eyes narrowed as a slow, burning anger began to ignite down deep inside him. There was no excuse for his stupid remark, but fair was fair. And Miri Shadmi had not played fair!

Saud, the night clerk, came in shortly before eleven. After a brief self-introduction and a friendly conversation, Brad heaved himself to his feet with a sigh. "Well, I'm ready for bed. I'm glad to meet you. See you tomorrow night." He started away and then, on a sudden impulse, turned back.

"Saud?"

"Yes?"

"Can you tell me a little bit about the Shadmis?"

A sudden wariness sprang into the Arab's face. "The Shadmis?" he asked slowly.

Sensing his hesitation, Brad leaned back against the counter and briefly explained how he had come to be the evening clerk at the Jaffa Hotel. "So anyway," he concluded, "it was very good of Mr. Shadmi to help me out, and I just wanted to learn a little more about him."

"Yes," Saud said, anxious now to help. "Mr. Shadmi is a very good man. They are a good family."

"Are they Jewish?" Brad asked casually.

"But of course," Saud said. "Nathan and Miri are what the Israelis call *sabras.*"

"*Sabras?*"

"An Israeli who is born in Palestine is a *sabra.* It comes from the Hebrew word meaning—how do you say it? Kahk-a-toos?"

The lack of comprehension on Brad's face was evident, so Saud tried again. "Kahk-a-toos. It is the plant with sharp stickers."

"Oh, cactus."

"Yes, kahk-a-toos. The Israelis call themselves *sabras* because like the kahk-a-toos, they are sharp and prickly on the outside, but the flowers and the fruit are beautiful and very sweet." Saud laughed, half to himself. "If you do not get stuck getting close to them. It is a good description of Israelis, no?"

Brad smiled ruefully. "It sure is, especially the first part." His nose still smarted from running full tilt into her spiny exterior. "Are there other children?"

"There was an older brother named David. He was killed in the Six Day War. So now there is just Nathan and Miriam."

"Miriam?" Brad asked in surprise. He hadn't thought about it being a nickname. Miri could pass for Arabic with a dumb American. But Miriam? No way! So Jewish as to be unmistakable. He threw another log on the growing fire.

"Well, thanks, Saud. I'd better get to bed. I'm still trying to adjust to Middle Eastern time, and my need for sleep has just caught up with me."

The latter proved to be an optimistic conclusion. Sleep didn't have a chance for the next hour and a half, as he lay in bed polishing off some very fiendish plots having to do with one Miriam Shadmi, former Arab and current kahk-a-toos.

Seven

It was perfect. The hallway was long and narrow, and there was only one entrance into the small linen room. And Miri had just gone inside.

He hadn't expected his opportunity to come so soon, but he was ready. A movie star, preparing to audition for the coveted role of the century, could not have rehearsed his lines any more thoroughly than Brad had prepared for this scene as he lay awake last night.

As he had come down from his room for breakfast and stepped off the elevator near the hotel's dining room, Brad had seen Miri start down the hall toward the linen room. Her back was toward him, and she hadn't seen him. Now he waited until she went inside, then walked softly down the hall after her, his tennis shoes making only the barest whisper on the tile floor. Stopping just short of the door, Brad leaned against the wall, trying to ignore the sudden tension winding up in him. The door was still open, and he could hear her moving around inside.

Suddenly the light clicked off, and she stepped out, her head half turned away from him as she shut the door. There was a stack of towels in her arm, which she nearly dropped as she turned and saw him and visibly flinched. The sharp intake of breath and the look of surprise were quickly noted, not without some satisfaction. Let her be caught off guard for once, Brad thought. He had been on the defensive long enough.

When Brad spoke, his voice was duly contrite. "Oh, I'm sorry. I didn't mean to startle you." Half truth, his mind noted. He hadn't really planned it that way, but to say he was sorry fell slightly short of reality.

Miri was quick. He had to grant her that. She recovered her composure almost instantly. "Excuse me," she murmured, and started to push by him.

Brad moved sideways and blocked her way. "Could I speak with you for a moment?"

Miri stepped back a step and looked at him steadily. Her head was tipped back slightly, her face bathed in the pale light of the hallway, her eyes unfathomable pools of black. She was beautiful, but it was the beauty of a cobra with its head raised. Admiration was possible, but only from a safe distance.

"Yes?" she said coolly. The cactus needles flicked out like a well-oiled switchblade knife.

"I would like to offer you an apology," he said in a soft voice.

It had the desired effect. He could visibly detect a slight lowering of her defenses, so he followed it up swiftly, his voice still dripping sweet innocence. "And then *you* can apologize to me."

Her eyebrows shot up in surprise, then dropped as her eyes narrowed to angry slits. "Apologize? What have I—?" Catching herself, Miri bit off the question. She lowered her head and tried to step around him. "If you'll excuse me, the maid is waiting for these towels."

He leaned casually against the opposite wall, cutting off her escape. "Oh, come now," he said. "Surely you can stay a moment. I have heard so much about the great warmth and friendliness of the *Arab* peoples."

Oh, how sweet it was! Even in the dim light of the hallway he saw her face flush. She looked up. "I—"

But Brad went on quickly, still holding the light, almost conversational tone in his voice. "Now, I've heard the Israelis aren't like that. More stiff and reserved. Almost rude sometimes. Tell me, from an Arab's point of view—are they really as bad as they say?"

He grinned easily into the wrath that blazed from her eyes. For a moment he thought she was going to hurl the towels into his face. She tried to push his arm aside, but he held firm.

"Please let me by." Her voice was like the low rattle of a coiled sidewinder.

"Not until you apologize for being prejudiced."

"Me?" she hissed.

"Yes," he replied. "I have detected a definite anti-American bias in you. But I have a forgiving nature. I accept your apology."

Miri stared at him, outrage momentarily overcoming the infuriated look on her face.

"Mr. Kennison!" The fury made her voice tremble. "We have a very large man cooking for us in this hotel. If you do not move your arm and let me pass, I am going to scream. You will find him to be a very unpleasant person."

Brad looked thoughtful. "Hmmmm!" he mused. "Just out of curiosity, do you plan to scream in Hebrew or Arabic?"

He should have felt some of the generous magnanimity that was expected of the victor, but it felt too good to find her suddenly and totally flustered, as he had been yesterday.

Stepping aside, Brad bowed politely and waved her through. "It must be a terrible thing to be the only Arab in an Israeli family, Miss Shadmi. Someday I would like to hear how you cope with that."

He turned and walked away, leaving her standing there, rigid as a steel fencepost. "Have a good day, *Miriam*," he called over his shoulder.

* * * * * *

When Brad entered the hotel lobby shortly after four that afternoon, he was hot and frustrated. A blast of arctic air rolled toward him from the direction of the desk where Miriam was working, though she appeared not to look up. He pushed aside the slight feelings of guilt he had felt after his ambush that morning. If she wanted a game of freeze-out, he was in the perfect mood. He strode across the lobby without giving her a second glance, then stopped as Levi Shadmi's voice boomed out.

"Brad, have you got a minute?"

Brad looked around and saw Shadmi's bulky figure in the office behind the hotel desk. Shadmi came out and stood next to Miri as Brad reluctantly turned back and moved to face them. If Shadmi noticed the frost in the air, he gave no sign as he smiled in greeting.

Miri was studiously reading the Jerusalem *Post* and was ignoring them both.

"Nathan tells me that you caught on very quickly last night," Shadmi said. "He thinks we were very lucky to get you." He glanced quickly at his daughter, who only lowered her internal thermostat a few more degrees without looking up.

"Thank you," Brad responded, pleased with what Nathan had reported to his father.

"Nathan said he did not show you anything concerning the gift shop," Shadmi went on.

"No. There were only three or four guests who wanted things from the shop last night, and Nathan said he figured I had enough new things to learn for one night."

"Well, it's not much of a shop, but our guests like to have something right in the hotel to supplement their other purchases. We keep it open until nine each night, so you had better learn the basics as soon as possible."

"Fine. Would you like me to do that now?"

"Oh, no," Shadmi said. "Go on down and get your dinner first. When you start your shift at five, Miri will take you in and show you how it works."

That was sufficient to break through her concentrated study of the newspaper. Her head shot up, and she gave her father an incredulous look. The only sign that he had noted her dismayed reaction was the glint of amusement in his eyes as he looked at Brad.

Shadmi turned and gave his daughter a light kiss on the cheek, oblivious to her withering stare. "I've got to go. I promised your Uncle Shlomo I would help him start ordering his equipment tonight. Tell your mother I should be home around eight." With that he plunged into the office, grabbed a small briefcase, and left with a wave.

"Well," Brad said, forcing a cheer he certainly didn't feel, "I will be back in a few minutes."

* * * * * *

Dinner helped his mood considerably, and by the time Brad returned to the desk he was almost looking forward to the next round of the Israeli-American war. The way he figured it, the score was now even, and if Miri chose to fire the first salvo, he was ready to up the tally to two to one, his favor. He smiled brightly at Miri, whose face was an inscrutable mask.

"Okay, I'm ready whenever you are," he said.

She nodded, came out from behind the counter, and walked across the lobby without a word. Once inside the shop, she began the orientation without preliminaries, her voice flat and expressionless. He smiled to himself. A mannequin would probably have elicited more warmth than he was getting. He leaned against the small counter and watched her, only half listening to her instructions. There was one bank of fluorescent lights in the narrow shop, and her hair gleamed under its glow. The scowl she wore couldn't quite obscure the fineness of her features—the high cheekbones and dark eyebrows, and, her most striking characteristic, the large brown eyes with their thick black lashes.

Miri wore a silver Star of David on a delicate chain, which further emphasized the soft line of her throat and the golden tan of her skin. She was wearing a navy blue skirt and a long-sleeved blouse of a pale blue silk, and

Brad couldn't help but admire the slimness of her figure. Without question, she was lovely. He felt a slight pang of regret that they were getting along like two bantam roosters competing for king of the barnyard.

Suddenly he jerked up, aware that she had spoken to him, "Oh, I'm sorry," he murmured. "What was that again?"

"Am I boring you, Mr. Kennison?" she asked.

"Oh, no, I'm listening." And then to quell her dubious look, he quickly added, "Olivewood statuary, prices on the bottom. Same with the brassware. Clothing is marked in the collar. Mother-of-pearl pins—large, three dollars; small, two."

He grinned at her. The army had honed his ability to listen with one ear while his mind wandered. "I'm sorry if I seemed inattentive. I was just debating about asking you a question."

"What?"

"Well," he said slowly, "I was wondering if you carry any weapons here in the shop."

"Weapons?"

"Yes, you know. Guns, knives, explosives. Just your usual stock of weapons."

"Of course not. Why in the world would we—"

"That's good," Brad interrupted. "Then I would like to make one more attempt to apologize to you. But after this morning, I didn't want to try it where you could lay your hands on something dangerous."

Brad thought he noted a momentary flicker of a smile, but if so, she squelched it quickly. "There is no need for an apology," she said.

"Maybe not, but I'd like to try. I promise, no blocking the exit this time. Okay?"

She folded her arms and looked at him, her eyes expressionless. But she didn't say no, so Brad plunged in.

"We have an expression in America. It's called putting your foot in your mouth."

"I am familiar with this expression."

"Well," Brad gave her a tentative smile, "my father says that I was born with a special talent for doing just that, and he thinks that since then, I've greatly increased my birthright."

That won him a smile. It was a tiny, reluctant smile, but it was a genuine smile nevertheless, the first he had seen. "I think your father sounds like a very wise man," Miri replied.

"Right. Well, anyway, I wanted to apologize for my statement yesterday about Arabs. I've said a lot of dumb, stupid things in my life, but that one tops them all. I know it sounds phony now, but I don't really feel that way."

"Then why did you say it?"

He hesitated a moment. "Because you got me so irritated. When you made your comment about the fact that I would rather face a terrorist than you, I knew you were trying to get even with me."

She tipped her head slightly to the side and looked at him quizzically. "Correct me if I'm wrong, but I thought originally that was *your* comment."

"Yes, I know. That is what my father means. Anyway, you threw me off guard, and I just blurted out that comment."

"And your remarks about Israelis this morning? Are you going to tell me that you really didn't mean those either?"

He smiled sheepishly. "No, I was just baiting you."

She looked puzzled. "Baiting me? I don't understand. What is 'baiting'?"

"It means to try to needle someone, to make them react the way you want. Kind of like waving raw meat in front of a hungry lion."

Miri nodded, her eyes mocking him. "I understand. And I was the hungry lion—or lioness. Correct?"

"Well, yes," Brad said. "And that is the second part of my apology. At first I felt terrible about offending you with that blunder. Then when I discovered you were Israeli and not Arab, I was just plain ticked off."

"You Americans and your expressions," she smiled. "I suppose that means you were angry with me."

"That's close. Anyway, I decided to get even and . . ." He paused, trying to choose his words carefully.

"And so you 'baited' me."

"Yes. And I apologize. That was unnecessary."

Miri lowered her eyes, her fingers tracing a pattern on the counter. "Perhaps unnecessary, but not undeserved. I don't know what prompted me to say that I was an Arab." She took a deep breath. It was obvious that apologies didn't come easily to her. "Your comment seemed so—so bigoted, so smug. So American. I reacted without thinking. It also was a stupid thing to say. But there are so many feelings between my people and the Arabs without having an outsider come in and be so smugly insulting."

Brad felt himself bristle and bit back an angry retort. Her words stung like pebbles flung into his face. But she was right. It was stupid, it was smug, and it was insulting. It said something for her that an Israeli should so sharply feel the insult on behalf of the Arabic peoples. "I know words are cheap," he said. "But I really don't feel that way."

"I hope not," Miri said, still seeming only half convinced. She straightened up and became very businesslike again. "Well, do you have any questions about the store?"

"Just one," Brad answered, letting his tone become as impersonal as hers. "You mentioned the mother-of-pearl pins were two and three dollars. Are all the prices in American dollars?"

"Yes, though they are in Israeli pounds also. Most guests from other countries either carry dollars or understand its exchange rate. We exchange all currencies at the desk, however."

"Yes, Nathan showed me the conversion tables last

night. I was just surprised at how common the dollar is, even here."

"Oh yes," she said, her voice again filled with bitterness. "The dollar, the fashions, the music, the politics. There is not much that America doesn't influence."

Brad nearly let the remark pass, remembering Nathan's explanation for Miri's caustic reaction to America, but recently he had gotten just a little tired of what seemed to be developing into a national and international pastime, and that was the "let's-run-down-America" fad. "Oh, I agree," he said, the sarcasm heavy in his voice. "Leave it to good old America and she'll pollute the world, right?"

Miri's head jerked up in surprise at his reaction, then her eyes hardened. "I didn't really mean it that way. But yes, I suppose that is not too far from being right."

"Is there anything at all you find acceptable about America?" Brad challenged.

"I think it is a beautiful country. The mountains, the lakes."

"Wonderful! Now if we could just get rid of the people."

"You twist my words." Her dark eyes flashed. "But if you must know, I lived in America for two years. I got to know your people."

"Correction. You lived in New York for two years."

"Ah, and New York is not America?"

"New York is only *part* of America. There is much, much more."

Miri's head was up, her fists clenched into tight little balls. "New York was enough. I found Americans to be narrow, materialistic, concerned only about themselves, and quick to tell other countries how they must live."

Brad shook his head in mock wonder. "You must have been a busy girl to meet all two hundred million of us in the two years you were there."

Her voice was tight and low, vibrant with the anger

that shook her. "I met some very nice people, but most of them were insufferably proud and arrogant." She tossed her head. "Very much like I find you, Mr. Kennison." She whirled around and started for the door of the shop.

"Tell me, Miss Shadmi," Brad retorted quickly, "why is it you find prejudice against Arabs so repulsive, and prejudice against Americans so attractive?"

If she heard him she gave no sign. She stalked across the lobby, yanked her purse out from behind the desk, and plunged out the door, her head high and her back rigid.

Eight

Brad was lost again. Once more the Old City had put him in his place. This morning when he had set out for the Wailing Wall and the Dome of the Rock, he had carefully studied the map of Jerusalem that Ali had given him. His destination was on the far eastern side of the walled city, and the street to it lay in an exact straight-line shot from the Jaffa Gate. Or so it looked on the map.

Frustrated, Brad looked at his watch. It was nearly one o'clock, and his stomach was getting as growly as his attitude. Something had to change. He was coming to the conclusion that if he was really going to see Israel properly, he needed help. He thought of Ali, and shrugged it off. His friend was too busy with the school to shepherd a green American tourist around. And the thoughts of trooping around with a package tour was more distasteful than being constantly lost. Yet even if he could find his way, he wasn't sure he would be satisfied. He felt a tremendous longing to understand this place, know its history, learn the stories and folklore that he was sure lay behind the sterile brevity of the guidebook. As little as he had seen, Brad felt the spirit of the Holy City, sensed that it was seeping into his soul and starting to purge out the frustration and irritability that had dogged him for the last four months. He hadn't come to any life-altering decisions as yet, but the pressured feeling, that sense of smothering in pointlessness, was now dissipating. He was aware of a growing hunger to capture more of the spirit of this land.

Suddenly an idea hit him, and he stopped in mid-stride, nearly tripping a heavyset Arab woman with a large tray of bread balanced on her head.

"Of course!" Brad said aloud, drawing suspicious looks from several people in the river of humanity that was flowing past the dam he had created in the middle of the narrow street. Liking his sudden inspiration more with every moment, he started looking for a young boy to lead him back to the Jaffa Gate.

Twenty minutes later he pushed into the delightful coolness of the hotel lobby. Miri was behind the front desk, but if she had seen him come in, she gave no sign. He walked up to her, amused at her sudden scrutiny of the molecular structure of the countertop.

"Good afternoon, Miss Shadmi," he said cheerfully. "Is your father in?"

"He's in the shop," she answered, not looking up.

"Thank you," he called as he turned away, too pleased with his idea to let her set him off the track.

Shadmi, holding a large piece of olivewood statuary, was jammed into one corner of the narrow shop, surrounded by three elderly women. They were speaking what sounded to Brad like German or Dutch. The hotel owner lifted his eyes in a combined expression of greeting and pleading for deliverance.

Brad studied the crowded shelves idly until the women had completed their purchases and squeezed past him. "Hello, Mr. Shadmi."

"Levi, please," he said with a pleasant smile. "How are things today, Brad?"

"Fine, thanks. Have you got a minute I could talk to you?"

"But of course. Let's go over to the office where we can sit down."

"Oh, this is all right," Brad said a little too quickly, thinking of Miri behind the desk. "It will take only a minute."

Shadmi smiled knowingly. "Whatever you say."

"I've just spent three hours lost in the Old City," Brad said, plunging right in. "No, it wasn't that bad," he added quickly in response to Shadmi's look of sudden concern. "I had a map and thought I could find my way."

"Ah yes," the older man sympathized. "Inside the walls is a different world, no?"

"Absolutely. Well, anyway, it started me thinking. I decided it might be of value if I had someone to show me around. Someone who knows the city—not only where things are, but the historical significance of them, the places of real interest. You know what I mean?"

"Of course. A guide."

"Yes."

"A very good idea."

"I know so little about Israel. After I get better acquainted, then I'll be fine on my own. It just seems like a shame to blunder my way around a city as significant as this."

"Yes, I agree. A terrible mistake."

"Well, I noticed the signs you have posted at the desk, about the guide service for either groups or individuals."

"Ah!" Shadmi said with sudden understanding. "Yes, that is a service we can provide for our guests."

"Can you tell me a little bit about it?"

"Well, we arrange whatever tour you are interested in. Usually we do this for groups, but occasionally some of our guests prefer to have a guide just for themselves or their family."

"Yes, that's what I'm thinking about. Is it terribly expensive?" Then noting the hesitation on the older man's face, Brad quickly added, "And no deals please. You have done far too much for me already."

Shadmi sighed. "Ali was right. You are too proud."

"I know, but I really mean that. What are the regular rates?"

"You can schedule either half-day or full-day tours. A

half-day is fifteen dollars. A full-day is twenty-five. We also have weekly rates.''

Brad hesitated, trying to keep the dismay out of his eyes. And yet, he thought, wasn't it just as foolish to spend the money to come over here and not get the full benefit? He was saving significantly on his board and room.

He nodded. ''That sounds good. About how far in advance would I have to schedule a guide?''

Shadmi laughed. ''At the moment, fifteen minutes. Most tourists come here on tour with groups and have all their arrangements already made. Our service merely fills the needs of a few like yourself who come on their own.''

''So, if I wanted to start tomorrow—?''

Shadmi shook his head quickly. ''Tomorrow is *Shabbat* and we do not provide the service on the Sabbath.''

''Oh, that's right,'' Brad said. ''We have church tomorrow too. So I couldn't go then either.''

The blue eyes widened a little. ''Your church meets on Saturday?''

''Only in Israel. The President of our Church gave the branch here special permission to meet on the Jewish Sabbath since otherwise people would have to get off work to come to church Sunday, and so on. So anyway, Sunday would be my first opportunity too. Would that be possible?''

The older man started to nod, then frowned slightly. ''There is one possible problem.''

''Oh?''

''You see, we have only two licensed guides. Nathan and—''

''Miri!'' Brad finished for him, the dismay evident in his voice.

''Right.''

Brad's mind was racing, looking for an out, as Shadmi went on talking.

''I know she was very rude to you, but it was because she worries so much about my finances. I am helping my brother Shlomo get a business started. I lent him some money, and she worries if we will pay the bills." He was watching Brad closely. "She is an excellent guide. Even better than Nathan. In addition to guide school, she has also graduated from the university in history and archeology. Miri has a great love for Israel, past and present. She would be very good—if you are willing."

Brad shrugged. There was no way he would offend this man after the great generosity he had extended. "That's fine with me. She might have some feelings about it though."

Shadmi brushed that aside. "It is nothing."

Brad choked on that one, grateful that her father didn't know about their last two encounters.

"Besides," Shadmi added, "a guide is not paid to take only people she likes."

A good point to be made with Miri, Brad thought. But he just nodded. "Then I'm willing."

"Let's go talk with her." Shadmi pushed past Brad and went out into the lobby.

"Miri!" Shadmi's deep voice boomed off the marble walls.

She had gone into the office and now came out, hesitating when she saw the two of them together.

"Do you have anything on the schedule for Sunday morning?"

"Just to be here to help you." The words came out slowly, as though a sudden sixth sense had warned her there was a trapdoor beneath her feet.

"Good. I can cover the desk for that long. Mr. Kennison would like a guide to show him around Jerusalem."

It was a credit to her that she was able to contain the anger that sprang to her eyes. Her voice was cool and polite. "Oh?"

"Yes, just the half-day tour. Is that okay with you?"

"Of course," she said, calmly.

Brad felt a tremendous surge of relief, which she instantly flattened.

"And what price has Mr. Kennison negotiated with you for *this* service?"

"Miri!" Shadmi snapped. "That is enough!"

"That's all right," Brad said. "You might as well confess. Tell her what we agreed upon."

It evened the score a little to see her triumphant look vanish as her father said, "Fifteen dollars per half day. Twenty-five for a full day's tour."

The lovely face was impassive as she nodded. "And what time would Mr. Kennison like to leave Sunday morning?"

"You're the guide," Brad shot back.

"Good! We'll leave the hotel at four-thirty A.M."

Shadmi hooted at the startled look on Brad's face. "Miri thinks the best way to see Jerusalem for the first time is from the Mount of Olives at sunrise."

"If you prefer to sleep in," Miri challenged, "we can leave at nine o'clock."

This one wasn't on the defensive very long. "Four-thirty sounds fine. As I said, you're the guide. Meet here in the lobby?"

She nodded, turned away, and stalked back into the office.

Brad held up his hand to cut off Shadmi's apology. "We'll be fine. Really. Now, let me ask you one other question. I'd like to learn as much about Israel as I possibly can. About the people, the history, the land, everything. Could you recommend some books and tell me where to find them? If I have slow time on the desk, that will give me something profitable to do."

"Say no more," Shadmi said, pleased at Brad's request. "I have many books that would be very good in that area."

"In English?"

Shadmi looked startled and then sheepish. "Some. Enough for now. I will call my wife and have her bring them when she comes to get me this afternoon. You can start tonight."

Nine

"We'll park and walk from here," Miri said as she opened the door of the hotel's Volkswagen van and got out. She didn't wait for him. She didn't even look around. These were the first words she had spoken to him this morning. Her eyes had stayed locked on the road ahead, her neck rigid.

She wore a softly tiered cotton skirt in a pastel floral print that fell gracefully around her tanned legs. Teamed with an embroidered peasant top, it gave her a charmingly cool look. Her feet were bare except for white sandals. She had a matching purse slung on her shoulder and carried a medium-sized notebook and a small Bible. Sunglasses were perched atop her head, nearly lost in the thickness of her dark hair. She was obviously used to Jerusalem's summer heat and dressed accordingly.

Brad watched as she strode away, totally unconcerned as to whether or not he was coming. Then he reached over the seat, grabbed his camera bag, and climbed out to trail after her. It was just now approaching quarter to five and yet daylight had fully driven away the last remains of the night. He estimated it was only four or five minutes to sunrise. A high stone wall that ran next to the sidewalk blocked any view of the city, and he quickened his pace slightly in order to draw even with Miri by the time they reached the place where the wall's height suddenly dropped in half.

Brad stopped in midstride and stared at the panorama

that suddenly lay before his eyes, letting out his breath in a long, slow expression of amazement. "That is incredible!" he whispered in awe.

Her sense of timing was precisely correct. Though they were still in shadow, being below the crest of the Mount of Olives, the entire Old City of Jerusalem lay across the valley, bathed in the first gentle rays of the morning sun. The burnished, golden sheeting of the Dome of the Rock dominated the entire scene, drawing the eye to itself like a selfish debutante who wanted to be the center of everyone's attention.

Brad reached instinctively for his camera, then slowly let his hand drop. Distraction was unwelcome at this point. He stood in silent awe, trying to let his mind soak up what his eyes were seeing.

"You were right, Miri," he finally said, unconsciously using her first name. "This is the only way to see it for the first time."

She nodded, pleased in spite of herself. "Each time of day has its own mood," she said softly, "but I love this one the best. The city opens herself to view, innocently, fully, as though she had nothing to hide."

"It is beautiful," Brad murmured. "This is what I came for."

Miri was watching him closely, searching for the slightest hint of mockery or sham, almost unwilling to accept the fact that he was as stirred by the sight as she hoped he might be. But it was evident that Brad was enthralled, almost unaware of her in his enchantment with the city before him. Her stiffness lessened slightly.

"The ancient rabbis had a saying: 'The Holy One of Israel, blessed be his name, created ten measures of beauty for the world. He gave nine of them to Jerusalem.' "

They stood, silent for a moment, and then Miri shook off the mood, remembering her resolve to maintain a quiet aloofness. "There is a place to sit a little further down. I will orient you to the city there, and then we will go to see it."

But before they sat down, Brad took out his camera. He had bought the best equipment he could find while he was in the Orient, and now he put it to its full use. He started with his wide-angle lens, the only one capable of coming close to embracing the full view. Then he went to his standard lens, clicking away steadily as he moved slowly from left to right trying to capture it all. When he switched to his telephoto lens, Miri let the professional guide in her take control.

"The corner of the wall, there directly across from us, is the pinnacle of the temple, the traditional site where Jesus was led by Satan and encouraged to jump."

Brad lifted his camera and focused in on the spot.

"If you wait a moment, there is a truck coming up the hill. When he is directly under the pinnacle, it will give you a better sense of perspective in the shot."

He followed her suggestion and was grateful immediately. The truck looked like a tiny bug laboring up the slope, dramatizing the massiveness of the walls. He clicked the shutter, then gave her a long look. "That was an excellent suggestion. Thank you."

That was the pattern for the next five minutes. She would raise her arm and point out things for him, explaining briefly what it was and why it was significant. He would nod, focus, and record it on film. To call it a cordial, warm partnership would have been a gross overstatement, but the tension that had filled the air on the way over from the hotel had largely disappeared.

Satisfied at last, Brad put the camera away and sat down. "Thank you," he said, sincerely meaning it. She had called his attention to things he would never have seen as important. "I'm ready for the orientation now."

To his surprise, she sat down next to him. It wasn't close enough to touch, but after their beginnings this morning, had Miri chosen a spot several feet away, it would not have surprised him.

For almost a full minute there was a comfortable silence, as Miri gazed at the panorama that lay before them.

When she spoke, her voice was low, emphasizing the huskiness of it. "Yerushalayim—or Jerusalem, as you say it—is a strange choice of names for this place. Its name is made of the Hebrew word *uru* or *yehru*, which means city or dwelling place, and *shalem*, which means peace."

"Like *shalom*?"

"Yes. It is the same word. To call it the dwelling place of peace is one of history's great ironies. There are probably few places in all the world that have seen more blood and less peace than the land that lies before us. The city itself has fallen to conquering armies twenty-six times in recorded history."

Brad gave a low whistle. "Twenty-six times!"

"It is a tragic history as well as a glorious one," Miri nodded. "The ground that you see before you has literally been irrigated with the blood of those who have died here." She held up her long, slender fingers and began ticking them off as she spoke. "Egyptians, Assyrians, Babylonians, Persians, Greeks, Romans, Saracens, Crusaders, Turks, British—each has come with its armies and left a trail of blood and horror in their wake."

Her eyes were saddened as she gazed out across the city. "And always they leave Jewish bodies broken and dead beneath their feet. Under the Romans in A.D. 70, the siege was so terrible in Jerusalem that the people turned to cannibalism. If they tried to escape, the Romans crucified them. At one point there were waiting lists for crosses even though they were crucifying five hundred a night."

Brad shook his head, deeply sobered as he pictured the fleeing refugees nailed to crosses, perhaps right on the very spot where they now sat.

Miri turned back to Brad. "Of course, Jews are not the only ones who have died. When the Crusaders conquered Jerusalem in 1099, they butchered thousands of Arab Christians. Since they looked like the 'infidel' Arabs, they were cut down even as they held up crosses and begged for mercy. Several thousand Jews fled into the main synagogue. These Christians—," the word was almost spat out in contempt, "promptly set fire to the building and drove anyone who tried to escape back into the flames at the point of the sword."

She stood up, suddenly restless. "When it was over, the Crusaders sheathed their swords and trooped off to the Church of the Holy Sepulchre. It was Sunday, and the Holy City was in Christian hands once again."

"Not Christian hands," Brad corrected softly. "Only hands that carried crosses. There is a great difference."

She turned around slowly and measured him with those somber eyes. The defiant set of her jaw relaxed, and he thought he detected just a flicker of admiration in her voice. "Yes, I suppose you are right."

Choosing his words carefully, Brad spoke again. "And it is not over yet, is it?"

"What do you mean by that?" she asked, her voice challenging.

"Jerusalem is still not ready to earn her name, is she?"

Miri took the sunglasses from their perch on top of her head and put them on, shaking her head once to rearrange her hair. The glasses hid her eyes, making it harder to read what she was feeling, but her face was sober. "You are right. The characters have changed, but the drama is still the same. Now it is the Arabs who encircle the city, and the Jews who wait for the final assault on the walls."

"While the world stands by, empty gasoline cans in hand, hoping all will turn out well in the end," Brad added.

To his surprise that brought a sad smile to her lips. "Exactly. At least well for them. And *they* grow impatient when the Israelis are so stubborn and uncooperative."

Brad spoke slowly and solemnly. "Now I personally have never met an Israeli who was like that."

Miri threw back her head and laughed out loud, a totally uninhibited and delightful sound. "Touché, Mr. Kennison. Touché."

71

Brad smiled back at her, relieved he hadn't triggered another explosion.

"Well." Miri picked up her purse and notebook and stood up. "Enough of this gloom. Let us stop looking at Jerusalem from a distance and go to meet her. She has seen much sorrow, but she has also seen much joy."

Shouldering his camera bag, Brad stood up to join her. "I am anxious to come to know her well."

* * * * * *

Thirty minutes later they stood inside the Garden of Gethsemane. It had been locked at this early hour, but Miri had found one of the Catholic priests she knew, and he had opened it for them.

The site lay in the bottom of the Kidron Valley, the deep, narrow ravine that lay between the Mount of Olives and Mount Moriah or the temple mount in the Old City. Beyond the walls of Gethsemane, the walls of the Old City loomed bright golden in the morning sun. A thick, bushy vine with violet and burgundy flowers hung over the stone walls that formed the garden's enclosure. The bright pink oleanders were thick clumps in each corner. Numerous flowers and small shrubs, set off by neat, stone-lined walkways, were well tended within the garden. But the eight olive trees were what arrested the gaze and invited the attention. They were grotesque, the trunks twisted and gnarled as though they too had suffered the agony of that night two thousand years before. Their silver-gray leaves stirred slightly in the morning breeze.

Brad stood quietly, awed to think that he stood near the spot where the Savior had knelt that night while his apostles fought against, and then surrendered to, sleep. Here Christ had bowed beneath the tremendous weight of the combined sins of the world and had suffered so intensely that his very vessels had ruptured under the strain and oozed blood from every pore. And now he stood here where it had happened. He was transfixed, touched, and moved more deeply than he had been for a very long time.

Miri finally spoke softly at his side. "Originally the olive grove was much larger than what you see here. The olive trees are very old, perhaps well over a thousand years old.

"They are—" Brad was going to say beautiful, but that was inadequate. He groped for a better word. "I don't know, awesome, I guess."

"The olive is a peculiar tree. When it dies or is cut down, the roots send out new shoots that grow into new olive trees. So if these trees do not date back to the time of Jesus, they spring from the roots of trees that were here when he was." She pointed out one of the nearest trees. "See, there you can see a new, young tree growing out of the parent root."

Brad nodded, still caught in the mood of reverence that gripped him.

"I suppose that is why the ancient prophets compared Israel to an olive tree," Miri mused. "So many times our enemies have cut down the tree and assumed we were dead."

Brad looked startled, remembering the allegory of the olive tree in the Book of Mormon.

"The Babylonians, the Romans, the Nazis. Each one has tried to kill the mother tree, and each has failed."

The aptness of the symbolism was beautiful and caught Brad's imagination. "And the modern state of Israel is the newest shoot," he said with understanding. "A new tree comes forth out of the old root."

Miri glanced at him sharply, the surprise evident in her eyes. "Yes, exactly."

"And I guess I can't blame Israel for getting a bit upset when she sees the world picking up their axes again," Brad said, meeting her speculative gaze. "But this time the tree itself will survive. It may take a few solid hits. But it will survive."

The expression on Miri's face was a study in puzzled thoughtfulness. But all she said was, "Would you like to go inside the church and see the rock of the agony?"

Brad shook his head. "Not now. Maybe some other time. The garden is what I came to see."

He fell silent again as he leaned on the fence and peered at the trees, trying to visualize what it must have been like on that night. Miri stood silent, sensing his desire for quiet. Finally he straightened up and nodded. "Okay. Shall we go?"

Ten

They had been on the temple mount for over an hour now, touring the majestic, almost awesome beauty of the Dome of the Rock, holy shrine to Moslem, Christian, and Jew. When they had left the Garden of Gethsemane, Miri had lapsed into silence, and Brad assumed she had retreated behind her wall of aloofness. But as soon as they had come through St. Stephen's Gate, she had warmed again. They became tourist and guide, he ignorant but eager, she knowledgeable and sharing. Soon there was an open interchange, like that between a tutor and pupil.

Now they sat in the shade of the huge eucalyptus trees that towered over the small grassy area just south of the Dome of the Rock. Two small Arab children were playing tag among the trees, and Miri watched them with amused eyes. She was half turned from him, her head tipped slightly back, her face in profile. Filtered sunlight made gentle patterns on her face as the slight breeze rustled the leaves overhead.

Suddenly Miri seemed to sense his gaze, and looked a bit startled. "I'm sorry. I was watching the children. Are you ready to continue?"

Brad shook his head.

"No?" she asked, her eyebrows lifting in surprise.

"No. It's lovely here." He turned and gazed at the Dome of the Rock, towering above them, its golden dome like a giant sun hurled down to rest on the blue-tiled walls that cradled it. "It really is an incredible building. It's magnificent inside and out."

"I have seen it a thousand times and yet, even now, it seizes the eye and leads it upward against its will."

"And to think that it is thirteen hundred years old," Brad marveled. "In the western United States, if anything is more than a hundred years old we say it is ancient. And then to think that just west of here are the remains of the original walls of Herod's temple. Those stones were here seven hundred years before the Dome was built."

"And just to the south of where we sit is Hezekiah's tunnel, carved through solid rock when the Assyrians laid siege to Jerusalem, seven hundred years before that!"

Brad was impressed. "This place literally breathes history. It's fascinating!"

Miri gazed at him steadily. "I am glad you sense it too. Americans usually jog through the holy sites, snapping pictures, dropping cigarette butts, and asking where the nearest restrooms are."

At first it was tempting to let that pass, but it was clear that she was taunting him for some reason. Brad picked off a blade of grass, stuck it in his mouth, and chewed on it reflectively for a moment.

"Yes," he finally mused, "I understand how you feel. When I was in the service we had a typical Jew in my platoon. His name was Samuel Goldstein. He had a big nose, smoked cigars, and was really quite obnoxious."

He ignored the sudden flash of lightning in her eyes and the sharp intake of breath. He turned and gave her a look of bland innocence, inwardly tensing for what was obviously building rapidly into an explosion equaling Vesuvius, Krakatoa, and the bomb at Hiroshima all together. "Actually, I had never known any Jews, and so I was glad to finally meet *one*." He emphasized the last word ever so slightly.

But it was enough. Gradually he could see the light dawn in her eyes, defusing the imminent eruption as swiftly as it had been armed. "Okay," Miri apologized grudgingly. "I get the point. Not *all* Americans are that way." Then she smiled. "Was there really a Samuel Goldstein?"

Brad nodded. "There really was. My bunkmate, Marvin Barnard, and I used to lay awake nights devising ways to deflate this guy's ego. One night Marvin asked me if I thought Sammy was typical of Jews. I was surprised. Growing up in Utah, I had never met any Jewish people, and I admitted that I hadn't even thought about Sammy being a Jew. I just thought of him as a first-class dork." He grinned at her. "Do you know what a dork is?"

"No, but I think I get the meaning from the context."

"Yes. Well anyway, Marvin looked at me kind of funny, and he just said, very quietly, 'Oh, that's good.' The way he said it made me curious, so I asked him why he thought it was good." Brad looked at Miri. "Do you know what he said?"

"That he was Jewish too?"

"Yes." Brad paused. "Marvin saved my life once in Viet Nam. He was killed three weeks later trying to help evacuate some wounded out of a mortar barrage. He was nineteen at the time. I consider it one of the privileges of my life to have known him."

"I stand rebuked," Miri admitted with no rancor. "I know that all Americans are not—" She paused, seeking for an appropriate term.

"Soft? Spoiled? Coddled?" Brad supplied.

Miri nodded. "You even have low-calorie dog food so your pets won't get too fat. Somehow that is a problem many people in the world have a hard time getting very concerned about."

"Guilty as charged," Brad said. "But we are not all that way. There are some who care, some who still stand for what is right. I'll grant you, there may not be as many as there should be. But there are many—a great many—who love their country and try to maintain her greatness." Miri didn't respond to that, and Brad decided to risk a comment of his own.

"If you want to comment on national character, the Israelis are not without their own problems. It would seem that little *more* softness on your part might go a long way to solving some of your problems."

"We are well aware of our own problems," Miri bristled, "but lack of softness isn't one of them. All of the soft ones marched to their death in the ovens of Dachau, Buchenwald, and Auschwitz."

"And now," Brad said softly, "here stands the invincible, tough-minded Israeli, a class of super-warriors, ready to tackle the whole world if necessary."

"Yes," she snapped. "And with the rest of the world frantically waiting at the base of the Arab oil spigots, we may have to stand alone."

"And so you trust only in yourselves," Brad said, knowing that this was rapidly getting out of hand, and yet not willing to let it drop.

Miri leaned forward, her brown eyes nearly jet black with anger. "You tell me—who else *can* Israel count on but herself? America?" She spat out the word with contempt.

Brad met her challenging stare and then slowly said, "When the barbarians were approaching Rome, someone said, 'The Roman world is falling, yet we hold our heads erect instead of bowing our heads.' "

Miri leaped to her feet, startling a group of tourists dutifully following their guide toward the Dome of the Rock. "Spoken like a true Christian," she said bitterly. "Turn the other cheek? Love your enemies? Tell that to the athletes who were butchered in the Munich massacre last year! Oh, wouldn't Yasser Arafat love that, because he's waiting with a razor at our throats to slash *either* cheek that turns to him."

She snatched up her purse and books and glared down at him, breathing hard. "Go out into the real world,

Mr. Kennison! Go out on the Golan Heights. Go into the Gaza strip. Go to the Sinai. You'll not hear hymns and prayers there. You'll hear the shriek of artillery shells, the screams of the dying, the cries of children as they huddle over the dead bodies of their parents. You go there and then talk to me about God and Christianity!"

Miri spun around, but before she could take a step Brad quietly said, "I've been there, Miri."

She turned back slowly, caught off guard by the quiet intensity of his voice.

"I've been there, and I'm ready to talk about God and prayer. Why is it you Israelis think you have the corner on suffering? Do you think death is any sweeter in the rice paddies of the Mekong Delta than in the sands of Sinai? Do you think Vietnamese children have no tears? Do American mothers receive their dead sons with any less grief?" He took a deep breath, getting just a bit angry himself. "And while we're at it, why is it that you can criticize and question and challenge my country and my religious beliefs, while if I so much as raise a tiny cloud of doubt about yours, you jump to your feet and storm off as if I've insulted everything you hold holy?"

Miri flinched visibly, and he could tell he had sent that one rocketing home. Her mouth opened and then shut again.

"Besides which," he said more gently, "it's not like an Israeli to run from a fight. If your convictions can't stand up to criticism, then they're not worth defending, right?"

"They can stand up to anything you can say," she retorted. But the anger in her voice was lessening, and she walked back over and sat down facing him. After a long pause she said, "You can be an infuriating person, you know." She was half daring him to take issue with her again.

"I know." He grinned. "It's one of my natural talents. And you—you really get kind of feisty when you're angry, don't you?"

"Now you're teasing me."

"Yes, I guess I am. But it's only my way of saying I'm sorry. I didn't mean to make you angry. Here we've gone a full three hours without a clash. I guess it was only natural that it just kind of boiled over again."

"My father says boiling over is *my* natural talent," Miri admitted, managing a genuine smile. It wasn't enough of a smile to bring in the photographers for, but it represented miles of progress from a few moments earlier. Then she grew serious again.

"Now that I have a little better control of myself, may I try to answer your question?

"Did I have the gall to ask a question in the midst of all that?"

Miri laughed, and Brad knew that for the moment at least they were back on safer ground. "Actually, it wasn't a direct question. But it was implied. You were asking why we don't turn to God."

"Yes, I guess I was."

She spoke in a low voice but one filled with intense emotion. "To what god would you have us turn? The god of the Hebrews who watched six million of his children go to their deaths in gas chambers and did not answer? The god of the Lutherans whom the Germans worshipped as the trains rolled eastward to the death camps? Or maybe the Catholic god who presided over the Vatican while they ignored the pleas of Jews begging for help to escape the Nazis? Tell me, Mr. Kennison, to which of these gods should the Israelis bow their necks?"

He started to answer, but she went quickly on. "For three thousand years we have been God's chosen people. For what are we chosen? Look at our history and there is only one answer. We were chosen to suffer. What a privilege, that God should select us! We waited all these years for God to help us. We went like sheep through the slaughtering pens. Now we will help ourselves. We have bowed the neck long enough. Now we bend the bow and unsheath the sword, and call on all Israel everywhere to die like sheep no more. If we die, we will die like human beings."

Gradually the passionate intensity faded. Her eyes focused, and she looked at him directly. "And that is the answer to your question."

Brad met her gaze and then said gently, "Why is it that we alternate between intense heat and bitter cold, you and I?"

His question took her back, and immediately her defenses went up again. "What is that supposed to mean?"

"Well, here we are scorching each other now, and yet in the car on the way over I nearly froze to death."

"Froze to death?" Miri looked puzzled, then laughed. "Oh, yes. Of course. I was very angry with you for making me serve as your guide."

Brad had a pained expression. "Somehow I had sensed you might feel that way. May I make a confession?"

"Of course."

"When I asked your father for a guide, I had no idea it was you. When he told me, I nearly died. I would have backed out except that after all he has done for me, I didn't feel I could."

"Well, that makes me feel better." She pulled a wry face. "I think."

"Can I make another confession?"

"I think I'm up to it."

"I'm glad I didn't back out. You are exactly what I was hoping for."

Miri raised an eyebrow. "You wanted the hot and cold?"

Brad laughed. "Well, it certainly keeps one alert. But no, that's not what I meant. I decided to hire a guide because I wanted to come to feel the spirit of this land. I told your father that, and he said you were the best." His eyes caught hers and held them. "And he was right."

Miri lowered her head, suddenly embarrassed by his sincerity. "Thank you. This morning I dreaded it, going through the day pointing out things to you while you taunted me, laughing at me behind my back."

"I have never laughed at you," Brad said softly. "Nor even felt like it."

"I finally realized that. I could sense you really did want to see Jerusalem. That made me feel better."

"Good. Then I have a proposal. What do you say to the idea of setting up an Israeli-American détente?"

A smile stole slowly over Miri's face, revealing even white teeth and a slight dimple in her left cheek. "Détente? Yes, it is a good word. The two hostile superpowers agree to seek more friendly relations." She stuck out her hand. "As you Americans say, 'It is a deal.' "

Brad took her hand, pleased at this sudden turn of events. "Yes, it's a deal. On one condition though. That you stop calling me Mr. Kennison. It's just Brad, okay?"

"Okay." She stood up and brushed down her skirt. "Then let us continue our tour. We have—" A horrified look suddenly sprang to her face. "*Oi vavoi!*"

"What's wrong?"

"*Oi*," she said again. "This is terrible. Can you wait here for a moment? I must make a phone call. I'll be right back."

"Can I help you?"

"No, no! I will only be a moment." She plunged away, leaving Brad to stare after her.

In three minutes she was back and obviously flustered.

"Brad, I'm terribly sorry," she burst out as she came up to him. "But I have a problem."

"Oh?"

She blushed but looked him directly in the eye. "I made an appointment this morning, and I forgot all about it until right now."

"Hey, that's okay."

"No, it's not. I made it deliberately yesterday so I

would have an excuse to end our tour as soon as possible." Her flush darkened. "I was afraid that by now we would both be ready to quit."

Brad checked his watch. To his surprise, it was ten after nine. "I only contracted for a half-day tour, and we've already been going for almost five hours." He grinned at her. "Was I really that fearsome?"

She was too embarrassed to return his smile. "I made an appointment to go shopping with a girl friend at nine o'clock. I tried to call her when I remembered, but she has already left. I am terribly sorry."

"If you're sorry, we're making progress." He smiled, his gray eyes teasing. "It's all right, really. In fact, I'd like to stay here on the temple mount for a while anyway. I'll just poke around and take more pictures. I can find my own way back." He pulled a face, remembering his last two excursions into the Old City. But there had proved to be an abundance of little Arab boys waiting to fatten their purses. "I'll be fine. Really."

"I feel badly about it," she said. "I promise it won't happen again." Her face dropped. "Oh, that is if you still want the guide service."

"Absolutely! Tomorrow if possible."

"Yes, tomorrow is fine." She touched his arm. "Thank you, Brad. I really am sorry."

"I know. Hurry now or you'll be even later. I'll be fine."

He watched her thoughtfully until she was out of sight, then hoisted his camera bag to his shoulder. "All right, Jerusalem," he said cheerfully, "here I come again."

Eleven

Ali finished the rest of his custard dessert and pushed back from the table with a satisfied sigh. "Though I protested heartily, thank you for your insistence that I join you for dinner, Brad. That tasted great."

Brad grinned. "For someone who said he wasn't really hungry, you tanked away a healthy amount of food." The hotel's Arab waiters knew Ali well and had brought out heaping servings of each course. Brad had finally surrendered after the roast chicken and rice, but Ali had had an extra helping of salad, two more rolls, plus a generous portion of dessert.

If Ali felt any embarrassment, he had it well under control. "Just be glad you aren't paying for it by the pound," he retorted, patting his stomach with satisfaction.

"It gives me shudders just to think of it."

"Actually, you shouldn't be paying for it at all. I didn't come here to get a free meal. So let me pay for my own lunch."

"Absolutely not. I am here in this hotel at a greatly reduced rate for my room and meals, I have a job, and I have a car to get around in, all because of you, my friend. Buying lunch is the least I can do."

Ali's face was split by that infectious grin that brightened everything around it. "Well, I always like to help a man do his Christian duty." He looked up and waved. "Hey, there's Miri."

Brad turned and waved too, then watched her come down the stairs with that easy, flowing grace with which she always moved.

"Hello, Ali," she said. "Hello, Brad. May I join you?"

"Sure." Brad pulled out the chair between them. "Have you had lunch yet?"

"Yes, I ate at home with Mother."

"It's probably just as well," Brad said, gesturing to the stack of dishes surrounding Ali's place. "There may not be much left in the kitchen."

Ali gave her a contented, lazy smile. "Brad was paying."

At that moment one of the waiters saw her and hurried over. "Would you care for some lunch, Miss Shadmi?"

Miri shook her head, but the waiter was anxious to please the owner's daughter. "Would you like some dessert, please?"

"No, thank you, Avraham. I'm fine."

"We have some iced lemonade. Very good."

"Okay," she laughed, giving up in the face of such persistence.

"Mr. Kennison?" he asked.

"Yes, that does sound good," Brad answered.

Ali held up a hand and forestalled the waiter before he could even ask. "No, thank you. I've got to get going. They are supposed to deliver the paint for the school this afternoon."

As the waiter moved away, Miri turned to the young Arab. "So how is the school coming, Ali?"

He beamed. It was his favorite subject. "Wonderful. I have all the furniture and equipment now. We found a building in Bethlehem. When we get it painted and fixed up, it will do very nicely. My brother Ahkmud and Brad have been helping me, so we should easily be ready in time for school. We will open on the third of September, not even two weeks from now."

"What you are doing is an important thing for your

people," Miri said, her voice warm with praise. "I hope it succeeds."

"How can it fail?" Ali asked. "Brad is going to teach for me."

"He is?" She turned to Brad in surprise. "You are?"

"Only because one Ali Khalidi twisted my arm," Brad growled good-naturedly. "And only until his regular Arabic English teacher can start around the first of October."

Avraham came bustling out of the kitchen with two glasses of lemonade on a tray and set them on the table, while Miri looked at Brad in astonishment. "I didn't know you spoke Arabic!"

"You bet," Brad intoned seriously. "I have it nearly mastered now. 'Yes,' 'no,' 'thank you,' 'you're welcome.' The rest is still coming."

"We're trying an experiment," Ali explained to her. "Like your *ulpans*, where you teach Hebrew to the immigrants through teachers who do not speak the immigrants' language. Only Brad will be teaching children six to fourteen who speak no English."

Miri gave Brad an appraising look, almost as though she saw him with new eyes, but she sipped her lemonade without speaking.

Ali stood up. "Well, I'd better get going. Thanks for lunch, Brad. See you tomorrow?"

"Right. Eleven or eleven thirty?"

"Fine." Ali waved, then turned and ran lightly up the stairs and was gone.

For a moment they both fell silent, sipping their lemonade. Miri watched his fingers as he traced the patterns in the tablecloth. She studied him quietly, keeping her eyes lowered, not wanting to draw his attention to her scrutiny. She smiled briefly as she thought of her first impressions and their first few encounters. They still had flashes of fire, but out of the tourist-guide relationship mutual respect and genuine friendship were developing.

His demand for knowledge about everything they saw constantly surprised her. He was like a desert wadi soaking up the first rains of winter. Equally surprising was his knowledge of the Bible. She had guided some Christian ministers who knew the scriptures thoroughly, but other than that, Brad's knowledge was a rarity.

She looked up and caught him studying her closely. Slightly flustered, she smiled, but then almost instantly became sober. She decided to go ahead with her purpose in coming down to the dining room.

"Brad, may I ask you something?"

"Of course," he said lightly. He became serious as he sensed her hesitancy. "Yes, go ahead."

"I do not wish to offend you."

"Offend me? Why would you offend me?"

"It is about your religion."

Startled, Brad nodded. "Okay."

"Father says you are a Mormon."

"Yes."

"Are Mormons Christian?"

"Yes. Actually Mormon is a nickname given to us. The formal name of our church is The Church of *Jesus Christ* of Latter-day Saints."

She was silent for a moment, digesting that. "Do you—I mean, does your church believe that Jesus was the Son of God?"

"Most definitely."

"In the literal sense, not just in a symbolic sense?"

"Absolutely. We believe that God was his literal Father, and Mary his mother."

"Doesn't that seem—" She stopped, the indecision clear on her face.

"Go on," he urged.

"Well," she said, still unsure of herself, "first maybe I ought to explain something. When I studied history at the university, I specialized in the period of the Second Temple—what you would call the Christian era. I was required to study much of the Christian literature of that period, including the New Testament. And, of course, to become a guide, we had to learn Christian history and study the New Testament quite intensively."

"Did that bother you?"

"Oh no, not in that sense. My grandfather, whom I never knew and who was an Orthodox Jew from Eastern Europe, would not even have allowed me to speak the name of Jesus in his presence. But he and his generation vanished into the gas chambers of Nazi Germany. Now all but the most Orthodox Jews are willing to accept Jesus as a great rabbi, though, of course, we reject the Christian notion that he was the Son of God, or the Messiah."

"I understand."

"There are many things in the life and teachings of Jesus that I like. I am fascinated with him as a man and a teacher. But the theology is very puzzling."

"In what way?"

"Okay. You say that you believe Jesus was the literal Son of God?"

"Yes."

"And Mary, was she divine too?"

"No, she was a mortal woman. In fact, I picture her to be very much like yourself."

Miri's head shot up, and she stared at Brad.

"Hey!" he added hastily, "I didn't mean to offend you."

"I am not offended."

"All I meant was that I picture Mary much like you—a young Jewish girl, a native of Israel. I suppose she didn't have to be, but I picture her as very lovely." He hesitated, then added softly, "Like yourself."

Her face flamed red as she lowered her eyes. "Thank you." She was silent for a long moment, then said, almost shyly, "Do you know what Mary's name is in Hebrew?"

"No, what?"

"It is the same as my name. Miriam."

"Ah."

Again there was a long pause. "You are not making it any easier to ask my next question," she finally said.

That surprised him. He thought he was being the model of cooperation. "I'm sorry," he answered, although he wasn't sure exactly for what. "Please go ahead."

She took a deep breath and plunged in. "Do you believe Jesus was a god before he came to earth to be a man?"

"Yes."

"And you don't find that peculiar? That a *god* has to become a *man* in order to save other men? If you told me it was the other way around, I might question the reality of the story, but at least it would be logical. Vice versa is profoundly illogical."

Brad toyed with his glass, nodding slightly, his eyes thoughtful. He remembered that the Apostle Paul had said that the Jews found Jesus to be a stumbling block. To say that Jehovah, the god they had worshipped for centuries, would divest himself of that majesty and glory, enter life through a stable, go about like other men, and, most incredible of all, allow himself to be arrested, whipped, spit upon, crucified! No wonder that Jesus as the Messiah caused them to stumble. Only the Spirit could render such a statement not only logical, but the only possible choice.

He looked up at Miri, knowing that a quick answer now was not what she needed. Groundwork had to be laid, foundational concepts established, before she was ready for the answer. And he was not prepared to lay that foundation properly. Not yet.

To his surprise, she reached across the table and touched his arm gently. "Now it is I who have offended you," she murmured.

"Oh no, I am not offended. It's just that your question is a good one, but a deep one. I was trying to think how best to answer it." He took a deep breath. "I'm not sure I can answer your question."

It said something for this woman that her reaction was that of disappointment rather than triumph.

"But," he went on quickly, "the problem is not that there are no answers, only that I am not prepared yet to answer you."

She nodded. "I understand. Thank you for your honesty."

"But I promise you this," Brad vowed solemnly. "I will get those answers and share them with you."

Twelve

Brad put down his paintbrush and pulled out a rag to mop his brow. "You know, I can't figure out whether the Lord put the Arabs in the Middle East because they like the heat, or whether they like the heat because the Lord put them in the Middle East."

Ali grinned down at him from the top of his ladder. "What makes you think we like the heat?"

"Well, look at you two. Here I am sweating like a polar bear in a sauna bath, and your foreheads aren't even damp."

Ahkmud made a face. He was obviously a Khalidi, though more darkly complexioned and at least twenty pounds heavier than his younger brother. "Allah has blessed you with poor eyesight and no sense of smell, my friend." He was sitting below the ladder on the floor, painting the baseboards of the schoolroom. "Ali smells like the unwashed colt of a donkey, and he is doing hardly any work at all."

"Ah!" Ali cried in mock outrage. "Only because I grow faint from the odor that rises from beneath me."

Ahkmud grabbed the ladder and rocked it wildly. "Silence, little pup, or I shall bring you down to where the air is more fair."

Brad grinned broadly, watching the two brothers. In the last few days as they painted the classrooms in Ali's new school, they had kept him laughing with their gruff insults and mock battles, which did not disguise the warm affection that lay between them.

Ali dipped his brush into the can and leaned out, holding it so it was directly over Ahkmud's head. "Your tongue is slick as a serpent's belly and black as a Bedouin tent. One more word and I shall paint it white and perform a great service for the whole of mankind."

At that moment a great drop of paint broke free of the brush and plummeted downward, hitting Ahkmud squarely in the center of his jet black hair. Ali was down the ladder in a flash and darting for the door. But Ahkmud was faster. He dove across the room and wrestled him to the floor.

"Ahkmud, no!" Ali wailed. "It was an accident. I didn't mean to."

With great deliberation Ahkmud reached up with his thumb and wiped the glob of white paint from his hair.

"Brad! Help me!" Ali screamed, but Brad couldn't have walked three steps, he was laughing so hard.

"People should be warned of a dangerous beast," Ahkmud said. He took his thumb and slowly ran it down the length of Ali's nose, leaving a broad white smear. "May all see you coming and get out of your way." He stood up and let Ali free.

Brad tossed his rag to Ali, still doubled over with laughter.

"Thanks a lot, American," Ali said, only half succeeding in wiping away the smear. "I ask for arms and miltary aid, and you send cotton goods."

"Hey, little brother," Ahkmud said, "one sends cotton to one who has cotton for brains."

"All right, you two," Brad finally managed. "If you don't cut it out, I'm not going to be able to sit up tonight at the desk. How do I explain to Levi that I can't work because my sides are too sore from laughing?"

"Which reminds me," Ahkmud said, "what time is it?"

Brad looked at his watch. "Almost twelve o'clock."

"Then I must go." He handed Ali his bucket and brush. "We have a delivery from Hebron coming to the store in half an hour."

"You only fear retaliation," Ali quipped.

"Ha!" his brother snorted. "The lion flees from the goat? No chance. Besides, you are almost done now."

"Ah!" Ali retorted. "Only with the painting and fix-up. We still have all the equipment and furniture to move in, and school starts on Wednesday. That gives us only three more days to have everything ready."

Ahkmud punched him lightly on the arm as he started for the door. "Only because you have let your Mormon ideas ruin a perfectly good workday tomorrow."

There was the slightest hint of criticism in Ahkmud's voice, but Ali ignored it. "The Sabbath is not a Mormon idea, my infidel brother," he said with a patient smile. "Originally, I think it was God's."

Ahkmud shrugged and headed for the door. Brad and Ali walked to the door after him and watched him climb into a maroon Mercedes sedan. They waved as he roared away in a spray of gravel.

Ali shook his head, but his eyes were warm and affectionate. "These Moslems," he said. "They are a stubborn lot."

Brad smiled and returned to his paint bucket. "I'd better hustle too. I told Levi I'd cover for him at the desk at two-thirty. Miri took that group from England on tour today, and he has an appointment somewhere."

"So that puts an end to your touring for awhile?"

"No, they are only here for a few days. She'll be finished with them today."

Ali gave him a long speculative look. "And how is your pocketbook holding up under all this?"

Brad stopped in midstroke and pointed the paintbrush at Ali. "What is that supposed to mean?"

"Mean? Nothing. I just figured at fifteen dollars a half

day, one of these times you might run out of money."

"Oh no," Brad said. "Don't play that inscrutable Arab bit with me. I know you too well already. What's really on your mind?"

The young Arab was meticulously studying the brush strokes as he painted the wall. "Well," he finally said, "it just seems that for two people who started out as the star participants in the Middle Eastern version of the gunfight at the O.K. Corral, you seem to be getting along famously."

"Ha!" Brad retorted with more vehemence than he had intended. "You ought to come on tour with us. This morning, for example, we really got into it over the Palestinian question. I was so foolish as to suggest that Israel had treated some refugees with gross unfairness and downright intimidation in order to take over their land."

"You are a foolhardy devil, aren't you?" Ali laughed. "You're lucky she didn't bite your head off."

Brad reached up and pulled his shirt collar down, baring his neck. "Care to see the teeth marks?"

Again Ali gave him that long appraising look. "Have you made any decisions about how long you are staying yet?"

Ali studied his friend, noting that the frustrated, strung-out air that had been so evident in Brad the first few days was largely gone. His tanned face was relaxed and broke into a smile much more easily than at first. The pinched look around his eyes had smoothed out, and the nervous drumming of the fingers whenever he faced inactivity was rarely seen now. The young Arab was deeply grateful for this American Mormon, and marveled that it had only been a couple of weeks since they had first met. It seemed as though they had known each other for years.

"Well," Brad mused, cutting into Ali's thoughts.

"I was just thinking of our conversation on the plane, why you said you were coming to Israel. As I remember, it was to find yourself, set some goals, stop smothering. I was just wondering how that is coming?"

94

Brad rested his brush on the paint-can lid. "Good question. I was asking myself the same thing just the other day."

"And?"

"And I don't know for sure, but I am sure that coming here was right. Dad said my problem was that after four years of mission and Viet Nam, I had spiritual battle fatigue. Suddenly I came home with no demands on my time, no real commitments. It left me dangling in a spiritual void."

"And do you agree with him?"

"I didn't at first, but now I think he knew me better than I did. I got so frustrated at home because I felt the pressures of everybody's expectations—including my own. But there was something deeper than that bugging me. I know that now."

"Like what?"

Brad shook his head slowly. "It is hard to explain, but I was torn. On the one hand, I felt this great need to do something, to launch my life, as it were. But on the other hand, the old goals, the former decisions were no longer acceptable. Like school, for example. Suddenly just preparing for a satisfying, good-paying job was not enough. Though I am just now coming to realize it, what I've been searching for is something really meaningful to do with my life, something that will require the same kind of intense commitment and wholehearted effort I've become used to during the past four years." He gave Ali a long, searching look. "That is why I envy you."

"Me?" Ali was genuinely surprised.

Brad picked up his paintbrush and waved it in a broad gesture. "I envy you this."

"What? An unpainted room with no furniture?"

"You know what I mean. The school. A life's work that is demanding, significant, and that absolutely enthralls you."

Ali finally nodded, with great soberness. "Yes. I hadn't thought of it quite that way before, but you are right. I

95

love it. The thought of spending the next forty years here thrill me."

"Exactly! That's what I'm looking for. And Israel seems to be a good place to do it. At least for now." He dipped his brush in the bucket and began painting again.

Ali began painting again too, and for several minutes the room was quiet. Finally Ali spoke. "And do your plans include continuing with your guide service?"

Brad looked up in surprise. "Yes. Why?"

Ali's face was a mask of bland innocence. "Oh, just wondering."

"All right, Khalidi. What is it you're driving at?"

Ali shrugged, and then, almost as an afterthought, he nonchalantly added, "I just wondered if you might have other interests in one Miriam Shadmi besides her qualifications as a guide."

"Don't be ridiculous," Brad shot back, just a bit too quickly. "She is an excellent guide, and I want to really come to know Israel."

"Of course."

Brad let out his breath in a sigh of exasperation. "Ali, Miri is just—"

"A very attractive young woman," Ali cut in, finishing for him.

"Oh, come on."

"And the fact that she is interested in Christianity and Mormonism throws the old missionary instincts into high gear. Right?"

Before Brad could respond to that, Ali went on quickly. "Hey, I'm not knocking it. I think it's great, although I don't think you stand much of a chance of converting her."

"Why not?"

Ali grinned. "That's what I thought. You are, aren't you?"

"I am what?" Brad said, realizing he had just gone over to the defensive.

"Lining her up in your missionary sights."

"Well, yes. I'd like to try. You ought to hear some of her questions. In fact, I want to corner President Marks after sacrament meeting tomorrow and ask him some things."

"Listen, my friend, I wouldn't discourage you for a minute. I've told you how hard the missionaries worked on me. But compared to a Jew, a Moslem is like the man who walks up to the missionaries and begs, 'Baptize me, oh please, baptize me.' We don't have two thousand years of persecution at the hands of the Christians to hang us up."

"I know," Brad sighed. "But in some ways, she is so open. I've got to try."

"Absolutely. But if she doesn't respond, then what?"

"What do you mean, then what? If she doesn't respond, she doesn't respond."

"And no further interest?"

"Well, we'll be friends, of course."

Ali nodded soberly and went back to his work, humming softly to himself. It took a minute or two for Brad to realize that he was humming the old tune, "It Seems to Me I've Heard That Song Before."

* * * * * *

Brad and Ali stood around after sacrament meeting, idly chatting with several students from the Brigham Young University Study Abroad program.

Brad saw the branch president finish with his counselor and start to put his scriptures in his briefcase. "President," Brad said, moving over to him, "do you have a minute I could chat with you?"

"Certainly, Brad. Come into my 'office.' " He motioned to the open space behind the table on which sat a homemade mini-pulpit. He pulled up a folding chair for Brad and the rickety piano bench for himself.

The branch "chapel" was a large open room in the basement of a small hotel in East Jerusalem. The facilities were less than adequate, but both last week and this the spirit in the meetings had been remarkable. Part of it, Brad sensed, was due to the man who sat before him now.

President Marks was a broad man in every sense of the word. Physically he was built along the lines of a touring bus. At first glance he gave an impression of obesity, but one had only to watch him move to see that flab found no place on his body. And yet he was a gentle man, radiating a kindness and sensitivity that seemed incongruous for such a large man. The previous week had been the first Sabbath in Israel for the BYU group as well as for Brad, and President Marks and his wife had been the sacrament meeting speakers. They had spoken about the land of Israel and how its destiny was interwoven with the destiny of the Latter-day Saints. Both had deeply impressed Brad. And today, in just a few brief words as he announced the sacrament hymn, he had set a mood that made the simple ordinance take on a new meaning.

Now he watched Brad out of clear blue eyes that sparkled with a hint of humor and yet at the same time a deep sense of concern. "How can I help you?"

"Well," Brad said slowly, "I need to ask you a doctrinal question."

"Hey, listen!" President Marks chuckled. "I'm just an old Idaho potato picker. If you have doctrinal questions, we ought to get Brother Spencer over here." Brother Spencer was the religion professor who had come as the BYU representative for the Semester Abroad program.

"I suppose we could," Brad said. "It's probably a dumb question."

The older man's smile broadened. "Well, now, if it's a dumb question, maybe I can help you. In college I was real good at asking those. Fire away. If we need Brother Spencer, we'll call him."

Brad took a deep breath, then let it out slowly, the frustration evident in his eyes. "What's the best way—I mean, suppose you have a Jewish person. You think there might be a slight—very slight," he added hastily, "chance they could be converted. What is the best way to approach it?"

The president looked at him, his expression half thoughtful, half concerned. "That is a tough one. You know that we cannot do any active proselyting in Israel, both by the laws of the government and by the directive from President Lee. It can be done only through association when a person asks."

"This person is asking."

"About Mormonism?"

"Not directly. Just about Christianity. But I figure she may as well get the best."

"True. Well, it is a special challenge. We have found that we even have to be careful of certain words we use with the Jewish people."

"Really?"

"Yes. Their only experience is with other Christian churches, and if you know anything about their history, you know that the Christian interaction with the Jews has been pretty sordid—persecution, torture, inquisitions, massacres. They don't find a lot in Christianity to attract them. Also, as you know, we have a special vocabulary of our own, and even take common Christian words and give them a special Mormon flavor."

"Such as?"

"Well, take the word *saint*, for example."

"Of course," Brad said. "I see what you mean. If a Jew were familiar with Catholic saints—"

"Exactly. Here are a few others. *Deacon, bishop, priest, stake center*—they think that's a restaurant. Talk about doing *sealing work* in the temple and they'll think you're painting the *ceilings* at the synagogue, which is what they call a temple. If another church converts a Jew, they turn him into a Christian. If we convert another Christian, we say that we have brought him into the house of Israel. Thus, when a Jew says *gentile* he means anyone not Jewish; when we say it, we mean anyone not Mormon." The president gave a wry smile. "Try explaining to your

Jewish friend that she's really gentile and see what happens."

Brad considered past encounters with Miri and decided that idea could wait for awhile.

"Do you understand what Zion and Zionism mean to an Israeli?"

"Somewhat," Brad replied.

"Zionism is the name given to the movement to establish Israel as a national homeland for the Jewish people. The state of Israel has been dominated by Zionists since its beginnings. That is why you'll often hear Arab leaders say that it is not the Jews they oppose, but the Zionists."

Brad nodded. "Which is a far sight different from what we mean by Zion."

"And that's the point. Converting a Jew requires a whole different approach from normal missionary work. I even try to refer to Jesus as the *Messiah* instead of as the *Christ*. Messiah is the Hebrew equivalent for Christ, but it doesn't have the same connotations in the Jewish mind."

"I see what you mean," Brad said, the discouragement in his voice hard to miss.

"But," President Marks said, "I have two suggestions, depending on how religious and how knowledgeable she is."

"Not very and very," Brad said quickly. "She says her family is not very religious, but she is a guide—that's how I came to know her." He stopped as he realized how true that was. "Anyway, she's read the New Testament a lot. She says she believes Jesus was a great rabbi, but she finds the theology very illogical."

"Well, that could be a lot worse."

"So, your two suggestions are?"

"First, if you find an appropriate moment—and I strongly suggest you heed the Spirit's guidance as to timing—give her the Book of Mormon. Remember what the title page says."

Brad probed his memory.

President Marks quoted, "It is for the convincing of *Jew*

and Gentile that Jesus is the Christ—the Messiah."

"Of course," Brad said, his voice excited. "It's a great missionary tool."

"And second, use the Old Testament."

Brad frowned. If expertise in the Old Testament were measured on a scale of one to ten, he would have to get a very low number.

"Once you know how to study it, the Old Testament bears powerful and consistent witness of the Savior. It is Jewish scripture. Convert them with it."

"But how? Give me some examples."

"Oh, there are hundreds. Take the Law of Moses as a case in point." Suddenly President Marks stopped. "Listen, I've got a better idea. Are you busy tonight?"

"Ali and I were going to come to the fireside, but I thought they announced that you were the speaker."

An apologetic grin appeared. "I am. But I haven't prepared anything yet. And that's my idea. Last year I made a presentation to the students called 'The Old Testament as a Witness for Jesus Christ.' This new group hasn't heard it."

Now Brad was really enthusiastic. "That would be super!"

"Even then I can only hit the highlights. But once you get the idea, you'll start reading the Old Testament with a whole new pair of eyes."

"That's great! Thanks, President. We'll be there."

"Thank you, Brad, for giving me a topic. I've been worrying about it all day. See you tonight. Oh, by the way. Are you and Ali going to be able to join us for the concert tomorrow night?"

"If you are sure you have enough tickets."

"We do. The Israeli Philharmonic is an outstanding orchestra. We try to get each Study Abroad group to at least one concert."

"Good. We'll plan on it. We'll meet you at the concert hall at seven-thirty."

Thirteen

It was a warm summer evening in Jerusalem, with a hint of a breeze stirring the air. Brad and Ali were standing with a small group of students taking their last farewells after the concert, when Brad saw her. She had just come out of the Convention Center and stood for a moment looking around. She was wearing a dress of black voile, its square neckline and long sleeves trimmed with a narrow band of lace. Black satin heels, which matched her dress perfectly, added to the look of simple elegance. Her black hair was pulled back away from her face, accenting the fineness of her features. It was the first time Brad had seen her really dressed up, and even at this distance, she was striking. His were not the only eyes that had lifted to watch her. Half the males in the area had stopped their conversations in midsentence, much to the dismay of their companions.

Brad stepped away from Ali and the group and started to raise his hand to wave, but he stopped abruptly and quickly rejoined his group as a tall, broad-shouldered man in a sports jacket and open-necked shirt stepped out of the doors behind her and moved to stand beside her. Much to Brad's dismay, Miri looked up at him, smiled, and slipped her arm easily into his. When they started moving in his direction, Brad quickly turned away and pushed deeper into the group of students, afraid Miri might see him. But it was a pointless worry. It was obvious that she was not seeing much of anything else as she looked up into the tall Israeli's face, eagerly taking in every word he was saying. Brad caught a quick burst of Miri's husky laughter as they passed him.

What did you expect? he chided himself. *A beautiful Jewish girl who gave guided tours during the day and then retired into a convent for the evening? Forget it.* But his eyes wouldn't obey his mind; they followed as the couple moved easily through the parking lot. It didn't help at all to see them stop at a gleaming, dark blue Porsche and have him open the door for Miri to slide in.

Brad yanked on Ali's arm, an idea suddenly striking him. "Let's go!"

Ali looked around, startled. "What?"

"Look, can we go? Now!" The Porsche had started with a low roar and was joining the line of slow-moving cars. "I'll explain on the way. Let's move it!"

The others in the group looked surprised as they said hasty goodbyes, and Brad pulled Ali into a trot, keeping one eye on the low sports car, which was making slow but steady progress toward the exit.

"What's the matter?" Ali asked, as Brad threw open the Volkswagen door, jumped in, and kicked the motor into life. "What's going on?"

"I want to see where someone is going," Brad muttered, smacking his hand against the wheel to make the little car stop sputtering from the sudden gush of gas to the carburetor. When the engine steadied, he spun out around a passing car, narrowly missing its right front fender. The line to the exit now stretched out twenty or thirty vehicles behind the Porsche, so Brad gunned the VW out around the back of the line, then rocketed forward, darting into a place three cars behind the Porsche that was barely big enough for a medium-sized Tonka truck. The angry honk that shrieked out behind him came as close to profanity as one could achieve within the limitations of an automobile's horn.

"Welcome to California!" Ali breathed, his hands pressed white against the dashboard.

"Sorry." Brad stuck his hand out the window and gave an apologetic wave to the car behind him.

"Just who is it you're interested in following?" Ali asked, regaining his composure.

"Oh," Brad said, trying to act nonchalantly. "That dark blue Porsche in front of us."

"Just the Porsche? Not anyone in it?"

"I thought I recognized someone," Brad stalled, suddenly feeling foolish.

"Who?" Just then the Porsche reached the street and turned right. For a brief second the passenger was revealed in the glare of the streetlight, and Ali answered his own question. "Miri!"

Brad nodded, feeling like a four-year-old who has just been caught standing over the fishbowl with a wiggling fish in his hand.

"Is the point to *catch* her or *run over* her?"

Brad laughed. "Good question."

"Who is she with?"

"Don't know him. A tall, good-looking dude."

"Oh." Ali managed to pack more expression into that one word than most people would achieve in a twenty-minute oration.

It was Brad's turn at the street, and he spurted out into the traffic, accelerating as rapidly as the VW could muster.

"Tell me, Kojak," Ali said in a deep rumbling voice, "have you done much tailing since you got into this line of work?"

"No."

"Then I suggest you not get too close. Not only are you in a car distinctive in its class, but it is one that would be instantly recognized by the suspect in question, one Miriam Shadmi."

Brad's foot came off the accelerator, and the motor immediately lessened its howl of protest. The taillights of the Porsche were still clearly in sight about a block ahead, but the evaporating distance between the cars steadied.

"In addition to which, unless you fixed the right front fender, you have only one headlight."

Brad groaned. "That's right!"

"Well, short of a neon sign saying, 'Hey guys! We're following you,' there's probably not a more effective way to give away a tail. Hang back and try to keep some traffic between you and him."

Brad obediently followed Ali's instructions, letting a taxi pull around between them. Then the Porsche caught a yellow traffic light and braked hard to a stop.

"What do I do now?" Brad asked.

"Keep the taxi in front of you and come up close behind him so it blocks you from view."

The light turned green, and the sports car moved out smoothly and swiftly. "Fall back at least two blocks," Ali commanded.

They drove for several minutes in silence, Brad occasionally spurting forward when he temporarily lost sight of his quarry. The Porsche took a quick left turn at the next intersection. As Brad approached, the light turned yellow. He stabbed at the brake, then realized such a delay could lose them, so just as quickly, he hit the gas and leaned the Volkswagen into the corner, taking the light at full red. A panel truck blasted its horn as Brad rocketed past him. If they were keeping score for the most unpopular driver in Jerusalem tonight, Brad had it going away.

Ali spoke up when the car had come out of the sliding turn and settled into the straightaway. "At the risk of sounding like a broken record and knowing I'm probably a hundred miles off target—" he stopped, searching for the right words.

"Go on," Brad said, sensing what was coming.

"All your protests last Friday about how casual your interest in Miri is seem a little hollow about now. You know that, don't you?"

Brad was silent and concentrated on the taillights ahead of him.

"Don't be ridiculous, right?" Ali said.

"I'm just curious about who she's with, and where he's taking her."

Ali grinned. "Some curiosity! We are not just out here risking life and limb in the Jerusalem Grand Prix. You might sell that to some dumb American kid, but with a brilliant, perceptive young Arab boy, it won't wash."

Brad nodded reluctantly. As usual, Ali, beneath that easy good humor, knew the score—even better than Brad. "All right, I guess I do find her very interesting."

"Interesting?"

"All right, you sadist. I find her attractive."

"That's more like it."

"You won't let a man have any illusions, will you."

Surprisingly, Ali grew very sober. "Speaking of illusions, are you facing the biggest one?"

"I know what you're driving at. But I'm working on her. If I could convert her, then—"

"Is this the cool-headed Mormon missionary talking? Or the young man who sees his girl with another man and jumps into his car in hot pursuit?"

Brad was silent, not knowing the answer to that himself. "I think there is more hope of converting her than the typical Jewish person. She really seems—"

"Oh, oh!" Ali cut in again, pointing ahead of them. "Your boy is turning left."

"So?"

"He's turning the wrong way into a one-way street."

They were headed north now, out of Jerusalem, and the traffic was thinning out rapidly.

"What do I do?"

"Don't follow him! Either he's made a mistake—and that seems unlikely, he's been driving as though he knows the city well—or he's on to us. You follow him the wrong way on a one-way street, and there'll be no question about what we're doing."

"Oh well, let's give it up. It's no big thing." The disappointment was evident in Brad's voice.

"Maybe we could out-fox the fox," Ali said a moment later as he peered down the street where the sports car had turned. It was dark. No taillights were visible.

"How?"

"Either he's turned off his lights, or he took a quick right to get off the one-way street. If he did that, there's only one major place he can come out. Hit it, and we'll see if we can be waiting for him."

Brad punched the gas pedal down as Ali directed him toward the likely intersection. Two minutes later he pointed to a spot along the curb that was deep between two trucks. "Pull in here. If he's coming out, he'll be coming out of that next intersection."

Brad pulled over and cut his lights. He smiled at Ali. "Crazy, huh?"

Ali shrugged. "Actually it's kind of fun. We had one class in surveillance techniques at the PLO camp. But we never got to do it for real. And I think," he said, trying not to sound too excited, "my instructor would be right proud of me. There he is!"

The Porsche eased out of the side street and then moved away, the rich, throaty roar of its engine clear even from where they sat.

"Okay, give him some running room and leave your lights off this time. If he sees this one-eyed beast following him again, he'll sprint like a scared rabbit. And this bug ain't no way going to keep up with his rabbit."

Brad obeyed, somewhat nervous to be driving without lights.

A few minutes later Ali spoke again. "I can't figure where he's heading. We are nearly out of the city and headed north for Nablus. Maybe he's going to take her on a quiet country drive in the moonlight."

"You're a real comedian," Brad growled.

"For a guy who's only curious, you sure are touchy."

A car was approaching from the other direction and, as

it came up on the VW, its lights clicked off and on twice.

"Oh, oh!" Ali said as it passed. "That was the police. You'd better turn on your lights, or we may have a three-some in this little party."

Brad reluctantly turned on the headlights and watched his rearview mirror anxiously. But the taillights receded rapidly and then disappeared.

"Now let's see if our man sees us and panics and runs," Ali said.

For the next several minutes the Porsche drove steadily. There was no increase in speed. They had left the city now, and only scattered houses, pale and ghostlike in the light of a half moon, appeared along the road. It was really quite pleasant, with the warm evening breeze streaming in through the open windows. *Yeah,* Brad thought. *A great night to park.*

Suddenly up ahead the right taillight winked a bright red and then winked again. Then both brightened as the driver braked.

"He's turning."

"That's odd," Ali said. "I don't remember any main roads out here. Maybe he's going to someone's house."

"Do I follow him?" Brad slowed down as they approached the spot where the Porsche had turned.

"Let's see what we've got. I'd hate to follow him into someone's driveway."

It wasn't a driveway. It was a road, though not much of one. As Brad turned, the sweep of the headlights showed that the pavement ended immediately. He stopped as he rolled onto gravel. A dirt track led on into an olive grove.

"Well, that settles it," Ali said as Brad brought the car to a halt. "You certainly can't follow him up that without being noticed. We may as well—"

A piercing white light exploded in Brad's eyes, and a deep voice bellowed a guttural noise in his ear. He jumped so hard his knees hit the steering wheel.

Stunned, he stared into the light. He couldn't see who was holding it, but he didn't have to.

"He says to get out very slowly," Ali said. "And to keep our hands in sight."

Brad had learned one thing about the military. A man with rank is to be obeyed without question—and this man had placed the flashlight so that it very clearly illuminated his rank—an M-16 rifle. He lifted his hands slowly and carefully, his heart pounding like an artillery barrage. The light moved back, and Brad's door was yanked open. Again the voice barked out a command.

"He wants me out too and both of us spread-eagled on the hood," Ali translated. "Move very slowly."

They obeyed. Brad squinted briefly into the light, then turned his head slightly so he could see their captor out of the corner of his eye. There was no question about it. It was the driver of the Porsche. But he was puzzled. Where was Miri? Probably hidden out in the trees somewhere.

Expert hands searched him quickly for weapons, then moved to Ali to do the same. Suddenly Brad understood and went cold. If I were an Israeli, and a beat-up old Volkswagen started following me late at night, what would I assume? Arab terrorists were too grim a reality to ignore. He admitted a grudging admiration that this man had taken action to protect Miri.

Then an even worse thought hit Brad. Where *was* Miri? What if she comes to see what is happening? He could picture the look on her face when she learned who her pursuers were. The Israeli stepped back, clearly visible in the light of the headlight. Brad and Ali slowly straightened and turned around.

From the look on his face, it was clear that his unsuccessful search for weapons had not greatly improved his mood. He lowered the flashlight, but the black muzzle of the rifle was set in stone. Again the flow of rapid Arabic came pouring out.

"He wants to know why we're following him," Ali

murmured. "That's a rough translation, minus a few choice terms."

"Well, don't tell him!" Brad hissed. "Think of something."

Brad grunted in pain as the snout of the rifle jabbed sharply into his ribs. The eyes staring into his were like two daggers of ice.

"Please *do* tell me why," he barked in rough but clearly understandable English.

Straightening again slowly and rubbing the tender spot, Brad spoke politely. "Look, we're sorry. There's been a mistake. We thought you were someone else."

"Shut up!" the Israeli barked. He looked at Ali. "You, Arab. You tell me why you follow me."

"Well," Ali said, giving Brad a quick glance, "we saw you at the concert with—" Brad cut off the critical word with a sharp kick to Ali's leg.

If he hadn't expected a reaction from the Israeli, the swift blow would have left Brad retching on the ground. As it was, he saw the sudden flip of the man's weapon, and dropped back as the butt of the rifle struck him solidly in the solar plexus. It made him gasp sharply, and he dropped to his knees.

"Hey!" Ali cried, diving for the weapon. The butt swung upward, catching Ali with a glancing blow on the chin. He flew backwards, hit the hood of the Volkswagen, and slowly crumpled to the ground.

Brad saw it all from his knees, but didn't turn his head. He gave one slow moan and toppled over onto his face in the gravel, where he lay trembling. His trembling was not faked, nor was it alone from the pain. Containing the fury rising in him was almost beyond him, but containment was his only hope. He groaned again as he clutched a handful of gravel beneath him.

"On your feet," came the command. Brad ignored it.

The feet crunched twice on the gravel, and Brad was yanked roughly onto his back. As he turned over he flung the gravel upwards, catching his opponent full in the face.

The Israeli howled in pain and grabbed for his eyes, jerking the M-16's muzzle straight up in the air. Brad sprang into a crouch, brought his two hands into a club, and swung with all the fury that was seething in him. It caught the tall Israeli right between the buttons of his sport coat and cut him down like a sapling hit by a Howitzer.

Brad staggered to his feet, breathing hard, and retrieved the rifle, leaving the Israeli where he lay, gasping frantically for breath. He moved to Ali and bent over him. An ugly red welt was visible on his jaw, but he was reviving. Brad helped him up to a sitting position. Even in the poor light of the headlamp, the gray undertone of his complexion showed he was still in a mild state of shock.

"Are you okay?" Brad asked anxiously, careful to keep the rifle trained on the Israeli.

Ali managed a wan smile. "Yeah. I'll be all right." He looked over at the sprawled figure, still twisting in agony. "I don't think he liked being followed. What did you do to him?"

"Evened the score for you." Sympathy was not one of Brad's more obvious virtues at the moment. But satisfied that Ali was going to be all right, he moved back to the Israeli. He grasped him by the belt and lifted him up and down several times as he had seen trainers do to football players when the wind was knocked out of them. Gradually the man's color began to return and his breathing slowed to a more reasonable rate. He hitched himself up and leaned against the Volkswagen, his eyes wary and full of hate, but not fearful.

Brad closed in on him, the muzzle of the M-16 in a position to suggest a strong hint. "Look," he said calmly, "I tried to explain to you that we meant you no harm, but you wouldn't listen."

"What *do* you want?" the man asked in a hoarse whisper.

"Nothing." Brad extracted the clip from the rifle and ejected the shell in the chamber. "We made a mistake. We're sorry. But next time you ought to give a man a chance to tell his story." Brad moved back, the rifle hanging loosely now. "We'll leave your rifle exactly one mile down the road on the right side."

Brad stepped back to Ali and helped him to his feet. "Let's go."

Suddenly a sharp voice rang out behind them. "Don't move!" The voice was firm and very impelling. "I have a pistol pointed at your backs. Drop the rifle!"

Brad obeyed, his heart sinking. He would have known that husky voice anywhere.

"Move into the light where I can see you."

Ali grinned weakly. "I think we had better obey the lady, don't you?"

Fourteen

It was past ten, and the hotel lobby was deserted and quiet. Brad was so deeply engrossed in his book that he wasn't aware of her until she was nearly at the desk. If someone had wired his chair with electricity and suddenly dropped the switch for a full charge, he wouldn't have come to his feet with any more dispatch.

"Oh, hello," he murmured.

Miri smiled. In his embarrassment, Brad couldn't tell if it was a smile of friendly welcome or more like that of a tiger as it eyed its intended victim.

"Hello," she said sweetly. "Brad Kennison, I presume."

Brad groaned inwardly. It was the tiger. But he decided to try a tentative smile. "How are you?"

"Well, as a matter of fact, I'm curious."

"Oh? About what?"

"Two things. First, are you still planning on coming to our home Saturday night? Father asked me to remind you."

Brad hedged. Levi had asked him last week to come to his home for an informal evening with some friends. At the time he had been very pleased at the prospects. Now . . .

"Well?"

"Well," Brad murmured, thinking rapidly, "I may have to—well, I'm not sure." He didn't want to offend the

Shadmis in any way. And yet how could he spend an evening making small talk with Miri after Sunday evening's disaster?

"I see," she said slowly. "That leads me to my second question. Why have you been deliberately avoiding me these past four days?"

"Well," Brad hesitated, "I've been helping Ali. School started yesterday. I have to prepare for that English class I'm teaching." He stopped, realizing how empty the whole monologue sounded.

"Uh huh," she said, her dark eyes holding just a hint of amusement. "And is that why you keep going through the hotel lobby as though you're making your way through an armed mine field?"

"Who, me?"

"And why you haven't eaten in the hotel except when you're sure I'm gone somewhere? Not even breakfast?"

"Well, we get an early start at the school."

"Oh really," Miri said.

He decided that the cat and mouse game had gone on long enough. "Listen, I am really sorry about Sunday night. I have never felt so ridiculous in my whole life."

Her expression was grave, but Brad had the distinct impression that a laugh was struggling to break its way to the surface. "Oh?" she said, her voice half mocking.

"I don't know why it is that whenever I'm around you, I keep doing these idiotic things," he finally said in exasperation.

"A girl loves to be told how she brings out the best in someone."

"I didn't mean *that*," he started, and then saw that she was playing with him. "Anyway, I *am* sorry. How's your friend?"

"He claimed he was fine. But I noticed that he walked me to the door very carefully Sunday night. What did you hit him with? He wouldn't talk about it."

"Nothing."

Her eyebrows shot up.

"I mean nothing that I picked up." Brad held up his hands, interlocking the fingers as he had done that night. "Just this. When I saw him club Ali, I'm afraid I lost my cool."

"How is Ali, anyway?"

"Fine. He's got a big bruise, but it hasn't slowed him down at all. He still talks a mile a minute."

"David felt a little better when I told him you were a Viet Nam veteran."

Brad shook his head, cursing himself for the hundredth time for deciding to follow Miri that night. "Does he always carry an M-16 and a .45 automatic with him on a date?"

She laughed lightly. "As you know, I can be very fierce."

Brad pulled a face at her. "Come on, be serious."

"David is in the military. He is a good friend of my brother, Nathan."

And of yours, Brad thought, remembering how she had looked up at him after the concert.

"Israeli soldiers are required to keep their weapons with them at all times," she added.

"I'll try and remember that."

"Now will you tell me what happened? As I told you, David refused to discuss it. Partly anger, partly hurt pride, I think."

"I don't blame him for being angry. What he did under the circumstances was very admirable."

"But to come to blows, Brad! Why didn't you explain to him? David is a kind man."

Brad smiled. That could be a good sign. Obviously she didn't know this fellow too well.

"Really, he is. Please, tell me what happened."

"How much did you see?"

"Nothing. David gave me the pistol and made me go hide among the olive trees. I waited for a few minutes and then decided to sneak down to see what was happening. I saw you standing over David with the rifle."

If compliments were being passed out for courage, this dark haired *sabra* could get in line. She had jumped into a potentially deadly situation to help David as swiftly as he had moved to protect her.

"Well," Brad said sheepishly, "Ali started to tell him that we were following you. I could just picture the look on your face when he asked you to verify our story. I just wanted to get out of there as soon as possible. When Ali started to explain, I kicked him in the shins. Your friend thought I was trying to stop him from talking. That's when he hit me and knocked me down."

"He hit you too?"

"I don't blame him. Anyway, Ali reacted and went for him, so—" He shrugged. "Will you tell him how sorry I am? It was really a stupid thing to do."

"I will tell David when I see him again. He went back to his unit on Monday."

For a long moment, she looked at him, her eyes unreadable and very disturbing. "And why *were* you following me, Brad?"

"We saw you coming out of the concert and—"

"I know. You said that Sunday night. But why?"

Brad had given that a lot of thought himself in the past four days. He decided to be perfectly honest and direct. "I don't know."

It wasn't much, but it seemed to satisfy her. "And you were so sure I'd be angry that you've been avoiding me these four days. I'm not sure that speaks very highly of your opinion of me."

"No," Brad protested quickly. "It was just that I felt so embarrassed about the whole mess that I didn't want to face you."

"Does that mean you'll be looking for another guide?"

He searched her eyes. "No, I hadn't planned on it. I just thought a few days' wait might not hurt."

116

"I'm offering discount rates this week." She smiled at his surprised look. "Fifteen dollars for a half-day tour, or fifteen dollars if you would like the full day. It is the best rate in town."

He stared at her, his eyes incredulous. "Are you serious?"

"Of course."

"I can't do that."

"I see. Then let's say ten dollars a half-day or ten dollars for the full day."

"Miri! You know what I mean!"

"Five dollars a day, and that's my last offer. My father won't let me take any less," she added with an impish grin.

"Okay, okay," Brad said, his expression still one of disbelief. "Fifteen dollars it is. But I provide the car. And definitely book me for the full-day program."

She put out her hand. "You drive a hard bargain, Mr. Kennison. When would you like to begin?"

"Well," he said slowly, holding her hand for just a shade longer than was necessary, "I've been very busy. I couldn't possibly leave before tomorrow morning. Is that too soon?"

She shook her head quickly and withdrew her hand. "Tomorrow would be fine. What about your class?"

"Friday is the Moslem Sabbath, remember? No school. How's that for luck?"

"Perfect," Miri said, the dimple in her left cheek showing as she smiled.

Brad was still half doubtful. "You're really not angry about Sunday night?"

She looked at him for a long moment. Then she lowered her eyes to avoid his probing gaze. "No, I think it is one of the nicest compliments I have had in a long time. And what shall I tell my father about Saturday evening?"

Brad gave her a thoughtful look. "Will David be on leave again?"

Miri laughed in delight. "No, of course not. But Nathan will."

"Nathan I can face. Tell your father I'd be delighted to come."

Fifteen

In addition to the four Shadmis and Brad, there were five others in the relatively small Shadmi living room. Miri's uncle, Shlomo Shadmi, whom Levi was helping to get started in business, was several years younger than Levi, but clearly cut from the same stuff as his brother. He had the squat build, the stiff wiry hair, and the piercing blue eyes. His wife, Ruth, was the perfect stereotype of a Jewish grandmother—pleasant brown eyes, a kindly warm face, steel gray hair pulled back in a bun.

Avriel Cohen and his American wife were neighbors of the Shadmis. He was one of the justices of the Israeli Supreme Court and every inch a gentleman of infinite refinement. According to Miri, his wife, Rachel, had been a high-fashion model in New York's finest salons. Watching her now, Brad didn't doubt it in the least. Though now in her early fifties, she was still a stunning woman. If he was every inch a gentleman, she was every bit a sophisticated woman. Brad felt almost intimidated by who they were and the very power of their physical presence, but they had quickly put him at ease. They were warm, gracious, and totally unaffected by their status.

The final member of the group was Sergeant Yitzhak Narciss, Nathan's driver, chief assistant, confidant, and friend. Brad marveled at that. In the United States Army sergeants didn't spend a social evening at their commanding officer's home, especially when he was a colonel. But he had heard that Israeli officers wore their rank lightly, earning the respect of their subordinates rather than demanding it. Narciss was solidly built and as lean and hard as Nathan. He was slightly balding and had alert, almost darting brown eyes. He had the look of a man very much in command of himself.

Brad arrived five minutes early, and Miri introduced him to her mother, an attractive woman who had given Miri her clear complexion, finely cut features, and deep brown eyes. Brad liked her immediately, and appreciated her efforts to help him feel comfortable as the others arrived. As she and Miri served glasses of wine to the others, it was Miri's mother who brought Brad a glass of orange soda.

"Levi tells me that Mormons don't drink alcoholic beverages," she murmured. "Do you drink soda pop?"

"Most definitely," Brad answered, grateful for her concern and consideration.

Bowls of nuts, dates, apples, pears, oranges, and tangerines followed, and very quickly the group launched into animated conversation—mostly in English for Brad's benefit, but with occasional lapses into Hebrew. It was comparable to being caught in a flash flood, and Brad struggled to keep his head above the conversational torrent.

The mood was intense, passionate, and fast-moving, and rarely focused on trivia. Current political events dominated—the latest developments in the Watergate crisis, the Arab oil embargo, Israel's soaring inflation, the latest artillery duel in the Sinai. There was no lull, the only ebb and flow coming when the group split into two or three sub-groups, all talking rapidly, intensely, gesturing emphatically.

Someone mentioned the name of Henry Kissinger and his increasing power in the United States government. For a moment there was silence. Then Avriel Cohen, the judge, spoke up, puffing thoughtfully on his pipe. "Mr.

Kissinger may have a chance to do more than advise Mr. Nixon on Mideast affairs. Speculation is heavy in the Knesset that Mr. Nixon is just looking for a graceful way to dump William Rogers, and then he will make Mr. Kissinger his Secretary of State."

Several of the group shook their heads sadly at that news, and Brad noted that Miri was watching him closely for a reaction. She had warned him yesterday that he might come in for some flak. "Israelis feel very strongly about things," she had said, "and they may ask you some very blunt questions. But you can be blunt with them also. You will never lose an Israeli's respect by speaking honestly of your feelings. He may grow angry and violently disagree with you—" At that point she had seen his grin, and they both laughed, remembering their own encounters. "We have a saying," she had continued. "Whenever you have three Jews come together, you will have four strong opinions. So do not be afraid to speak up."

Rachel Cohen looked over at Brad and shook her head in mock sadness. "You must forgive them," she said. "Israelis have three national sports—soccer, war, and criticizing America."

Brad smiled. "I'm learning that."

"But do we criticize without cause?" the sergeant asked, leaning forward and speaking with his hands. "America tries to tell Israel what she can and cannot do."

The justice's wife smiled sweetly at him, then turned to Brad again. "You must understand, Brad. What Yitzhak is saying is that Israel wants America's help, but only if it is money. No suggestions, please."

"Some of us," Nathan spoke up, "wish that Israel would stop taking America's money for that very reason."

"That is easy to say now," Rachel shot back. "If it weren't for American dollars—federal aid as well as private contributions—there would be no Israel today, and you know it."

Nathan's father broke in. "What Rachel says is true. It

121

is a great dilemma for us now that America is changing."

"Brad has a better solution," Miri said, catching him totally by surprise. Everyone turned to look at him.

"I do?"

Mira nodded. "Brad thinks Israel should trust only in God for its defense."

"That's not what I said," Brad said, as he shot her a devastating look. But she only smiled. It was almost as though she wanted him to challenge the others in the same way as he had challenged her.

"I said I didn't think Israel is wise to trust only in herself. I don't think she's wise to trust only in America either. It just seems tragic that the people who gave the world the idea of one true God no longer look to him in what may be the hour of their greatest need."

"Only because God no longer looks to us," Nathan said quickly.

"Nathan!" his mother said sharply. "Do not speak like that of God."

"Why not? Offer me one proof that God still cares for us as a people."

"The state of Israel," Brad said softly. "Here you are in fulfillment of prophecy."

"No!" Nathan shot back hotly, "not because of prophecy. Because of determination, because of sacrifice, because we refuse anymore to die simply to please the God who chose us."

The rest watched the two young men, and Brad was suddenly tempted to back down from an open confrontation. After all, he was the guest here. But then he remembered Miri's advice about speaking his mind. He took a breath and plowed in.

"That is one of the great ironies I find in this land. Israel is the only country in the world that uses the Bible as a textbook in its public schools. Your children know the history. They know the sites, they know the stories, and yet you ignore the most important thread of it all—that

122

God is behind your history. God *is* your history! How can you ignore the hand of God in bringing Israel into being? In 1967 you fought what could easily be the most miraculous war in history. People call it the 'incredible' war. Can't you see divine help in that?"

Yitzhak and Nathan both started to speak simultaneously, but Yitzhak prevailed. "No. I see the help of brilliant planning, careful strategy, and flawless military execution of that strategy. The Six Day War was incredible because of the way we did it, not because of God."

Levi Shadmi cleared his throat, letting the tension ease slightly, and then spoke. "Do not be too sure, Yitzhak. David faced Goliath because he had great confidence in the power of his sling. But he said to the giant, 'You come to me with a sword and spear, but I come to you in the name of the Lord God of hosts.' Perhaps that is a lesson we should not forget."

"Brad is a Mormon," Miri interjected. "Mormons take their religion very seriously." She smiled at him. "They call themselves Israelites too. They believe they are descendants of the tribe of Ephraim."

That surprised Brad completely. He and Miri talked almost constantly about Christianity, but he had hardly said a word to her yet about Mormonism. Where was she getting her information from?

That interested the others immensely, and for the next twenty minutes they threw question after question at him. Brad talked of living prophets, the Word of Wisdom, the Mormon concept of temples, the members' special feelings for Judah. He talked about the great apostasy and the need for a restoration.

"I am well aware," he continued, in response to a question from Miri about the apostasy, "that so-called Christianity has been responsible for many of the Jewish persecutions down through the ages. That is not the natural product of Christianity, but of apostate Christians. No true follower of Christ would seek to persecute the Jews.

That is why there had to be a restoration of the truth."

Miri's mother spoke up. "So Mormons do not think the Jews crucified Jesus?"

Brad took a deep breath. He had been expecting that question from Miri and had thought about his answer a great deal. There was no sense trying to duck it. "We accept the New Testament as a historically accurate record, which means—"

"Which means the Jews were responsible," Nathan broke in.

"The Romans actually carried out the execution, but the Jewish religious leaders were responsible for it," Brad admitted. "But," he went on hurriedly, "that is something quite different from saying the Jewish *people* are responsible. One group of Jews—evil men—rejected him and conspired to bring about his death. But another group—which included people like Peter, James, John, Mary Magdalene, Matthew, Nathanael—all of them were also Jewish, and they accepted him. Christianity was totally Jewish in the beginning. It would be as foolish to say that the Jews—as a people—are to blame for Christ's death as it would be to say that the Jews—as a people—are responsible for Christianity."

Something was still digging at Nathan. He lit a cigarette and turned to Brad. "So you reject the idea that God has been punishing the Jews for the death of Jesus for the last two thousand years."

"In the sense you mean it, yes. I reject that. We do not believe that God punishes one person for the evils committed by another."

"Do you believe the god of the Jews is the god of the Christians? Of the Mormons?"

"Yes."

"Then why has he allowed the Jews to suffer so much down through the centuries? Our people have committed themselves to him above all others. They have worshipped him for three thousand years without fail, while all around them the Gentiles have worshipped frogs and crocodiles. And who has suffered? The Gentiles? Not on your life."

"The Mormons have suffered too," Miri said, again surprising Brad with her knowledge. "They were persecuted, driven from state to state in America. Their first prophet was killed by a mob. Six thousand Mormon pioneers died when they were driven out by their enemies and had to cross the plains to Utah."

"Six thousand is far short of six million," Nathan snapped, obviously irritated at his sister's interruption. "Have you been to Yad Vashem yet?" he demanded.

Brad looked blank.

"We are going there tomorrow," Miri answered for him. Then to Brad she added, "It is the memorial for the Jews killed in the Holocaust."

"Enough of this bickering over who has suffered the most," Cohen broke in. "Six thousand or six million, either is a great tragedy. I wish to hear Brad's answer to Nathan's question. If you do believe in God and say that he is not punishing today's Jews for killing Jesus, then how *do* you explain the sufferings of our people?"

Brad looked at the judge, then at Miri, and then around the group. How did he get himself into these situations? He liked these people. They were good people, and he had no wish to offend them. And yet, for Miri most of all, it had to be said.

Brad took a deep breath. "I can only answer in terms of what I believe. You may find my answer foolish or perhaps even offensive."

"We may not accept your answer," Cohen said with an encouraging smile, "but we shall not be offended."

"All right," Brad went on, choosing his words more carefully than he had for a long time. "We believe that God cannot or will not force himself on anyone. Either one comes to him freely or God allows him to go his own way."

125

"That's a reasonable conclusion," Levi Shadmi said.

"Second, we believe that knowing about God and the principles he teaches brings a special responsibility with it. When a people have the truth, they become more accountable to God than a people who do not."

Again several nodded as Brad paused. That was the easy part. "Since the Jews knew God and his laws, they were under a special obligation, which none of the Gentiles were. God had special expectations of them. And when they went into apostasy—that is, when they rejected him, they brought the natural effects of disobedience upon themselves. That is the whole story of the Old Testament. When Israel was faithful, she had tremendous power. No enemy could touch her. No problem could overwhelm her. But when she turned from God, she immediately lost his power and protection. And the result? Suffering, conquest, captivity."

He looked at Miri, whose face was attentive but impassive. "In a religious sense, I believe the Jewish people are still in that same state. They have not turned to their God with all their hearts. And so they continue to endure problems, sufferings, and persecutions."

They were all attentive, so Brad plunged ahead. "Israel and the Jews are not the only people who are turning from their God. Most of Christianity is in the same state. Some Mormons are slipping into the same pattern. They go through the motions of their religion, but God is not the highest priority in their lives. To the degree that a person abandons God, to that degree he will experience sorrow, misery, and suffering. The same is true of nations or peoples." He sat back, his gray eyes somber. "That's what I meant when I told Miri that Israel needed to trust less in herself and more in God."

Nathan raised his glass of wine and spoke, his voice tinged with bitterness. "God, Kissinger, and the United States. Courage, brothers, we have nothing to fear."

Sixteen

Brad pulled up in front of the Shadmi apartment and turned off the motor. Miri must have been watching, for the door opened immediately. To Brad's surprise, Nathan came out with her, a travel bag and rifle in his hand.

Miri came over to the car, leaned down, and smiled in at Brad through the open window. "Do you mind if Nathan rides with us?"

"Of course not."

"He has a staff meeting in Tel Aviv at noon. I thought that after we've seen Yad Vashem, we could start seeing things out away from Jerusalem. We could visit some places today in Jaffa and Tel Aviv, and then drive up the coast to Caesarea and see the ruins there. Does that sound all right?"

Nathan leaned over to join her. "Good morning, Brad." If there was any feeling over their conversation last night, he showed no evidence of it. His greeting was warm and friendly. "Listen, it's no big thing if this is a problem. I can just hitch a ride."

"No problem at all," Brad responded. "Today is Sunday. I don't have to work, and I don't teach my class. And Miri's the guide. If she suggests Caesarea, Caesarea it is. Hop in."

Miri climbed into the back seat, and Nathan handed her his bag and weapon and got in next to Brad.

"Where am I going?" Brad asked, putting the VW into gear.

"Straight ahead and then left at the first intersection," Nathan commanded. He glanced at Brad as they started to move. "Would you mind if I join you at Yad Vashem?"

"Of course not."

"Good. I want to see your reaction."

* * * * * *

Brad's reaction was one of profound somberness and a growing sense of horror. He had seen his share of Nazi war movies and even a documentary or two on the Jewish persecutions, but this wasn't the movies. There were no Hollywood trappings to glorify things, just the grim documentation of an incomprehensible tragedy.

They had walked up the long driveway to the memorial in the bright sunshine, already hot at eight o'clock. It belied any sense of tragedy that Yad Vashem—"The Hill of Remembrance"—might hold. But when they entered the modern building that housed the archives of the Holocaust, the awful reality of the Nazi nightmare began to hit Brad.

They stopped in the entry foyer, where a huge relief sculpture took up the entire wall. Miri briefly explained its symbolic significance, and then they entered the museum itself. "This is the 'Hall of Warning and Witness,'" Nathan said quietly, and he stepped back to let Brad enter first.

The walls, ceilings, and numerous partitions were painted black. Only the enlarged photos and documents and an occasional display case broke the solid blackness. It was all there. Brad was quickly absorbed as he moved slowly through the hallways, reading every document, studying each picture.

The exhibits were arranged chronologically, starting in the early 1930s with Hitler's rise to power. Even madness is implemented step by step, Brad thought. At first there were "minor" harassments and persecutions—the call for Germans to avoid the Jewish shops, the amusement of the

128

soldiers as they cut the beards and earlocks of the Orthodox Jews or made them scrub streets on hands and knees. Then came the book burnings, the requirement that all Jews wear the yellow star of David on their clothing, and Hitler's brownshirts racing through Berlin smashing windows and burning synagogues.

It took Brad nearly an hour to come to the mid-1940s, and his mind was reeling under the shock. Virtually every photo now stunned the senses with brutal savagery. A line of naked men, standing in front of a trench already filled with the dead, patiently awaited the next volley from the firing squad. Ten limp bodies hung from a gallows, the star of David on their coats. A mountain of emaciated, twisted corpses of Dachau waited for the lime pits. Two grotesque figures hung on the barbed wire of Auschwitz, having preferred the swift suicide of electrocution to the "shower rooms" with their Zyklon-B gas. A storeroom was crammed with eyeglasses and shoes, spoils of the victors. A woman exhibited an eight-inch gaping wound in her leg, surgery performed without anesthetic by Nazi doctors in "scientific research" to see how much pain the human body can tolerate. A father huddled over his six-year-old son as an S.S. officer put a pistol to the back of his head.

Brad found himself swallowing hard as he read the eyewitness account of a German engineer who witnessed a mass execution in October 1942. "The people—men, women, and children of all ages—were forced to strip by order of an S.S. wielding a horse whip or dog whip. The people undressed without a cry or tear, stood together family by family, kissed each other and said goodbye, and waited for a signal from another S.S. man who stood near the trench, also whip in hand.

"During the fifteen minutes I stood there I did not hear a single complaint or plea for mercy. I looked at a family of about eight people, a man and his wife, both about fifty, with children with them, aged one, eight and ten, and two grown-up daughters aged about twenty and twenty-four. An old woman with snow white hair held the year-old child in her arms, singing to it and tickling it. The child laughed with pleasure. The husband and wife watched them with tears in their eyes. The father held the hand of a boy about ten and spoke to him gently; the boy tried to keep back the tears. The father pointed toward heaven, and stroked the child's hand, and appeared to be explaining something to him.''

Brad turned away, deeply touched. He thought of his own family—of Susan, his older sister, and her toddler who gurgled happily whenever he saw Brad; of Kathy, now at BYU; of Craig, a sophomore tailback at East High School; of Jimmy, proudly ordained to the Aaronic Priesthood just three months ago; of Barbara and Brenda, so much like twins even though they were six and eight. Brad had baptized Brenda the week before he left. And he thought of his parents, herding them all naked to an open trench, and he felt physically ill.

Neither Nathan nor Miri commented when they moved to the hall documenting the world's response to this horror. There was no need to. Brad felt the shame in every fiber of his soul. The document in front of him read: ''We knew in Washington, from August, 1942, on, that the Nazis were planning to exterminate all the Jews of Europe. Yet, for nearly eighteen months after the first reports of the Nazi horror plan, the State Department did practically nothing. . . .'' It was signed by Henry Morgen-thau, U.S. Secretary of the Treasury.

It was a sober threesome that finally walked to the car. Miri quietly directed Brad to the freeway to Tel Aviv, but other than that they were silent, lost in their own thoughts.

As they pulled onto the four-lane freeway and started down the steep canyon that led to the Mediterranean plains from Jerusalem, Nathan began to speak. He was staring out the front windshield; his voice had a faraway quality, almost as though he were speaking to himself. He spoke softly, and Brad had to strain to hear him. Miri leaned forward so she also could hear.

"After the Six Day War, I was sick in my soul. My eyes had been filled with the blood and horror of battle. My heart was full of sorrow for David, my brother, who was killed in the Sinai. I needed to get away, to let my spirit heal."

Brad glanced quickly at Nathan, noting that his hands were clenched into tight fists.

"I went to Europe. I began in Scandinavia, absorbing the beauty of the mountains and the fjords, and then I worked my way south until I came to Germany."

He stopped. The silence stretched on for so long that Brad decided he wasn't going to finish. But finally the soft voice continued.

"I found myself walking around Germany. I felt so strange there, because on the one hand it was a beautiful country, but every German sound, every German voice reminded me instinctively of the movies I had seen of the Holocaust. The discipline and the order of everything frightened me. Everything was neat and clean and in its place, with no mistakes. I saw the soldiers at the airports dressed exactly as in the pictures you just saw at Yad Vashem."

Nathan's voice had an almost ghostly quality to it, and Brad could tell he was deeply moved. "I felt very strange, as though I had gone back in time to World War II. I went to Munich and visited Dachau, where my grandfather died. And I was shocked. It was not horrible. It was not ugly. It was like walking around a Japanese garden. Everything was white, surrounded by green grass, with little stones lining the paths—everything fixed in its place. The gas chambers were all cleaned and painted. And there was a room over by the gas chamber—white and neat."

Nathan stopped again and swallowed hard, angry at himself for his emotions. "It was the room where they made the Jews strip naked, and prepare for the 'showers.' In the room was a group of tourists from Italy. They stood quietly, not speaking or saying anything."

Brad glanced back at Miri, who stared at her brother, totally captivated by his words. Her eyes were shining, her mouth tight, and Brad knew she was hearing this for the first time too.

Nathan sighed, a sound of tremendous inner pain. "And I felt very bad at their silence, that no words were being spoken. I felt like crying. But instead I shouted, 'If you don't hear the blood of my brothers screaming from the earth in this neat garden and from this neat room, I will scream so you will hear!' And I screamed out with all my heart, 'Hear, O Israel, the Lord our God he is one God.' It is the prayer of every dying Jew. And then I turned and ran. I ran into the gardens. I wanted to get away, but the fences were still there."

For the first time he turned to Brad, staring at him, his dark eyes like pools of immense sorrow. Finally he spoke. "And I raised my face there in that garden. I looked into heaven, and I shouted again. And this time I shouted 'O God of Israel, why do you not hear the cries of your people?' And then I knew. I knew that if there is a God up there, he couldn't hear." There was a long pause. "Or he didn't care. I left Dachau, and I left Germany. I came home to Israel, where every Jew is welcome, where every Jew can hold up his head with pride, where our children will never again wear the yellow star. I came home to Israel, where we do not wait for help from a god who neither hears nor cares."

Seventeen

For most of the ten-minute trip from Bethlehem to Jerusalem, the conversation had been light, rambling, and punctuated with smiles and occasional laughter. Now as they crested the last hill and the walls of the Old City lay before them, the color of a field of autumn wheat in the late afternoon sunshine, Brad, Ali, and Miri had all fallen silent.

As he guided the battered old Volkswagen through the light Sabbath-day traffic, Brad estimated they were about three or four minutes from the hotel where the branch held its sacrament meetings. He felt the faint tuggings of nervousness in his stomach. He checked the rearview mirror to see Ali's face, but his friend was gazing out the car window with almost hypnotic concentration.

Miri gave Brad a warm smile as their eyes met briefly, and Brad decided she didn't share his concern about the next couple of hours. Her hands were lying quietly in her lap, her long fingers toying absently with the ring she wore on her right hand. In a cool mint-green dress of soft crepe, Miri was as lovely as Brad had ever seen her. She had brushed her hair until the soft curls had the sheen of polished obsidian, and her tanned skin glowed like amber honey in the sunlight. A tiny star of David hung at the base of her throat on a delicate filigree chain. She wore it often, but now he wondered if she had not subconsciously chosen it to visibly maintain her Jewish identity in a crowd of Mormons. With that thought he fell to worrying again how the branch members would receive Miri, how she would react to the sacrament meeting, what she would say when it was over.

Suddenly he was aware of soft chuckling from the back seat. He glanced in the rearview mirror and caught Ali's eyes, sparkling with amusement.

"What's so funny?" Brad asked.

"You two."

Miri half turned in her seat and looked at the handsome young Arab. "Us two? What is so funny about us two?"

"The way you are both playing it so cool and casual. Why don't you just admit how nervous you are? Look at me, for example. I keep telling myself, 'Ali, so what if this is the first time you've ever spoken in sacrament meeting. There is nothing to be afraid of. Relax.'"

"And does it help?" Brad asked.

"Of course. Instead of being absolutely petrified, I'm only in a mild state of sheer terror!"

"Okay," Miri said, "I admit it. I am very nervous."

"You are?" Brad exclaimed in surprise.

"Yes, I am."

"Listen, Ali won't be that bad. He has prepared for this talk for the last ten days."

"Yeah, thanks a lot, Miri," Ali chimed in. "Nothing like a solid vote of confidence with which to send a man into the jaws of death."

"If he really bombs," Brad said soberly, "we'll sneak out the back and pretend we don't know him. He can catch a taxi home."

"Stop it you two," she cried. "You know that's not what I meant."

"Then why *are* you nervous?" Ali demanded.

The smile gradually faded, and she gave Brad a long, searching look. "Because I have never attended a Christian church meeting before."

Brad's eyes softened as he nodded. "I know, Miri. I know." Then the teasing note crept back into his voice. "I understand that Daniel felt the same way about going to the meeting with those Babylonian lions."

"You are hopeless, Brad Kennison!" she laughed.

"I came to the same conclusion weeks ago," Ali said. "But being greatly given to Christian charity, I have reluctantly agreed to work with him a while longer."

"Ha!" Brad snorted. "Some charity."

Miri watched the two friends as they bantered on for a moment more, sensing the deep affection that had developed between them. As they stopped for the signal at the Damascus gate, they both fell silent, and Miri quickly turned to Brad.

"And what about you?"

"What about me?"

"Come on. Ali laughed at both of us for pretending to be so nonchalant. I have admitted I am nervous about going to a Christian meeting. Ali confessed he is worried about his talk. What about you?"

Brad grinned in surrender. "I haven't had butterflies like this since I played the part of a potato bug in the third grade school play."

"Really?" Miri said, her eyes widening. "Why?"

He pondered that for a moment, and finally a slow, almost boyish smile played at the corners of his mouth. "Because," he said gently, "I have never taken a Jewish girl to a Christian meeting before." *Nor tried to convert one to Mormonism*, he added to himself, which, had he been totally honest with himself as well as Miri, was the greatest cause of the butterflies doing power dives in his stomach.

* * * * * *

But if he had planned the entire meeting himself, manipulated the setting in every way possible, and orchestrated every word, Brad could not have asked for a more appropriate introduction to Mormonism for Miri. The

Jerusalem Branch met in the basement of the Jerusalem Star Hotel, since they had no building of their own as yet. Brad had not noticed before how simple and unadorned the room was until he walked inside with Miri, worrying how she would respond. But the branch members gave her no chance to study the surroundings. Brad had been tempted to warn them about Miri's visit, but now he was grateful he had not.

The Jerusalem Branch had about ninety members. There were sixty or so Study Abroad students who rotated each six months from BYU, and five families—almost all Americans—who were permanent residents of Jerusalem. The response to Miri was spontaneous and warm without being overdone. Within two minutes President Marks engaged her in a conversation more like that between close friends than recent acquaintances.

The opening song and prayer were normal enough, but as the congregation began the sacrament hymn, a change took place. It was at first very subtle, elusive, almost undefinable. Later Brad decided it was the result of the sunrise service earlier in the day.

The BYU students—with Ali and Brad joining them—had met in the Garden Tomb at six o'clock that morning. They had moved quietly to the eastern end of the lovely garden in the center of Jerusalem and had stood somberly gazing at the small hillock known in Hebrew as Golgotha, "the place of the skull." And indeed the small cavelike holes in the face of the cliff did look like the gaping sockets of a human skull. Here the Master had come, infinitely exhausted from his ordeal during the night when blood had oozed from every pore, when a kiss had betrayed, when Jewish hands had buffeted and pummeled him, when the Roman lash had left his back criss-crossed with bleeding stripes, when a Procurator had sought in vain to wash away the stain of guilt. Here the nails had been pounded home. Here the cross beam with its agonized burden had been lifted into place. Here the spear had been thrust deep into his side. A God had come to earth, and here men had tried in vain to put him away from them for good. Here Jesus Christ had died.

Deeply sobered, the group had moved to rows of benches overlooking the tomb cut into the side of a limestone hill. From where he had sat, Brad could clearly see the stone track cut to hold the massive sealing stone. For the next half hour, with President Marks leading them, they had immersed themselves in the scriptural accounts of that morning when crushing, devastating despair had turned to incredulous, blazing, overwhelming joy. The sunlight had filtered through the trees, and behind them a bird greeted the morning with joyous abandon, as though this were the very morning of the resurrection.

President Marks had closed the Bible slowly, and after a long pause, had turned and gazed down at the tomb. "There, in that small, insignificant grotto of stone, they brought Jesus and hastily wrapped his body for burial. Little did they know that within a few short hours, he would be back for that body, would raise it up from the cold stone, fold up those burial clothes, and lay them aside."

He had turned back and searched the eyes of those who sat before him. "And because Christ did so, someday you and I will come back to where our bodies have lain in wait, put there with care by those who love us, and we too shall rise up and put aside our burial clothes."

Now, as the congregation began the sacrament hymn, "I Stand All Amazed," it began to happen. What had begun as ninety separate voices singing a hymn accompanied by a rather tinny and slightly out-of-tune piano was suddenly transformed into a single heartfelt cry of supplication that sent chills coursing up and down Brad's spine. *I tremble to know that for me he was crucified.* The image of Golgotha, with its haunting face of death, flashed into Brad's mind. He could almost hear the chilling ring of the mallet as it drove the nails home, and the tortured voice crying at that moment when others cursed and raged at their executioners, "Father, forgive them." *That for me, a sinner, he suffered, he bled and died.* The chorister stood with tears streaming down her cheeks. The voice of the boy next to him suddenly faltered and dropped into silence.

I marvel—Brad bit his own lip as his heart poured out the words with all the fervency of his soul—*that he would descend from his throne divine to rescue a soul so rebellious and proud as mine.* He ducked his head, blinking rapidly, unable to say the last few words.

Oh, it is wonderful! The small room reverberated with the song of praise, but Brad could not join in—not until the middle of the third verse. *Such mercy, such love, and devotion can I forget?* The question was like a flame in his soul. *No! No!* he sang, his voice a fierce whisper of intensity. *I will praise and adore at the mercy seat, until at his glorified throne I kneel at his feet.*

The feeling of reverential supplication did not end with the hymn, and even the few small children present were subdued while the bread and water—on simple plates from the hotel's dining room—were passed down the rows. Brad finally risked a glance at Miri as she passed the bread without partaking of it. In profile it was hard to see her expression, and he wondered if she could sense any of what the group was feeling.

When Ali finally stepped to the makeshift podium, clutching his notes tightly, Brad smiled his encouragement. Oh, how grateful he was to know this young Arab with the flashing grin and ready wit.

"My brothers and sisters . . ." Ali stopped and for a long moment stared down at his papers, visibly struggling for control of his emotions. He took a deep breath and tried again. "When I think what it means for me to call you brothers and sisters, I get a little overwhelmed. And so—" He held up the notes for all to see, his familiar smile flashing briefly. "In spite of the fact that I have here what is undoubtedly the best prepared sacrament meeting talk in Mormon-Arab history, I would like instead to tell you how I came to be your brother. And more importantly," he said, looking directly at Miri, "I would like to tell you how I came to accept Jesus Christ as my elder brother."

* * * * * *

By the time they had dropped Ali off in Bethlehem and returned to Miri's apartment, it was dark, and the cool air held the slight nip of September in it. Brad turned off the lights and the engine; the nervousness he had felt earlier was suddenly back. After dropping Ali off they had been content to ride quietly. Now he knew it was time to talk.

Brad took a deep breath and cleared his throat, but before he could speak, Miri laid her hand on his arm, her face soft and radiant in the faint light of a streetlight a few yards away. "Thank you, Brad, for a very special day."

He nodded, marveling at her loveliness, keenly aware of some feelings stirring deep inside him that he had never felt before. "Thank *you*! I think it really pleased Ali that you would come." He shook his head slowly. "Why should Ali get all the credit? *I* am glad that you would come." He took her hand, hesitantly, almost shyly, but she slipped her arm through his and returned his gentle squeeze.

"Good. I went to hear Ali, of course, but mostly I went for you."

Immensely pleased, Brad searched her eyes, deep pools of almost liquid blackness, for clues to her inward feelings. "And?" he finally asked.

Miri's eyes dropped beneath his probing glance. Her lips, soft and full, pulled down slightly in an expression of thoughtfulness. Finally she shook her head. "I don't know how to describe it. As you know, my family is not religious. We do not go to synagogue except on special holy days. The holy-day services are times of great emotions—solemnity, rejoicing, mourning—but I don't think we ever have the kind of feeling in our meetings that you had in yours."

His brow furrowed as he considered that. "We try to have feelings of reverence and devotion in all of our meetings, but I've got to admit that today was very special." His expression softened as he stared down at their hands. "It was the most meaningful sacrament meeting I have ever attended."

Miri studied his face in profile, wanting suddenly to touch his cheek. Instead she squeezed his hand as she spoke, her voice husky and low. "I know, Brad. I could tell."

His head came up, his eyes wide and searching.

"Your religion is very important to you, isn't it," she said.

The memory of the sacrament hymn and the feelings that had washed over him as he sang returned to his mind. "Yes," he agreed. "Not nearly important enough, but it is the single most important thing in my life."

"And for Ali too." It was a statement, not a question and Brad just nodded.

"What he said today—" Brad unconsciously held his breath as she searched for the right words, "was very interesting." She gave her head a quick shake of impatience. "No, not interesting." She searched again, her face intense with concentration. "I don't know the best word. Ever since his return I have wondered what would cause a Moslem to become a Christian. Ali talks about it so easily all the time. I would never have guessed that he went through such a struggle."

"I knew it hadn't been easy for him, but today was the first time I had heard about that final battle with himself—the fasting and prayer, and his wrestle with the Book of Mormon."

Miri nodded, then leaned her head back against the seat and closed her eyes. The dark lashes lay gently on her cheeks, her face a study of quiet repose. Brad watched her for a long moment, again keenly aware of the stir of emotions he felt in her presence. He gently withdrew his hand and turned in the seat to face her more directly.

"Miri?"

"Hmmmm?" Her eyes opened slowly, and her lips parted in a warm contented smile. Then she sat up and grew sober as she looked at Brad, sensing his sudden nervousness. "What?" she prompted again when he hesitated.

He had rehearsed the moment a dozen times, yet he still felt a quickening of anxiety. He took a quick breath and plunged in. "Today Ali talked about the Book of Mormon."

"Yes."

"And how it became the pivotal question for him."

"Yes." She was watching him closely now.

"Well, while that book has great significance for a Moslem, or anyone else for that matter, it was written by *your* people. It is a record of Jews who left Jerusalem. And more important, I guess, it was written *for* your people." He reached under the seat and withdrew the book. "I would like you to have a copy."

When Brad had first thought ahead to this moment, he had obtained a small paperback copy of the Book of Mormon. But the more he considered it, the less satisfactory that became. Then one day while in the Old City he had had a flash of inspiration. Olivewood was one of the most common tourist items of the Holy Land, and Bibles with olivewood covers were popular. From there it had been easy. Akhmud, Ali's brother, was a major buyer of olivewood, and the manufacturer in Bethlehem was more than anxious to please him.

The Book of Mormon Brad handed Miri now was a large, hardbound edition with thin sheets of gleaming, highly polished olivewood bonded to each cover. "Miriam Shadmi" was engraved in small letters in the lower corner.

She took it from him slowly, her eyes finally raising to search his face. "Oh Brad, it's lovely," she whispered. She touched the cover, her fingers lightly caressing the smooth surface, then slowly opened it. She read softly what he had written inside. "To Miri, whose friendship I have come to treasure more each day, I offer this gift, which I have come to treasure more than life itself. Brad."

When she finally looked up at him, her eyes were swimming. "Thank you, Brad."

He smiled and took her hand in his again. "Hey," he said, keeping his voice light, "I just wanted to do something for the best guide in Jerusalem."

Eighteen

Brad looked at the eager faces, tapping the chalk against his fingers. "Let's see, what else can I show you?" he said to himself. His students sat at their desks, brown faces attentive, dark eyes sparkling with pleasure at their success. There were sixteen of them, nine boys and seven girls, the best of the school, according to Ali. But then Brad suspected that Ali thought all of his students were the best.

Brad hadn't mastered all of their names yet, but nearly. He walked closer to their desks, watching them, feeling a great affection for these Arab children. Natasha, the oldest at fourteen, sat straight as an arrow, her jet black hair pulled back from her face and braided into two long pigtails. Abou, just barely seven and the youngest, sat next to her, squirming in anticipation, his cheeks round, his eyes sober. He was usually the first to shoot out an answer. Mahmoud, his older brother, usually tried to appear bored, but nearly always failed when Brad started challenging them. Nimra, Arabic for "tigress," was very unlike her name. She reminded Brad of a darker version, almost a carbon copy, of his sister Brenda. Nimra was his favorite, with her shy little smile. But he had quickly grown to love them all: Ibrahim and Faisal, unable to stop poking at each other unless they were separated; Mohammed, his large dark eyes so expressive; Wojiha, at twelve already a lovely young woman.

Suddenly Brad had an idea. "Okay," he said, pointing to them, "new word." He turned to the chalkboard and sketched hurriedly, painfully aware of his lack of artistic talent.

Before he had even finished the drawing on the board, the class erupted into a cacophony of sound. The older boys jeered at him and started pounding their desks. The younger children made faces as they yelled and shook their fingers at him.

Brad was stunned. His pupils had been alert and attentive just a moment earlier, each intent on being the first one to answer his next question. Suddenly he had a miniature Arab riot on his hands. They were all shouting at him in Arabic, but gradually the older boys prevailed, and the whole class joined in, slapping the flat of their hands against the desk tops and chanting *"La! La! La! La!"*

That much Brad understood. It was Arabic for "no." But no what? He stood looking bewildered, trying to determine what had broken the floodgates.

The door opened, and Ali stuck his head in. It was like pulling the plug on a blaring stereo. One instant there was ear-throbbing sound. The next a pin would have sounded like an amplified thunderclap.

"Mr. Kennison," Ali said sternly, winking at the children as he entered. The older ones grinned, the younger ones squirmed in anticipation. Teacher was in trouble. "Your firm hand of discipline seems to be losing its grip. Do you have a problem?"

Brad held up his hands in a gesture of bewilderment. "I don't know. The only thing I can understand is that they keep saying 'La! La!'"

Ali nodded sagely. "Somehow, it was my impression that you were supposed to be teaching them English, not them teaching you Arabic."

"Come on, Ali. Find out what I did. Why are they so upset?"

The young Arab principal turned to face the sixteen

144

eager faces and spoke briefly in Arabic. Someone plugged in the stereo again. They all waved their hands, jumped up and down, and explained the problem simultaneously. Ali plugged his ears and pulled a face at them. Gradually bedlam subsided. Ali selected Natasha and spoke to her. She responded briefly, pointing at Brad.

"I didn't do it," Brad wailed as Ali turned and walked up to him, "and if I did, I was insane at the time."

Ali gently pushed Brad aside, revealing his artistic handiwork on the board. "Um humm," he mused, his head cocked to one side. "And may I ask who is responsible for this masterpiece?"

"What? The pig? I drew it. We are working on vocabulary. If you think that is bad, you should have seen my horse. What are they, half-pint art critics?"

Ali looked at the class and shook his head, his face long and sober. "Mr. Kennison," he said in great solemnity, "do you have any concept of what a pig means to a Moslem?"

Someone turned on the light in Brad's attic. "Oh," he said with a long drawn-out sound. "So that's it. I knew that the Jews—but I didn't realize—Moslems, too, huh?" He erased the board quickly.

Ali nodded, unsuccessfully trying to suppress a smile.

"Would you apologize to them for me? I didn't mean to offend them."

"Actually, to call someone a pig is a gross insult—not quite profanity, but close. They thought you were calling them a pig."

"Oh no," Brad said in dismay. "They were supposed to say 'This is a pig.' I was just trying to teach them some new words."

Ali turned to the class and again spoke briefly. "Ah," said the group almost as one. They smiled and waved their forgiveness.

Ali turned back to Brad. "Class is about over. Shall we dismiss them? I need to talk with you anyway."

"That's fine." Brad stepped forward. "Attention," he commanded them, coming to a ramrod stiff position.

"Ah-ten-shun," they echoed, following his example.

"Can we show off a little?" Brad asked.

"You bet," Ali responded.

"I am—" Brad pointed to himself.

"Tee-chur," they called out, aware that they were performing for the principal.

Brad's sweeping gesture included all of them. "You are—"

"Stoo-dents." Again their eyes were bright and shiny.

He picked up the objects on his desk one by one, and they called them out in unison—apple, pencil, book, orange, shoe, and so on. Then he turned to the board and wrote one word after another—*this, that, is, are, will, I, you, me, we.* Again, usually before Brad finished writing, they called the words out.

He gave a little bow and applauded. "Very good." He dismissed the children with a wave. *"Salam aleichem."*

"Salam! Salam!" they cried as they burst for the doors.

"Hold it!" Brad bellowed, freezing them in their tracks. They didn't know those words yet, but the tone was in a universal language.

"La, salam," he said sternly, shaking his head. *"La! La!"* he waved again, *"Salam aleichem."*

This time they remembered, smiling. "Goodbye," they said as one.

"Very good," Brad nodded. "Goodbye."

They were gone like a shot.

"Well?" Ali said, pulling up a chair and dropping into it.

Brad sat on a corner of the desk. "Well what?"

"How is the experiment going?"

Brad gave an audible sigh. "I don't know. If I could speak even a little Arabic so I could explain things to them. It's like trying to communicate with a very small child. I have to repeat and repeat."

146

"When did you learn to speak English?"

"All right, as a baby, but—"

"Funny thing. That's how I learned Arabic too. Maybe you're onto something with this 'new' method of yours."

"Well," Brad conceded, "I do feel as though they're making some progress. They can understand and make simple sentences now. Anyway, it's fun. Have you heard from your other teacher yet?"

"Yes, she finishes her other job this week. She'll take over from you starting Thursday."

Brad nodded, a little sad to know he wouldn't be continuing. "I am glad we changed the class to morning instead of afternoon, but I still feel guilty only teaching them four days a week."

Ali shrugged that off. "Friday is their day, Sunday is yours. You came to Israel to see Israel, not to spend your time in a classroom."

"I know," Brad replied. "But this has been a delightful experience for me. I can see why you feel so strongly about your people. They are really special."

"There are a few exceptions to that, but all in all I would have to agree with you."

"You said you wanted to talk to me," Brad reminded him.

"Oh, yes. Miri called."

"She did?"

"Yes. She wants you to meet her here instead of at the hotel. She had to be out this way anyway."

"Does she have a ride here?"

"I guess so. She didn't say."

"Okay. What time?"

"Ten."

Brad glanced at his watch. "That's right now."

"I know. That's why I came in. That, and to put down a small insurrection. By the way, how is she coming?"

Brad shook his head in discouragement. "You know Miri. She wants to know, and she seems to accept things,

147

but I keep getting this feeling that it's only an intellectual acceptance. I think she finds Mormonism attractive in the same way that a person finds Plato's philosophy more attractive than Aristotle's. It's an intellectual preference, but there's no spiritual commitment."

"I don't know," Ali mused. "She's constantly asking me questions. Every time I deliver something to the hotel, she corners me for fifteen minutes or so and quizzes me."

"I know," Brad laughed. "She keeps saying 'Ali said this or Ali said that. What do you think?'"

"Maybe we'd better start checking our answers beforehand. I mean, I'm hardly an expert on Mormonism."

"But what fascinates her about you is that you, a non-Christian, should decide to join the Church. Miri has told me that several times."

"How did she react to Brother Spencer's talk the other night?" The BYU faculty advisor had spoken on the prophetic relationship between Ephraim and Joseph, using Ezekiel, chapter thirty-seven, as his theme. He knew Miri was there, and he hadn't pulled any punches. He had defined the stick of Judah as the Bible and the stick of Joseph as the Book of Mormon, and then had talked about the significance of their being joined together.

"I don't know. Why don't you ask Miri?" Brad suggested.

"Ask me what?" Miri said, as she came into the classroom.

Both Ali and Brad jumped. "Hi," Brad called, aware of the sudden excitement he always felt when he saw her.

She smiled brightly, then turned to Ali. "So? Ask me."

"We were just wondering how you felt about the fireside Saturday night."

She laughed. "You two and your conspiracy to make me a Mormon. What hope have I?"

"Only one," Ali replied soberly.

That caught her off guard. She had expected a light response in return. "What's that?"

"There is a Church policy against baptizing unconscious candidates. Otherwise we would have knocked you over the head and dunked you in the River Jordan weeks ago."

Brad watched the two of them as they continued to banter back and forth, envious of Ali's easy manner concerning the topic. Brad knew he always reacted too intensely to any hint of progress or any sign of rejection. And he knew why he reacted that way. There was much more than a convert baptism at stake for him.

"So stop stalling," Ali said. "Answer the question."

Miri sat down on the desk next to Brad.

"Well, I read all those references he gave us again last night. The one big question in my mind is whether Mormons really do represent Ephraim. But," she went on quickly as both Brad and Ali started to speak, "the thing that really bothered me was his interpretation of Ezekiel. He made such a point of the fact that the sticks were books—the stick of Joseph was the Book of Mormon, the stick of Judah the Bible."

"Right." Both Ali and Brad spoke as one.

"When I got home I got out my Bible in Hebrew and read that passage."

"And?" Ali asked impatiently as she paused for a long moment.

"At first I was really bothered. The Hebrew word for 'stick' doesn't mean book at all. Its basic meaning is wood. The meaning clearly seemed to be two staffs or rods on which the names of Judah and Joseph were written. It is a prophecy that the two tribes will be reunited, but it has nothing to do with books or records. But Brother Spencer made such a point that Joseph Smith claimed it was a book. I felt sure that your Mormon prophet was in error. He should not have spoken out on a Hebrew text without knowing Hebrew."

"Sometimes a prophet knows more than a linguist," Brad said stubbornly.

149

Miri smiled. "Another assumption that one must take on faith. But," she added quickly, cutting off Brad's protest, "let me finish. Before challenging you on this, I wanted to be absolutely sure. So I went to the Hebrew University this morning. I got out some Hebrew dictionaries and lexicons. I found out a couple of interesting things."

"What?" Brad asked eagerly.

"Well," she said, "to make a long story short, I finally ended up in the office of one of my former professors, one of the foremost archeologists in the Middle East. I won't go into all the archeological trivia, but the professor told me that the Babylonians used *wooden* writing books to make records."

Brad got the first glimmer. "So—"

"So," Miri continued, "the Babylonian word for these wooden boards is close to the Hebrew word for 'stick.' My professor thinks a better translation of that verse would be: 'And he took one wooden writing tablet and wrote on it for Judah.'"

"So it *is* a record," Brad said, surprised at her information, and even more amazed at her.

Miri nodded. "I must admit I was very impressed. Your Joseph Smith has a remarkable record." She looked at Ali. "So to answer your question about Saturday night, I am impressed, I am troubled, I am intrigued. In a word, I don't know."

"Grab your club, Brad," Ali said happily. "This girl needs to be baptized, conscious or not."

"Oh no," Miri protested quickly, "Remember, one 'stick' does not a convert make."

"Oh, ho ho!" Ali said, making a face at her. "Very punny. Very punny indeed."

Miri bowed her head, acknowledging her just dues. "Thank you." She looked at Brad. "I need to call the hotel and talk to my father before we leave. I'll be only a minute or two. May I use your phone, Ali?"

"Sure thing. It's in my office at the end of the hall."

For almost a full minute after she had left, both men were silent, wrapped up in their own thoughts. Finally Brad spoke.

"She really is something. If she ever does convert, she will make a super Latter-day Saint."

"And one heck of a wife," Ali added.

Brad had learned that trying to hide his feelings from Ali was like trying to appear inconspicuous in a business suit on the beach. "I agree," he admitted. "*If* she will join the Church. That's still a very big if."

"And if not," Ali asked softly, "then what?"

"Then old Brad packs his bags and heads for home."

"Just like that?"

"No, not just like that. But he'll do it. It won't work any other way. Besides, what are we talking about? I don't even know if Miri is interested in me. She hasn't said a word."

"Oh, brother!" Ali groaned. "If you are that dense, drawing pigs on the blackboard may be the highlight of your life." He walked to the door and leaned against the frame, where he could see Brad and look down the hall too. "If you can't see her feelings for you in her eyes, you're the only one who can't. Even her father can see how she feels."

Brad's head shot up. "What's that supposed to mean?"

"Levi quizzed me the other day about you two."

"He did? What did he say?"

"He wanted to know what I thought your intentions were—if you liked her, et cetera, et cetera."

"And?"

"And what?" Ali asked innocently.

Brad scooped up the eraser and hurled it at his friend, missing his head by at least a millimeter. "You know what!" he exclaimed. "Come on, what did you tell him?"

"That you were madly in love with his daughter, seriously considering an elopement, but that you would be back in time to cover your evening shift and not to worry."

The shoe on the desk used for vocabulary training followed the eraser, only this time Brad's aim was true. It whacked Ali solidly on the shoulder.

"Ouch!" he hollered. "All right, all right," he cried as Brad picked up the orange. "I surrender! I surrender!"

"So what did you say?"

"I told him the truth. I told him nothing formal was happening, but that I thought you were both starting to develop some deep feelings for each other."

"And what did he say to that?"

"Not much. I think Levi has mixed emotions. He has concerns about Miri marrying a non-Jew, and a non-Israeli, and yet he really likes you. Her mother really likes you."

"I really like them. They are good people."

Ali gave Brad a long, searching look. "Actually, I think Levi is more concerned about her relationship to Mormonism."

That brought Brad up short. "Oh?"

"You know, it's funny. The Shadmis claim that they are not practicing Jews, and yet those traditions die hard. Levi grew up in an Orthodox home. If theirs was an Orthodox home now and Miri converted to Christianity, there would be a formal funeral. Her name would never be spoken in the home again. That would be true even if she married you and didn't convert."

"Do you think they would react that strongly now? Levi seems to have some positive feelings about Mormons himself."

"I don't know. I really doubt they would kick Miri out of the home, but it would, I think, introduce a serious strain into their relationship."

"And that would be tough," Brad murmured glumly. "They are a very close family. And yet now that I think about it, they were noticeably cooler when I picked up Miri for church that day when you spoke."

Ali nodded, his dark eyes thoughtful. "Not that it would stop Miri. She has a mind of her own. If she decides for baptism, she'll do it no matter what."

"*If* she decides." They both fell silent, considering the chances of that happening.

Finally Brad shrugged, his face long. "Well, that's a secondary worry, anyway. First we have to get her converted, and that is a big enough task for the moment."

Nineteen

Masada! Its very name meant mountain stronghold, and that it was. It was a superb natural fortress, its sheer cliffs towering thirteen hundred feet above the lowest spot on the face of the earth, the shores of the Dead Sea. Brad and Miri were climbing up what Josephus, the ancient historian, had called the "Serpentine Path." It snaked its way up the eastern flank of the boat-shaped mountain, each sharp switchback becoming steeper and narrower as it came up under the lip of the cliffs that ringed the top. Brad let his eyes follow the path upward, awestruck at the choice of the Jewish Zealots some two thousand years before. A six-year-old with a basket of grapefruit-sized rocks could defend the final fifty or sixty feet from a thousand troops. Fifteen thousand of the Tenth Legion, the best Rome could field, were held at bay by a few ragtag rebels, probably less than three hundred actual fighting men. No wonder this spot had captured and fired the imagination of the Israelis. It personified their own struggles against incredible odds.

Miri pointed to a small bench where the trail made yet another switchback. "Shall we take a break for a few minutes?"

Brad nodded, and they plopped down, grateful for the small patch of shade provided by a thatched overhang. They had been climbing steadily for close to half an hour and were still barely two-thirds of the way up. The Dead

154

Sea shimmered azure blue in the searing heat, a mile or two to the east and a thousand feet below them. Even though it was late September, the sun could still blister the skin, and it left the air hot and oppressive.

Brad unhooked his canteen and offered it to Miri, watching as she tipped her head back and drank. Even in the fierce heat of the Judean wilderness, she looked cool and lovely. A light cotton blouse, sky blue and sleeveless, with matching shorts emphasized the slimness of her figure and the graceful line of her legs. A bright yellow scarf protected her head from the sun.

"Tastes good," she murmured, then leaned back against one of the thin metal poles that held up the protective covering. She was right about the water, but only because out here water was at a premium. It was tepid and tasted faintly of aluminum.

Brad studied her face, calm now in repose, and felt again the tug of conflicting emotions. He leaned over, picked up a pebble, and rolled it back and forth in his hands. Yesterday his hopes had soared when she had discovered on her own the meaning of the two sticks prophecy. At other times they crashed in hopelessness. This morning as they had driven down from Jerusalem, Brad had thought she was asleep, her head back against the seat of the car, her eyes closed. Suddenly she had said, "I just cannot accept it. It doesn't make sense."

"What doesn't make sense?" he had asked.

"That God would let his own son be killed to save all men, when the vast majority don't want to be saved anyway."

Brad had started to explain, but it soon became clear she had been thinking out loud and did not want any intrusions in her thoughts. So he had lapsed into gloomy silence.

He flipped the rock away and watched it arc downward until it hit the mountain, making a little puff of dust. Miri opened her eyes.

"Are you ready to go?" she asked.

He shook his head. "No way."

"Good," she murmured lazily. "Neither am I," and she closed her eyes again.

He watched her, knowing that soon he had to make some commitments of his own. He had left home in a state of turmoil and frustration. He had been without purpose, rudderless in the stream, irritated at his own inability to decide what to do. Those feelings were gone now. In his quest for ammunition to combat Miri's incessant questions, he had found himself. He knew now what he wanted to do with his life, and the desire to embark on that path was becoming more and more powerful. Some of the greatest events of history were starting to unfold, and those events were intimately connected with the Mormons and the peoples of Israel—Arab and Jew. Brad wanted to learn everything he could about those intertwining destinies, and then teach it to others, ignite them with the flame that consumed him. He had been so overjoyed when he realized he'd found the answer he had been looking for, that the next morning he had spent several hours at the Hebrew University, checking out classes, programs, possibilities. By noon, however, he knew that he couldn't get what he wanted there. He would have to become completely fluent in Hebrew to get a degree in Jerusalem, and that would take a year or more in addition to his studies. And back home, with the Middle Eastern Center at the University of Utah, he had one of America's finest facilities right in his backyard.

He studied Miri, then shook his head. Only one thing held him here now—this beautiful dark-haired Israeli who sat next to him, totally unaware of his frustrations. How much longer should he hang on? He had money enough yet for several months. But every dime spent here now was robbing the achievement of his goal. And what if Miri converted? Would she be willing to marry him and go to America?

That thought surprised even Brad. *Hey, c'mon Kennison*, he said severely to himself. *This girl is a nonmember. A Jew. And you're thinking about marriage? It's time to wake up and face reality. Just tell her goodbye, get on the plane, and go home before you're in this over your head.* He shook his head. *Who are you kidding? You're already in this up to your eyebrows and—*

"Hey, you!" Miri's voice startled him out of his thoughts. "Anybody home in there?"

Brad smiled, slightly embarrassed. "Oh, hi! Haven't we met somewhere before?"

She nodded, only half smiling. "What in the world were you thinking? You've been frowning as if you were sitting on a thornbush or something."

He searched for a quick reply. Then the rumble of the gondola broke in. The bright red car passed overhead, full of tourists who waved down to them. Brad waved back and pulled a face at Miri.

"I was thinking about those poor unfortunates who only get to ride up to the top in five minutes instead of experiencing the exhilarating pleasures of a forty-five-minute hike in the bright and delightful sunshine."

Miri pulled a face at him. "You're the one who said you wanted to—"

"Don't remind me. Tell me again how much money we're saving by climbing up."

Her dark eyes were thoughtful. "Was that really what you were thinking?"

"No," he admitted after a long pause. "Actually I was thinking about how fooled we can be sometimes."

"Fooled?"

"Yes. Like the Dead Sea." He pointed to the panorama before them. "From a distance she holds out so much promise. She is beautiful from here. You might think at first you could satisfy all of your needs at her shores." Brad looked into those sober, probing eyes for what seemed like an interminable moment, then finally looked away. "But when you get closer, you find the promise is not real. You have deceived yourself into thinking she can solve your problems. And you go away more thirsty than before."

The gondola reached the top, and in the stillness they could hear the laughter and chatter of the group as they disembarked and climbed the last few feet to the top.

Finally Miri spoke, her voice soft, her eyes reflective. "But such is not always the case. Sometimes the promise is fulfilled."

Brad glanced at her sharply, wondering if she had sensed more of his feelings than he thought. But Miri turned and gazed out over the valley and water below them so he couldn't see her eyes.

"From the hills above Tiberias," she continued, "the Sea of Galilee looks very much like the Dead Sea does from here. But when you come closer, you find no deception. The water is clear and sweet, the shore is lined with trees and shrubs, the depths are filled with fish. She fulfills all of one's expectations. If one did not know there was a difference between the Dead Sea and the Sea of Galilee, one might never come down to drink and be satisfied."

A moment earlier, she had asked him what he was thinking. Now he would have given far more than a penny to know her thoughts.

"Miri, I—" He stopped and then shook his head. What would he say? What *could* he say?

Again those deep, unreadable eyes probed his for a long moment. Then she brightened and smiled. "Which reminds me, how would you like a free trip to the Galilee for three days?"

"The Galilee sounds great, but not for free."

"Hey, Mr. Proud, just listen for a moment. You've heard me speak about my good friend, Sarah Millstein."

"The one who teaches school on the kibbutz?"

"Yes. She is taking the children on a *tee-yool*—an out-

158

ing. Oh, there's no really good English word for it. It's kind of like a tour, a field trip, as you would say. Only in Israel it's more like our national pastime. We love to see our land and our country."

"I understand."

"I promised Sarah I would serve as their guide. They leave next Sunday."

"That sounds good, but I still insist on paying my way."

"Just listen, please. The men of the kibbutz are just finishing up the harvest. They can spare only one sixteen-year-old to guard the children. They prefer two guards."

That was one of the sobering realities of Israel that Brad had noticed. Every group of children was accompanied by armed men or women. The terrorists had no respect for age, and the Israelis knew from grim experience that they must protect their own.

"They just happen to be offering about fifteen dollars a day for someone who could accompany them. That would cover your guide's fee."

Brad laughed. "You are an incorrigible liar, for which I am grateful. Tell Sarah she has a guard."

"Good. We'll—"

"Oh," Brad exclaimed in sudden disappointment. "I have to work for your father those nights."

Miri blushed slightly. "I've already talked to him about it, hoping you would accept." The blush deepened. "I mean, assuming you wanted to see the Galilee. Father said that was fine."

"You're sure?"

"Yes, I'm sure. He said at the beginning he promised you time off whenever you wanted it, and you haven't asked for any yet. Sarah will hold classes for the children each afternoon and since we'll be staying mostly on local kibbutzim, the children will be safe. I could then take you to the Christian sites, if you'd like."

"I would like," Brad said firmly. "The whole thing sounds great. Ali's new English teacher should be here Thursday, so I'll be finished at the school."

"Fine." Miri stood up. "Then enough of this decadent American laziness. Up, we must press on to the top."

Brad groaned and stood up to join her, hoisting his camera bag to his shoulder. "And you criticize the Romans for being such terrible taskmasters."

Three hours later they sat in the quiet coolness of the giant cistern on the southern tip of Masada. *Cistern* was a deceptive word if one thought of a well or similar storage facility. This one, hewn out of solid rock, was approximately the size of a small chapel, and in Roman times it held over eighty million gallons of water. Now it was dry and dusty, the aqueducts that fed it long in disrepair. The only light entered through the three or four openings near the ceiling, where the water had originally been funneled in. It was dim and gloomy, appropriate to the mood of Masada. They had explored the ruins on the top: the bath house, the storage buildings, the synagogue, the incredible "hanging palace" of King Herod, which clung to three levels of the northern face of the cliff.

Miri had told him the story of the last days in the fortress, back in the first century A.D. She talked of the huge dirt ramp built in the searing desert heat by Jewish slaves to provide a place for the Roman siege machines to batter the walls, of the shift in wind that drove the Roman fire into the wooden braces of the Jewish wall and signaled the collapse of their last defense against Rome. Miri's voice grew subdued and husky with emotion as she told of the Jewish leader, Eleazar, and his impassioned plea to the defenders to cheat the Romans of their victory after three years of siege. If it was God's will they perish, he demanded that they do so by their own hands.

Miri described those final moments when the men had embraced their wives and children and then, weeping, cut them down with the sword. The men had then drawn lots. Ten were chosen to kill the others who lay down next to the bodies of their families and bared their throats. Those ten next drew lots. One, whom fate chose, executed the other nine, set fire to the buildings, and then ran himself through.

Now as Miri and Brad sat on the bottom step of the flight of stairs hewn out of the walls of stone, Brad was keenly aware of the soft touch of her arm against his own.

"There were seven survivors," she said, picking up the narrative without a break. "Two women and five children. They told the Romans what had happened. They had hidden in one of the cisterns—I like to think it was this one, where we are now—when the suicide pact was carried out."

She looked around the giant cavern as though looking for traces of the seven. "Some scholars believe that two of the men didn't have the courage to kill their families, or that the women fled here with their children to avoid death. But I believe Eleazar appointed them to survive so they could testify that the Jews would rather die than fall into Roman hands."

She fell silent, and the gloom of the cavern seemed to permeate her mood as well as Brad's. He started to speak, but just then six tourists started down the stairs into the cistern. Brad half expected Miri to leave, but she stood up and moved away from the stairs, smiling politely at the intruders, then waited quietly as they oohed and aahed and flashed their cameras. When they were gone she moved back to the stairs and sat down again. Brad joined her.

"Some people accuse us of having a Masada complex," she said.

"What is that?"

"They say we view it as a national shrine. We bring all of our new military cadets up to the top of Masada to swear their oath of allegiance. They end it by saying, 'Masada shall not fall again.' It has become the motto, the cry of Israel."

"Yes," Brad said, "I've heard that."

"The Western press says we have the same complex. We are so afraid of defeat that we would rather commit suicide as a nation than give in. They say Israel has a death wish, a suicide fixation."

"Perhaps the Western press has never walked through Yad Vashem," Brad answered quietly.

Miri gave him a long look. "It is hard for others to understand," she finally said, choosing her words with great care, "but this land is part of me. It is a land with many difficulties and many challenges. Taxes are incredibly steep, the highest in the world, because one half of our budget goes for defense. Inflation is out of control. The Israeli pound was worth two dollars and eighty cents in 1948. Now it is worth twenty-three cents. Nearly every couple works two jobs to make ends meet. We call our children the 'key children,' because they wear their apartment keys around their necks since their parents are rarely there when they come home from school. We are a land of almost unbearable tension, a land of soldiers and war. Men and women are drafted in Israel, and all men stay in the reserves with three weeks of summer training until they are fifty. Childless women stay in the reserves till age thirty-four. There is hardly an apartment building without its war widow. We are a country of armed guards and barbed wire, of night patrols and terrorist attacks."

Brad nodded, wanting her to know he understood, and yet not wanting to interrupt her.

"Some have come here, and they cannot stand living on the edge of the knife as we do. They go back home. I do not condemn them. Sometimes I long for peace, for relief, for rest. But if we fail here, now, if Israel falls again, then who will save my people when the next fuehrer comes to power?"

She stared at Brad almost defiantly, daring him to speak. Then gradually her face softened into a quiet smile. "That is the passionate speech of a guide who has forgotten her place. It will not cost you any extra."

Brad smiled. "Do you know what I think?"

She shook her head.

"I think if you had been asked to be one of the two women survivors of Masada, you would have refused."

To his surprise, she flared up at that. "Was life as a slave in Roman hands more sweet than death?" she said fiercely. "I think not."

"Hey!" Brad said, taking her gently by the shoulders. "Put away your sword, Eleazar. I meant that not as an attack, but as a salute."

And when he felt her stiffness slowly relax, he pulled her to him and gently kissed her. For a split second she started to resist, but then came willingly to him, her lips warm and responsive.

Miri pulled away and stared at him for a long moment. Then she put her arms around his neck and kissed him back, a soft, lingering kiss. Pulling away again, she shook her head, almost sadly. "This wasn't supposed to be part of the guide service either," she said, her voice very soft.

And then to his surprise, she stood up, turned, and ran swiftly up the stairs into the sunlight, leaving him to stare after her.

Twenty

They stood under the deep shadows of a poinciana tree, Miri close to him, her head against his shoulder. The chirp of an occasional cricket was the only sound louder than the slight rustling of leaves when the breeze stirred. The bright orange-red flowers of the tree, now barely visible in the light of the moon, poured their rich fragrance into the air around them.

She shivered slightly in the evening cool, and Brad put his arm around her shoulder. "Cold?"

"Not now."

"Want to go in?"

"Not yet. It's so lovely out here."

"It's been a lovely three days. I can see why Jesus loved the Galilee so much," Brad said. "The whole area is beautiful. And the children have been delightful, Miri. I'm glad you needed some help with them."

"So am I," she murmured. "It's been a wonderful time for me."

"Miri?"

"Hmmmm?"

"Sometime we have to talk about some things."

She nodded, reaching up to touch his hand on her shoulder. "I know."

He was silent, torn with indecision. Three times he had decided to tell her about his decision to return to America. Three times he had turned away, unable to bring himself to say it because it committed him to a course he still fought against.

She looked up at him, then put her finger gently to his lips. "Not tonight. I know it is time we talk very honestly with each other. But not tonight, not now. Tomorrow we go back home, back to life and reality. Tomorrow is soon enough, okay?"

"Okay," he agreed, pulling her around to face him. She looked up expectantly, but as he bent his head down to kiss her, Brad suddenly remembered Mordecai, the sixteen-year-old from Sarah Millstein's kibbutz who had accompanied them on this outing as the other guard. Because it was located close to Lebanon, the kibbutz posted a nightly guard, and the young man had insisted he take his turn.

"What is the matter?" Miri asked as he pulled back.

"Mordecai."

"Mordecai?"

"Yes, he's on guard duty right behind us."

Miri giggled. "Don't you think he's ever seen a man and woman kiss before?"

"Well, I know, but—"

Her own kiss cut off his words.

"Oh, for heaven's sake," Miri said, still sensing his hesitancy. "He can't see us that well here in the shadows." She stood on tiptoe and peered over his shoulder. "Besides, he's not even there now."

That surprised Brad. The young man had been standing under the yard light when he and Miri had strolled by. They had spoken to him briefly, and then stopped here under the tree. Brad turned around and studied the large parking area of the kibbutz.

"Maybe he went off duty," Miri suggested.

"No," Brad said, scanning the area with his eyes, aware of a sudden sense of foreboding. "He told me he was to stay on watch until midnight. He was very proud to be doing it, and very conscientious."

Miri clutched at Brad's arm, sensing his sudden concern. "Do you think something is wrong?"

"I don't know," he said, his voice barely audible. He pushed her gently aside and reached for the carbine he had leaned against the trunk of the tree. He had carried it almost religiously for the last three days.

Brad touched Miri's arm. "He may have just walked over to talk with the other guard, or maybe he got embarrassed eavesdropping on us, and stepped around the corner of the building. Stay here. If I'm not back in five minutes, sound the alarm."

She nodded, gave his hand a quick squeeze, and stepped back deeper into the shadows.

It took Brad just one minute to reach the spot where Mordecai had been standing. He moved in a crouch around the perimeter of the open area, using the shadows of bushes and vehicles as cover. Even if nothing was wrong, he didn't want to startle a trigger-happy kid.

But Mordecai was never going to be startled again. Brad found him around the side of the building face down in the dirt, a large dark spot staining his T-shirt in the center of his back. Fear hit Brad like a wave of icy water. He stood motionless, knowing from experience that it was the initial burst of adrenalin racing through his system. Every sense in his body was straining to read the night.

A minute later he was back with Miri. "Mordecai is dead." He went on quickly, ignoring the sharp intake of her breath. "The fence has been cut, so they're somewhere inside the compound."

"Oh no!" she cried. "The children!"

Brad lunged for her as she started to dart away and jerked her back. "Listen!" he said urgently. "They can't have gotten far yet. We saw Mordecai just two or three minutes ago." He raised his arm and pointed. "They'll head for the dormitories, and if we try and warn the others, they'll see us."

He gripped her shoulders and noted that while her

eyes were wide, they held no panic. "Keep to the cover of the bushes and buildings. Go to the back gate and get the other guards. Tell them to watch out for me. I'll see if I can delay these guys. Be careful!"

Sprinting away across the grass, Brad heard her one desperate whisper, *"You* be careful."

As he cut around the equipment shed, Brad's mind raced. All the old instincts jumped into life, and his mind clicked with deadly cool precision. The prime question involved how many there were. Three to six, he guessed. There was no question about their target—the two long, low buildings that housed the occupants of the kibbutz. Terrorists sought psychological shock effect, and blowing up empty sheds and stables was hardly the most effective way to achieve that.

As Brad dropped quietly to his belly and slithered around the corner of the kibbutz dining room, he saw the first man. The dark figure was crouched down over a bundle of some kind, fiddling with the flap. His rifle lay on the ground alongside him.

The terrorist was scared or an amateur, or both, for he had chosen terrible field position. The dim light from one of the windows left him in clear silhouette. His back was turned to the one most likely source of attack, and he had set his rifle down. The critical question was whether someone else was covering for him. There was no time to wait and find out. Once that bundle was armed, Brad didn't want to be handling it. He leaped to his feet and darted toward the huddled figure.

Whether it was Brad's footsteps that caught the attention of the terrorist or the sudden blast of automatic rifle fire that exploded the silence of the night didn't make a lot of difference. The young Arab spun around and grabbed for his rifle about two seconds too late. Brad hit him with a sweeping blow from the rifle butt as he flew by him and dropped into a tuck and roll, slamming up behind the cover of the main steps.

The second terrorist who had opened fire may have been scared, but he was definitely not an amateur. The bullets tracked Brad's path with deadly accuracy, chipping cement off the stairs, then whining away in angry ricochets.

Suddenly the whole compound erupted. Automatic rifle fire opened up behind him, then more blasted away to his left. He suddenly felt sick. Had Miri stumbled into them? Shifting his weight, Brad prepared to make a dash for better cover, but he was directly under the light over the front step of the dormitory, and his assailant could obviously see every twitch he made. He frantically jerked himself into a tight ball behind the steps as a hail of bullets bracketed his position like a furious swarm of hornets.

Slowly he inched over onto his back, and with one blast from the carbine he took out the light above him. Again he hugged the earth as the deadly hail sought him out.

Suddenly the front door squeaked loudly.

"Stay back!" Brad shouted, but if the man understood English he paid no attention. The door exploded outward, and a dark figure hurtled over Brad, clearing the steps completely. It was utterly courageous and utterly suicidal. The man came out of his dive and got three steps into a darting run when the "hornets" found him, jerked him violently around twice, then cut his legs out from under him.

"Can you hear me inside?" Brad hissed, now painfully aware that the lights from the doorway left him as exposed as before. "This is Brad Kennison," he tried again. "I'm with Miri Shadmi. Can you hear me?"

"Yes." It was a guttural whisper, urgent and commanding. "Cover me! I'm coming out!"

"No!" Brad shot back, but he could have saved his breath. The man near the dining hall opened up again, and the bullets slamming through the open doorway provided a far more convincing command than Brad's.

168

"Cut the lights!" Brad called softly, not daring to raise his head.

There was a short bark in Hebrew, and the lights went dark. But there was still sufficient light in the area to make lifting one's head a very foolish move.

"How many are there?" the deep voice whispered.

"Two here. One is down. The other one has an automatic rifle over by the dining hall. Can you throw something out the side window to distract him?"

There was another unintelligible grunt, and a moment later a muffled scraping from the inside. Then, "Ready?"

"Ready!" Brad swung his carbine around and tensed his muscles.

The shattering crash of glass brought a vicious response from across the grass. Brad popped up, saw the muzzle flashes coming from a clump of bushes near the building, and snapped off four quick shots. He grunted in satisfaction as he dropped back down and heard a sharp cry of pain and brief thrashing in the bushes.

"I think it's clear," he called in through the door. "I'll cover you."

The Israeli kibbutzniks came tumbling out of the doorway like skydivers out of the belly of an airplane. A barrel-chested man with no shirt barked commands in Hebrew. Two men ran to their downed comrade while four more darted for the two downed terrorists. Brad had hit the second man in the upper thigh and high in the chest. He was bleeding badly, but he was still conscious. The Israeli had not been as lucky.

The owner of the guttural whisper nodded once to Brad; then, amenities over, his face hardened. "It sounds as though the others are down by the dairy barns. Let's go!" Again the short, barked commands in Hebrew sent the men running, this time Brad with them.

It was short but vicious. Three other terrorists had fled to the animal sheds when their surprise had been cut short, and now they fought like cornered wildcats. But the

Israelis had a fury of their own. When two of the three Arabs went down in a withering cross fire, the third screamed wildly and tossed out his rifle.

The sudden quiet was almost as deafening as the previous bedlam. The big man jerked his head, and the terrified Arab was led away by three grim-faced farmers. "Come!" he said to Brad. "It sounds as if it is over. Let's assess the damage."

But the Israeli was wrong. As they came around the last dormitory building, they saw a large crowd milling around in a wide circle. Sarah Millstein turned and saw them, then burst into sobs. "Brad!" she cried. "He's got Miri!"

With the large man clearing a path like an angry bull, Brad plunged into the crowd. Suddenly he understood why the milling group had formed such a large ring around the two central figures. A young Arab boy, eyes wild with terror, had Miri around the throat with one arm and was waving the encircling Israelis back with the other, which held a hand grenade clenched in white knuckles. The Arab, clearly not much older than Mordecai had been, was screaming at the crowd in hysterical Arabic.

Brad stared for a split second, his stomach a hard knot, then grabbed the big man's shoulder. "What's he saying?" he demanded.

A man next to them spoke up. "He's saying he'll let go of the pin on the grenade unless we stand back and let him out of here."

"Okay," Brad said, yanking on the big man's arm. "Tell him we'll do it. Tell the people to move back and let him go."

The man thrust Brad's hand away and shook his head. "We don't allow hostages to be taken," he said bluntly, turning away.

Brad spun around savagely. "Listen," he hissed, "I

know where they cut the fence and came in. Is there any other way out of here besides the gates?"

"No. And they are locked."

"All right. I'll meet him at the fence. Don't let anyone follow him and panic him. I think he'll go out the way he came in unless he's cornered."

The Israeli looked doubtful. "What if there are others?"

"This makes a total of six. I think that's it. If not, I've got this." He waved the carbine.

The Israeli hesitated. "Well—"

"Come on, man!" Brad cried, wanting to shake him violently. "If he sees me leave, he'll know what we're up to. I've got to go now."

"Okay. Go!"

"Don't let *anyone* follow him," Brad commanded. As he turned and ran hard for the perimeter of the kibbutz, he heard a man's voice start to boom out in Arabic.

Fortunately, the terrorists had picked their point of entry well. It was one of the darkest portions of the fence, and the cut lay between two large overhanging oleander bushes. Brad surveyed the setup quickly, then squeezed in against the fence behind the bush. It was tight, severely restricting his freedom of movement, but it was the only place of concealment that would give him a shot at the man's hand. The rifle was useless in these close quarters, and he propped it under the oleander's branches. Then he concentrated on trying to settle his breathing down to where it didn't whistle like a force-six gale. He didn't dare think about Miri with the Arab.

It didn't take long. He heard the scrape of their feet on the gravel first, then the sharp commands in Arabic. Brad breathed a quick sigh of relief when they rounded the corner of the equipment shed and came past Mordecai's body toward the cut in the fence. The young man's back was to Brad as he watched for possible pursuit, but his grip on Miri was iron-tight. Everything depended now on how this terrified Arab decided to make his exit through the fence. He and Miri couldn't go through together, and he wouldn't dare let go of her for an instant.

He pushed her through first, holding tightly to her wrist, cursing her in a steady flow of Arabic. Brad heard Miri gasp as the cut edge of the fence scraped her arm. As the young terrorist crouched down to follow her through, the hand with the grenade arched back toward where Brad huddled in the bushes.

Brad lunged forward, clamping both hands tightly over the grenade. "Run, Miri!" he shouted, jerking the thin young body backwards and breaking his hold on Miri's wrist. She fell backward, then leaped up and darted away. Brad saw her go and then promptly forgot about her. The Arab was onto his back like a terrified cat, scratching, clawing, screaming, pounding. Brad held on desperately to the boy's fist and the grenade with both hands and hurled himself backward. They fell heavily against the shed, Brad's body crushing the boy between it and him. The air whooshed out of the Arab like a popped balloon, and the flailing instantly stopped. Stunned himself, it took Brad almost a full second to realize that he was squeezing an empty hand. The grenade was gone!

With no idea where it had dropped, Brad jumped away in three mighty leaps, then dove for the ground, feeling searing pain as his face skidded in the gravel. The blast roared out behind him, peppering the building and fence with shrapnel.

Dazed, Brad got slowly to his feet, vaguely aware that there was still a very dangerous young man out here with him. He shook his head and tried to move into action. Then he saw the dark mass huddled up against the building and moved slowly toward it. Cautiously, he turned him half over, then felt sick. Like Mordecai, this boy would have no more surprises. The hand grenade had fallen within three or four feet of him, and he had caught a major portion of the blast full in the chest. Brad let the boy slump back again and stood up wearily.

"Miri!" he called, a great relief washing over him. He was dimly aware of the pounding of feet behind him. "Miri! It's Brad. Everything is okay now."

He held the fence back as she came running, stumbling out of the dark. She crawled through and threw herself into his arms.

"It's all right," he soothed, holding her tight, as great sobs racked her body. "Everything's okay. It's all right now."

Twenty-one

Dawn was just starting to lighten the eastern sky when Miri peeked into the TV room off the main dining hall of the kibbutz. "There you are," she said to Brad, her voice full of relief.

Surprised, he stood up. "Hi, what are you doing here? You're supposed to be asleep."

"So are you."

"Fat chance," he said. The uproar had not finally died down until after two in the morning, with police, military, and press swarming the place. Brad, painfully embarrassed at being the hero of the hour, had finally pled exhaustion and gone to his room. A doctor had forced a sleeping pill down Miri two hours before that, and had sent her to bed. Once it was quiet, Brad had slipped in here and had been staring at the walls ever since, thinking about two young boys—one Arab, one Jewish—and about a dark-haired, dark-eyed Israeli *sabra*.

Almost shyly, Miri looked up at him. "Do you mind if I join you?"

"I'd like that."

She came and stood before him, then reached up and gently touched the angry red scratches on his cheek. "How do I ever say 'thank you'?" she said, her eyes suddenly welling up with tears.

He reached out and pulled her to him. "Teach me how to dive into loose gravel and not lead with my face." Then the image of the young Arab boy who hadn't dived at all flashed into his mind. "It isn't much," he murmured.

"You know what I mean," she said, struggling to control her voice. "Me. The children. They told you about the explosives?"

He nodded soberly. There had been sufficient to level a good portion of the two dormitories. Brad reached down and examined the four ugly red welts that ran across Miri's arm where the fence had caught her.

"If I can't take better care of you than that, you'd better shop around for a more efficient bodyguard."

"Oh, Brad," she cried, throwing her arms around him and clinging to him fiercely. "When I think—" She shuddered and held him even more tightly.

"Hey! Hey!" he said gently, tipping her head up and wiping the tears away with his hand. "I'm supposed to be the soft-hearted American, and you're the stoic, brave Israeli. Remember?"

"I know, just give me a minute, okay?"

"Sure," he said, and held her close to him.

Finally she pulled away and looked up into his eyes. "It's tomorrow now."

"It is?" he asked, not following the sudden switch in the conversation.

"Yes. We said we would talk tomorrow. Can we talk now?"

Brad nodded, and they moved over to a couch and sat down. He took her hand and began tracing the lines on her palm lightly with his finger. For the last two hours he had been asking himself if he could really leave this woman and return home. And yet the reply followed quickly. Can you be happy setting aside your goals and staying in Israel with a nonmember wife? After two hours, he was less certain of the answers than when he had started. "You know, Miri," he said, trying to keep his voice light, "in some ways this could be even harder than what we've just gone through."

"I know, Brad," she said softly. "So let me start."

Gratefully he nodded.

Miri took a deep breath and let it out slowly, then put her hand over his. "I love you, Brad Kennison."

If she had jabbed him with a pin he wouldn't have jumped more visibly. Completely taken by surprise, he stared at her.

"I know what you're thinking," she stammered, finding it very difficult to explain her feelings. "But it is not just because of what you did last night. It didn't take a hand grenade to convince me of my feelings for you. I have known I love you for two weeks now. Last night only convinced me that I can't hide it from you—or from myself—any longer." Once again the dark eyes threatened to spill over. "When that young Arab grabbed me, I was terrified, of course. But over and over I kept thinking, if I die Brad will never know how I feel. So . . ."

"Miri," Brad began, still half surprised, half overjoyed, "I—"

"No," she said quickly. "I want to finish. If I don't say it now—" She shook her head, her face determined. "I have finally had to face the fact that I feel something for you that I have never before felt for anyone. Remember David?"

"Do I ever!" Brad said, pulling such a face that it caused Miri to laugh. But the smile disappeared almost instantly.

"I thought for a while that I was falling in love with him. He's handsome, charming—"

"Wealthy," Brad added sourly.

"Yes. He is an Israeli girl's ideal. He is a decorated war hero, has a brilliant career ahead of him. Then you came along."

"Yeah. Poor, klutzy, abrasive."

She touched his cheek. "And brave and gentle and kind. And so intensely committed to your convictions." Her eyes were luminous as she looked into his. "This isn't supposed to happen, you know. Guides don't fall in love with their clients. Israelis don't fall in love with Americans. And," she paused, "and Jewish girls most certainly do not fall in love with Christians."

Brad took her face in his hands and pulled her to within an inch of his own. "And good Mormon boys don't fall in love with non-Mormon girls, Jewish, Catholic, or Anglo-Saxon Protestant. And yet I did. I have." He kissed her, a long, gentle kiss that was returned fully and completely.

"I'm so glad," she whispered, leaning against him snuggling in against his shoulder.

"Are you really, Miri? All things considered?"

She nodded. "Loving you is creating some real problems. But to not have you love me back would be infinitely worse."

He thought about that, knowing she was right, wishing she weren't. They sat quietly for several minutes, lost in their thoughts and basking in the warmth of their discovery. Finally she spoke.

"Tell me about marriage in the temple."

Once again she brought him bolt upright.

Miri blushed furiously. "Oh," she stammered, "I didn't mean it that way. I wasn't suggesting—" She stopped, thoroughly embarrassed.

Brad put his hand over her mouth. "Shhh!" he said gently, kissing her on the tip of her nose. "I didn't take it that way. What I want to know is how you know about temple marriage. I've never said a word about it." His eyebrows furrowed. "Has Ali been talking to you?"

"Only after I asked him about it," Miri admitted.

"Then how—?"

"I read about it." Seeing the question on his face, she continued. "There is a book in the library at Hebrew University called *Meet the Mormons*. It said that Mormons believe in marriage for eternity and that it is performed in their temples."

Brad suddenly remembered Miri's surprising knowledge of Mormons at the party in her father's home. "Is that all it said?" he asked.

"Yes." Her eyes had that gentle teasing look that he was beginning to recognize. "But President Marks explained it in much greater detail." She looked up at him, waiting for his reaction.

"President Marks!" Brad had been up now for twenty-four hours—and an exhausting twenty-four hours at that. That was the only explanation for how sluggishly his mind was working.

"I've been meeting with President Marks for the past two weeks," she confessed.

"You've what?" If she had just announced that Moshe Dayan had become a Franciscan priest and entered a monastery, he could not have been more surprised.

"I wanted to ask some questions," Miri explained quickly, "and I couldn't trust my reaction to you anymore. I couldn't be objective. So I called him and asked if we could talk. Does that make you feel bad?"

"Bad? No, I'm delighted, Miri."

Miri stood up, walked over to a chair across from Brad, and sat down facing him. "I said I wanted to have my part first in this little talk, so let me say it now."

Brad nodded, noting the tension in her hands, the stress in her face.

She sighed, then plunged in. "I know it was terribly presumptuous on my part, but once I began to see that our relationship was getting serious—" She shook her head impatiently. "No. Why beat around the bush? Once I realized I loved you and thought that you might come to love me too, I began considering what that meant for us. I suppose I shouldn't have. But I kept thinking, 'What if this works out? What if we get married?'"

"Don't apologize," Brad said softly. "That 'what if' has been one of the primary things on my mind for the past two or three weeks. I'm glad you've thought about it too."

She smiled her pleasure at that. "I remembered what I had read in the book about your marriages, so I asked Ali about it. I asked him not to mention it to you, for obvious reasons."

"He didn't."

"From Ali I learned that temple marriage is not just a light thing, not just a slight preference for one kind of ceremony over another. That is when I called President Marks."

She looked down at her hands as she went on. "He was very kind, but very direct. He said that if you were any kind of a Latter-day Saint, and he thinks you are, then there would be no option. Either I become a Mormon or we could never be married." She looked up. "He was a little more diplomatic than that, but the message was clear."

She gave him a long, searching look. "Are you any kind of a Latter-day Saint, Brad?"

There it was, the question he had been hurling himself against for the past two hours.

"Our only hope of working this thing through, Brad," she said as he hesitated, her voice almost a whisper, "is if we are both totally honest."

"I know, Miri. I know." He took a deep breath and began. "All of my life there has never been the slightest question in my mind about my church commitment. Until you, I've never even dated anyone who wasn't an active Latter-day Saint. I suppose it says more eloquently than anything else I could say about how much I love you that for the first time in my life I have seriously considered abandoning that position." He gave her a rueful expression. "Thou art a sore temptation, Miriam Shadmi."

"For that much at least I am glad," she said, her eyes soft.

Brad's expression was morose. "I guess what it all comes down to is, do your convictions guide your life or not?"

"So when all is said and done, Brad, what you're saying is that President Marks is right. There is no other acceptable option for you."

Brad nodded, his expression bleak. "I guess not, Miri. It sounds so selfish that it has to be done my way. But I can't accept any other choice and live with myself. I can't."

"In a way, I suppose that makes me glad. That's the very thing I admire the most in you. But it puts me in a very strange position. It's like emotional blackmail. Now I want to accept Mormonism for that reason alone, so I won't lose you."

"I would never want that," Brad said quickly.

"I know, I know," she said. "But don't you see? Now I want it, not just because it may be good or true, but because it gives me access to you."

"That would be a sell-out for you, Miri, just as marrying outside of the temple would be a sell-out for me."

"Exactly," she said, grateful for his understanding. "So I have a suggestion, a proposed bargain, as it were."

"I'm listening, eagerly."

"For my part of the bargain, I will try to find out for myself if Mormonism is all that you say it is."

Brad felt his heart leap with elation. "Great!"

"In the past, I have wanted to know what you believed, to understand it. Now my studies will take on a whole new purpose and dimension. I don't just want to know it, I want to know *if it is true*."

"I wouldn't ask for any more than that," Brad said, thrilled at her words.

"In fact, I have already started. That's why I've been meeting with President Marks. I've been reading in the Book of Mormon you gave me. I'm now up to—how do you say it? Mos-ee-ah."

"Moz-i-uh," Brad corrected softly. "That is tremendous."

"I have even started to pray about it and the whole

idea of Mormonism. Do you know how strange and difficult that is for me, when I'm not even sure whether I accept the reality of God?"

Deeply touched, Brad got up and went to her, pulled her to her feet to face him. "You make me feel ashamed that my belief comes so easily. If you are doing that, what is my part of the bargain?"

"I'll tell you in a moment," she said, holding his hand tightly. "But I must say one other thing. Remember, we promised to be honest."

"Yes."

"Don't let your hopes rise too high, Brad. I could find it very easy to accept Mormonism. So far I find the Book of Mormon very plausible, and the idea of Joseph Smith as a prophet is not difficult at all. Your religion is very logical and has many parallels to Jewish life. But—"

"But—" Brad repeated, knowing what was coming.

Miri shook her head slowly, her dark eyes deeply troubled. "The idea that Jesus was the Son of God strikes against everything I believe. Every portion of my soul cries out against the sheer illogic of the concept that a god had to become a man to save everybody. That a man who is born of God—*is* a god—would allow himself to be nailed to a cross while men jeer and spit upon him—it's so absolutely contrary to what I can accept. I don't know if I ever can change that, Brad. Not ever."

"Miri," he said quietly, "will you pray about that too?"

"To a god who let six million of my people go to their deaths in Germany and Poland?" she asked, the tears welling up in her eyes. "Can't you see, that is what makes this so difficult for me. You accept a god with feelings and concerns, a god who listens to prayers and answers them. But how can I ask for an answer myself, when he refuses to listen to the cries of my people?"

She wiped the tears away with the back of her hand. "I'm sorry," she said, struggling to regain her composure. "But I want you to know that this whole thing may not work, Brad. And if it doesn't, if I give it my honest sincere effort and it fails, I don't want to lose you."

Brad enfolded her gently into his arms and held her to him. "It won't fail, Miri. I'll be praying with you, for you. I'll help you."

Slowly she pushed away from him. "That's your part of the bargain. I don't want you to help me," she said softly.

"But why?"

"I am going to ask you to not push me on this in any way. I promise you I will try to find an answer with all my heart. I ache for you. I want so badly for this to work out that if you start asking me, encouraging me, getting anxious about my progress, I'll cave in. Your love is pressure enough."

"Miri, I won't pressure you, but I just have to help!"

"Please!" Her eyes were pleading. "If it happens, I've got to know it was not just for you. I have got to find it myself. President Marks has agreed to meet with me and to answer my questions. And he's given me some other books to read. Please, Brad. It has to be my way!"

"Does that mean I can't see you?"

"Oh no," she said, quickly. "I'm not that noble. Just don't press me on this. Let me find my own way."

Brad kissed her then, hard and long.

"Does that mean 'yes'?" she asked breathlessly.

"That means yes. You've got your deal."

"Thank you for understanding." She put her arm around his waist as she looked at her watch. "It's nearly five. The kitchen crew will be arriving any moment now. We'd better go."

He kissed her one more time, and they moved to the door.

She stopped and turned to face him. "Brad?"

"What?"

"You know how they have a canopy at Jewish weddings?"

"Yes." Brad had been doing some reading of his own. "And do you know why?"

Surprised, Miri answered. "They say it represents the tabernacle that Moses built in the wilderness."

"Exactly. And the tabernacle was the portable temple for the Israelites. In other words, though you don't know it, you believe in temple marriage too." He smiled.

"The parallels really are quite remarkable, aren't they?"

"Anyway, I didn't mean to interrupt you. Go on."

"Well," she said, her dark eyes sparkling now, "*if* this does happen to work out and I join the Church, and *if* we then decide to get married, could we have a canopy? I mean, I know we'd be married in the temple. But at the reception, could we?"

Brad took her by the shoulders and looked her in the eye. "Miriam," he said, "*if* this works out, you may have dancing elephants and the whole Israeli army at our reception, if that is what you want."

* * * * * *

Brad glanced at his watch, his face lined with exhaustion. It was nearly ten o'clock, and he was beat. Since he and Miri had parted in the TV room early that morning, it had been one long, frantic day. They had delivered the children back to their kibbutz west of Jerusalem shortly after eleven, but by the time they had accepted the profuse and often tear-filled thanks of three dozen parents, it was after noon before they had started back to Jerusalem. Much to Brad's dismay, a horde of reporters, photographers, and the curious were waiting for him in the hotel lobby. At first, grateful that he had dropped Miri off and saved her this, he stood patiently, embarrassed as they pressed him with questions and praise. But he quickly tired, feeling the drain of the last thirty hours catching up with him.

At that point Levi Shadmi had bustled in and driven the crowd out like a bull skinner handling a team of balky mules. When it was quiet, he had turned to face Brad. His normally piercing blue eyes suddenly grew moist, and Brad's spine nearly cracked under the crushing bear hug that was thrown around him. "To bed with you," was all that Shadmi had finally managed, his voice low and raspy.

But three hours later, Brad had awakened with a start. The huge Arab in his nightmare had leaped through the fence, pulling it closed behind him, then had tossed Brad the hand grenade, his mouth twisted in a wicked grin. Over Levi's vehement protests Brad had come downstairs and insisted on taking his evening shift at the desk. Now he knew that had been a foolish mistake, for the phone had rung incessantly, and two more reporters had sought him out.

Brad groaned inwardly as he heard the lobby doors open again, but then brightened as he turned and saw it was Ali. "Hi," he called, pleased to see his friend.

Ali snapped to attention, executed the perfect imitation of a drum roll with his tongue while he tapped his invisible sticks, then lifted both hands to form a mock trumpet and tooted out a fanfare. "Welcome home, the conquering hero!" he called out in his best herald's voice.

"All right," Brad growled in embarrassment. "Knock it off."

Ali strode over and stuck out his hand. "Allow me to shake the hand of the man who made the front page of today's Jerusalem *Post*." He stepped back so as to get a better view of the unseen newspaper hanging in the air in front of him. "Viet Nam Veteran Battles Terrorists," he intoned.

"Hey, come on, Ali. It's bad enough as it is, without you chiming in. I even got a call from my folks this evening. It made the wire services in America."

"No kidding? Not only nationally famous, but internationally as well. That is really something."

"No it's not. I've been hounded all day. And my

mother! I kept telling her there was no danger here. Somehow I have lost my credibility."

"Not with Levi Shadmi," Ali said, coming around the counter to sit next to Brad. "He was in the shop picking up some things today. He could hardly talk about you without choking up."

"That's only because of Miri," Brad said modestly. "He thinks about what could have happened."

"How is Miri, anyway?"

"Fine. She went through a real shock, and she got some bad scratches on her arm, but she's incredible. Today you wouldn't know anything had happened."

"She really is a remarkable person," Ali said, then squinted at Brad. "How are things going with you two? Last night probably didn't hurt, did it?"

"I'm very encouraged." Brad told Ali about their early-morning talk concerning her study of Mormonism and about their bargain, but left out Miri's confession about her feelings for him.

"Good," Ali said, obviously pleased. "If she'll give it an honest shot, I think you've got her. And President Marks is super. But can you really stay out of it?"

Brad shrugged. "I don't know. I'm going to try, because she is right. If she joins, it can't be for me."

"So how long do you wait?"

Brad let out a long sigh. He had asked himself the same question several times today. "I don't know."

"And if she finally does decide against joining the Church? Are you really going to just walk away?"

"*Just* walk away? No, I won't *just* walk away. But I will go. At least I've come to that. I will not marry out of the temple."

"And what about your decision to return home and get started on your schooling there?"

"It goes into a holding pattern for now," Brad said glumly.

Ali touched his shoulder softly with his fist as he stood

up. "I don't envy you. You've got your plow stuck in some hard ground. But listen, I've got to get going. See you tomorrow," he called as he headed for the door.

"Hey!" Brad shouted. "I almost forgot." He left the counter and joined Ali at the door. "What did you decide about the Sinai trip?"

"Oh," Ali said, his brow furrowing. "I forgot about that in all the excitement. Tell me again. When are you leaving?"

"A week from next Monday, October the first. We'll be gone five days, Monday to Friday. All you need is a sleeping bag and personal items. Miri and Sarah have planned out the menu. You won't put any meat on those Arab bones, but you won't starve either."

"Sarah?"

"Yes, Sarah Millstein. The schoolteacher we were with this week. You and she could talk shop. I think Miri is hoping something will develop between Sarah and Nathan."

"Nathan's going?" Ali said slowly.

"Yes, he's got a week's leave for the Yom Kippur holiday. He was stationed in the Sinai in '67. He really knows the area." Suddenly Brad sensed Ali's hesitancy. "What's the matter?"

"Does Nathan know I'm going?"

"I don't know. And frankly, I don't care. I'm paying for the majority of this trip. It's my idea. It is the only part of Israel I haven't seen. So if he doesn't like it, tough! We can find our way around without him."

Ali still looked unconvinced.

"Anyway, I thought you got along fine with him."

"Oh, I do. It's just that . . ." He sighed. "With Miri I don't think of her as Jewish, and I don't think it occurs to her that I'm Arab, unless she really thinks about it. We're just people who like each other and do business together. I think the same is true of Levi. But I don't think Nathan can ever quite forget it. I suppose being in the military is part of it. It might add strain to the trip for you."

"I'll chance it," Brad said firmly. "So I say, let Nathan be hanged. I want you to come."

Ali nodded slowly. "And I would like to come. Count me in."

Twenty-two

The monastery of Saint Catherine lay near the southern tip of the Sinai Peninsula, nearly two hundred and fifty miles south of Jerusalem. The monastery looked more like a fortress than a center for meditation and prayer. Tucked up beneath the incredibly sheer granite cliffs of Mount Sinai, from a distance it looked unreal, almost toylike, like a model built by an architect to sell a client on his design. But when one stood at the base of the massive walls, six to eight feet thick and almost a hundred feet high, and saw that they enclosed an area about the size of Temple Square, any feeling of smallness was instantly dispelled.

In the harsher light of day one might agree with Ali's dry comment that since the Emperor Justinian's workers had left thirteen hundred years ago, nobody had touched the monastery. But now as Brad slipped out of his room, the arches and domes of the various buildings were lovely, almost ethereal in the pale light of the half moon that gleamed out of a stunningly clear sky.

Neither Nathan nor Ali nor any of the other six tourists in the men's dormitory stirred as Brad carefully dressed and slipped out. He tiptoed past the windows of the women's dorm-style room where Sarah and Miri lay sleeping and went down the stairs to ground level. Only then did he sit down and put on his tennis shoes.

The air was still biting cold with the desert night's

chill, and he shivered in his light windbreaker. The cold didn't concern him, however, for he had before him nearly two hours of hiking with a vertical ascent of almost three thousand feet. He would quickly warm to the task.

Of greater concern to Brad was Nathan's reaction when he awoke and found Brad's note. Though it was supposedly Brad's tour, Nathan had taken charge and wanted to be on the road by six this morning. They had a lot of hard, bone-jarring miles to drive across the Sinai. Brad knew he couldn't climb up and back in the three hours left till six, but he thought if he pushed himself he could make it in four, maybe four and a half. Yesterday, the five of them had taken nearly seven hours for the round trip up and down Mount Sinai. But they had set a leisurely pace and had spent over an hour on the top, plus another hour eating lunch on the way down.

The heavy iron door blocking the only exit through the high walls was shut and padlocked. For a moment Brad felt cheated but then he checked his watch and saw he was a few minutes early. He had told the Bedouin gatekeeper three o'clock, and he was confident his promise of some *baksheesh*, a little green on the palm, would bring him.

As he waited in the moonlight, aware of the immense stillness and the soft fragrance of some unknown blossoms, Brad wondered again why he was doing this. The climb to the top was a man-killer, especially the last portion, where the steep slopes gave way to imposing granite cliffs. The only access to the top lay in a narrow cleft, breached by seven hundred crude rock steps made by the monks. But yesterday, when he stood on the top of Mount Sinai, he knew he had to get up there again alone. In every direction the upthrusting fists of granite mountaintops punched into the incredible blue-black sky. No trees softened the grandeur and majesty of the convoluted, jagged rock. Breathtaking was a gross understatement. *Spirit-taking*, if there were such a word, would come closer. It was inspiring, and Brad felt a desperate need for some inspiration.

He heard a shuffling sound and saw the little man with the wizened old face appear from out of the dark.

"*Shukran*," the Bedouin said softly, as Brad slipped him three one-dollar bills, the universal trading medium of the Middle East.

Brad left the monastery quickly and settled into a steady pace that would eat up the distance without exhausting him, and yet leave his mind free to agonize over his dilemma. Two weeks ago he had been ecstatic over the prospects of Miri's conversion. Now he didn't know what to think. Miri had said virtually nothing about her quest. President Marks reported that they were still meeting regularly, and that he was pouring it onto her straight and undiluted. But when Brad pleaded with him for some indication of hopeful signs, the president just shook his head. "I don't know, Brad. I just don't know."

If that worry hadn't been hanging over him like the threat of a coming doomsday, Brad's life would have been glorious. The cactus spines of his *sabra* were completely retracted, and each new day he saw more of the tenderness, more of the inner flower unfolding. Cautiously, almost shyly, she opened herself more and more to him. He found a woman of great strength and yet gentle tenderness, sparkling, almost teasing humor, and yet profound solemnity. She was vitally alive, and he found her physical presence distracting to the point of madness. Yet they could sit for hours talking, touching ever so softly, and not have the physical blot out the wonder of discovering each other.

Brad had bitten his lip nearly a dozen times to stop himself from violating his part of the agreement, and so far he had been faithful to it. If she sensed his growing frustration and despair, the only sign she gave was in her fierce longing as she clung to him when they kissed. More and more he questioned his ability to hold out in his resolve. More and more he rationalized that if she couldn't commit before marriage, then after she surely would. More and more he asked himself what he would do if she came back at last and said, "I'm sorry, Mr. Kennison. I love you, but I can't abide your religion." Brad hunched his shoulders and increased his pace. Maybe if he punished his body sufficiently, it would let his mind rest.

The moon was now low in the sky, the stars glittering like a thousand thousand diamonds spread out on a vast expanse of blue-black velvet. He stared up into the heavens for a long moment. *Oh Lord*, he cried out from the depths of his heart, *Moses came to this mountain and received a law to govern Israel. I come to find answers to direct my life. What shall I do?*

Moses and Brad Kennison were not the only ones who had come to the top of Mount Sinai. The sky in the east gradually paled from the deep velvet of dawn, through the pink of coming sunrise, to full light. Brad was puffing heavily up the last fifty or so steps, his thigh muscles feeling like beef jerky that had been left out in the sun too long, when he raised his head and saw her.

She sat at the apex of the granite summit, her arms hugging her legs, the first rays of the morning sun burnishing her black hair with highlights of gold. Her head was cocked to one side, the dark brown eyes filled with—what? Pleasure? Amusement?

Brad stopped and stared at her. "Miri?"

"Hi," she said cheerily. "What took you so long?"

He shook his head. "What are you—?" He stood there, panting heavily, unable to believe what he was seeing.

"Hey, old man, when you get your breath, come on up. It's a gorgeous view."

He left the trail, scurried up the steep slope of rock,

and dropped down beside her. Miri reached over and brushed a damp lock of hair away from his forehead, then kissed him gently.

"Are you going to be okay?" she asked, as he took in huge gulps of air.

Brad glanced at his watch. One hour and a half. He had really pushed it. But to heck with that! He turned to her. "How in the world did you get here?"

"Rented a helicopter." Little flickers of amusement danced in her eyes.

"Come on!"

"Would you believe a friendly caravan?"

"Miri!" he said in exasperation. "How long have you been here?"

"About fifteen minutes." Gradually her smile faded away and she grew serious. "I overheard you talking to the gatekeeper last night, making arrangements to get out this morning." Her eyes dropped, and her fingers touched his arm. "I know you wanted to be alone, Brad. But I—" She sighed unhappily. "Do you mind terribly?"

Brad put his hand over hers and gave it a quick squeeze. "Of course not, I'm delighted. But when did you leave, for heaven's sake?"

"I slipped out at two-thirty, but I was afraid you might catch up to me, so I came up the front way. I wanted to surprise you."

"Well, you succeeded in that." Brad shook his head and stared at her, still unable to believe she was here. There were two ways up Sinai, the long circular back route Brad had taken and which most others took, and the much shorter route the monks had carved right up the face of the mountain into the rock. Virtually that whole way was like the last seven hundred steps Brad had just conquered. It was steep, precipitous, and, counting those last seven hundred, consisted of over three thousand steps of rock and dirt, some of which had a vertical rise of eighteen inches or more. They had gone down that way yesterday, and by the time they had reached the bottom, Brad's knees were throbbing. And that was going down!

"You came up the steps?"

Miri nodded.

"And you sit here looking like you've been in a beauty shop all morning. That's disgusting."

She grimaced, as though she were clenching her teeth in pain. "It's all show. Actually you will have to call for a stretcher to get me off the mountain. I left my legs behind somewhere on the way up."

Brad put his arms around her and hugged her to him. "You are something else, do you know that?"

"No, tell me," she murmured, putting her head against his shoulder.

Brad started to chuckle, and she looked up in surprise. "What?" she asked.

"Oh, I was just thinking. In Salt Lake City the kids drive up above the state capitol building or into the mountains so they can have a beautiful and private place to neck. But this is ridiculous."

"Neck?" Miri asked, puzzled for a moment. "Oh yes, that peculiar American expression. I never could understand how it got its name." Then she smiled. "If those are your intentions, Mr. Kennison, then maybe I'd better leave."

"Hey, remember, I had no idea you'd be here."

"I know. I've worried about that all the way up."

"Well, stop worrying. We haven't had a moment alone since we left Jerusalem. This is a delightful surprise." Suddenly he groaned. "Except Nathan will be furious. He'll think we planned this together."

"No, I told Sarah the situation last night. She'll tell him. Don't worry about Nathan," she added. "He likes to think he is much more intense than he really is."

"Sounds like someone else I once knew—no names mentioned, of course."

Miri dug him in the ribs with her elbow, then leaned

against him again and sighed, a sound that Brad couldn't decipher. Was it a sigh of happiness and contentment or of frustration and longing? He touched her gleaming black hair softly, aware that he was unable to untangle his own emotions, let alone hers.

"Brad?" They had been quiet for several minutes, both absorbed in their own thoughts.

"What?"

"Why *did* you come up here?" He had come to recognize that particular husky throatiness in her voice as a sign that she was struggling with her emotions.

"Oh," he said, wondering how much to admit, "mostly to see this sight again." His sweeping arm included the panorama before them. "It is really quite incredible."

"Mostly?"

"And to think," he added.

"About me? About us?"

Brad nodded.

"And so?"

"And so I found you here," he said, touching her nose with his fingertip. "You know I can't think when I'm around you."

"Brad, please!" Her brown eyes were full of pleading. "Tell me."

"How can I? We have an agreement."

"I know," she whispered, her eyes filling up. "And I know how hard it has been for you to keep it. You've been wonderful about it."

Now it was Brad's turn to sigh. "My part is no harder than yours," he apologized.

"So I'm lifting the restrictions for a moment. I may impose them again, but please tell me what you've been thinking these past few weeks."

He stared out across the granite peaks parading away before them. "I just wonder how it is coming for you. I wonder, and question, and yearn, and pray."

194

"And fast?"

Brad looked at her in surprise.

"I've been checking up on you," Miri admitted. "I ask the cook in the hotel dining room if you've eaten there."

He winced slightly. "Sometimes I eat at Ali's or somewhere else."

"Sometimes," she agreed. "I asked Ali too. He finally told me that you both were fasting and praying for me." The tears brimmed over, and she wiped at them angrily. "I love you, Brad," she whispered fiercely. "You are so good. Too good. How can I ever deserve you?"

He touched the wet streaks on her cheeks. "Too good for me? Only when it comes to hiking up mountains. If we get married, you will definitely have to restrain yourself."

"*If* we get married. And what if I don't find my answer?"

"I don't know," Brad said, his voice as full of sorrow now as her own. He began to trace a pattern with his finger on the dark tan of her forearm. "I think about not having you and I get this sick feeling in the pit of my stomach. I don't know, Miri. I don't know."

She nodded, sniffing back the tears. "I understand."

"Isn't there any hope, Miri? Are you getting any answers?"

Her dark hair rippled in the sunlight as she shook her head. "Sometimes I feel very encouraged. I'm nearly through the Book of Mormon now. It seems true. I want it to be true. But the other, it is like trying to pierce solid rock with a sword made of tin. I cannot seem to penetrate."

"Jesus?"

"And God, and the Atonement! Why can't I get an answer?"

"Have you tried fasting?"

Miri ducked her head and nodded almost imperceptibly. "I'm fasting now."

Brad suddenly remembered that at dinner last night

she had pleaded that she wasn't feeling too well and hadn't joined them. "And you're climbing Sinai? Miri, that's not wise."

"I've missed only one meal so far. If you care that much, then how can I not fast too?"

"The answers will come then," he said, holding her close, fiercely proud of her, and yet unable to shake the nagging fear that she might not be able to accept the answers when they came. Maybe they were coming now and she refused to soften. Was the Jewishness so deep that it could not be rooted out? "They have got to come!" he said ardently.

She shook her head sadly and touched his cheek. "I so much envy you that deep faith, that burning knowledge."

"It will come, Miri," he promised, taking her hands. "Keep trying. Please keep trying."

"I have not given up. And yet, it seems hopeless. President Marks said you believe that Jesus in his premortal life was the God of the Old Testament."

"Yes, he was and is Jehovah."

"The same God who delivered Israel from Egypt?"

"Yes."

"Then if he was powerful enough as *God* to save Israel from bondage, why did he have to become a *man* to save other men from the bondage of sin?" Her eyes were liquid and close to overflowing again. "I know you don't have any trouble with that, but can't you at least see how illogical it sounds—that a god has to become a man in order to save others?"

"I can understand," Brad said, trying to mask the discouragement in his eyes. "But there had to be someone who was like us, and yet free from our condition. If he had not been mortal and faced temptation, how could he say that he had triumphed over sin? And yet, if he had not been a god, he would have sinned too and then been in the same state as we are. How can a man locked in chains deliver others from captivity?"

Miri stood up, pulled Brad up to face her, and put her arms around his neck. He kissed her, pouring all the frustration and impatience and all the longing for resolution of their conflict into the embrace. She returned it, giving herself to him fully and without reservation. But when they parted, the barrier between them dropped back into place.

"I want to believe, Brad," she whispered. "Why won't God answer me?"

"I don't know," he admitted. "Maybe he is testing you."

"And how long must I wait? Two thousand years, like my people? Why doesn't your God listen to the cries of a Jew?"

Before he could answer, she shook her head. "I'm sorry. I didn't mean that."

Brad had an unexpected idea. He took both of her hands and brought them up, clasping them tightly. "Miri," he said, "will you pray with me?"

She looked startled. "Here?"

He smiled gently, his face full of love for her. "If it was good enough for Moses . . . We could go a short distance back down and find a place where we won't be seen if someone does come."

She hesitated. "I don't pray very well. Will you do it for us?"

"If you like."

They found a small hollow in the granite, well off the path, about fifty yards below the crest. As Brad smoothed away some of the rocks and pebbles and folded his windbreaker to offer some protection to their knees, he cried out in his heart for help. *Oh Lord, give me the words that I can say. Help me now. Please!*

They knelt side by side, Miri suddenly shy and reserved. Brad took her hand, interlocked their fingers, and bowed his head. There had been three times in his life when he had raised prayer from a level of communication

197

to a level of communion: at sixteen when his father was diagnosed as having cancer of the stomach; in the mission field when he and his companion had converted a Christian minister after a terrific struggle; and during that first night on the perimeter of the outpost of the Mekong Delta when he had sought for the courage to stay in his place throughout the night, though he had nearly bitten his lower lip clear through as he fought to control the terror.

On the top of Mount Sinai, Brad achieved it for the fourth time. The yearning reached the very core of his being, an intense burning fire of desire that started as an unspoken plea for himself that the Lord would make it possible for him to have this woman as his wife. But as he began to pray, to his surprise he found his heart changing its focus. Suddenly he felt the inner anguish of Miri's soul, her doubts, her tortured questions about God's love and indeed His very existence, and Brad's yearning became hers. His words were not particularly profound; there were no forced dramatics, no straining to sound sincere. The words simply poured out of him as he pled with the God who was his Father and hers, to the God who so loved that He gave the world His most prized possession. He pled for light, for understanding, for courage.

When he finished, there was silence for a long moment. Then he started to rise, but Miri held him, pulled him gently back down beside her. Tears were streaming down her cheeks.

"For the first time, I *feel* Him, Brad. I feel as if He's here. I want to pray now too."

Brad nodded. He put his arm around her shoulder and pulled her close. Her voice was barely a whisper.

"O God—" She stopped, then began again. "O Father, I thank you for this day, for this man you have brought into my life. Please help me. I want to know what he knows, to feel what he feels."

Again there was a long pause as Miri struggled with

her emotions. "I want to know if your Son was really the Messiah. And most of all, help me to understand Him— what He did, and why. I *want* to understand." Her voice caught and she went on slowly. "But I can't yet. Please help me, Father. Help me to understand you. I want to know you and to love you. Help me to know. Amen."

Brad got slowly to his feet and pulled Miri up to him, holding her close. She put her face against his chest and hugged him fiercely. He buried his face in her hair. "I love you, Miri Shadmi," he whispered.

"And I love you," she responded, raising her face to him. "Don't give up on me yet."

"Give up?" Brad nearly shouted, his joy spilling over. "Are you kidding! We're going to make it, Miri! It's going to work. I just feel it." He kissed her, long and hard and joyously.

When they parted, both a little breathless, she was smiling through the remains of her tears. "Do you really think so?"

He picked her up and swung her around and around. "Yes, Mrs. Kennison, I really think so!"

Twenty-three

Miri and Brad arrived back at Saint Catherine's just before eight that morning. To describe Nathan's reaction as cool would be to do great disservice to the art of under-exaggeration. He had the Volkswagen bus packed, and he, Ali, and Sarah were sitting inside, Nathan's fingers beating a steady tatoo on the steering wheel.

"Well, well," he said in parody of cordial welcome. "I hope we didn't rush you two."

"No, not at all," Miri smiled, giving Sarah an excited squeeze on the arm as she climbed in the back seat.

"It's my fault," Brad apologized as he climbed in beside her.

Nathan started the engine, slammed it into gear, and left a spray of gravel, which is no mean trick with a Volkswagen bus.

"It was so incredibly beautiful up there, I wanted to go back," Brad said.

Ali and Sarah both nodded, sensing a happiness in their two friends that deeply pleased them. Nathan just grunted. He mumbled and continued complaining about the delay until finally Miri quietly reminded him that it was Brad who was paying for the bulk of the trip, and if he wanted to climb Mount Sinai again, that was his right.

Thereafter the comments stopped, but it was evident from the way Nathan pounded the bus across the washboard roads that he was going to make it miserable for all of them, one way or another.

Nor did the blowout on the left rear tire cause him to ease up much. Miri again was the only one who had the courage to suggest that it was the direct result of his driving habits.

"Listen, little sister," he snapped as he undid the lug bolts on the wheel, "we have got the rest of today and then tomorrow until sundown to get home. Or had you forgotten that tomorrow night begins Yom Kippur, and that our family will be waiting for us to go to Tel Aviv with them to spend the holiday with Aunt Esther? Sarah also has a family waiting for her."

"No, I hadn't forgotten," Miri answered calmly. "We left only two hours later than you had planned. I find that hard to accept as quite the crisis you seem to make of it."

"We've got approximately a hundred and twenty miles to El Arish, a good portion of that on gravel roads worse than these, and another hundred to Jerusalem—long, slow miles. Now we've got to go over to Abu Rodeis, at least thirty miles out of our way, to get this tire fixed. We don't dare drive out here without a spare."

"Not the way you're driving," Miri retorted. "That's for sure."

Look," Brad interjected, "I really feel bad that I've caused all this. I shouldn't have gone up there this morning. But we can make it up. All of us can drive. Let's go as far as you planned to get by tonight, no matter how long it takes us."

That seemed to mollify Nathan somewhat, but the sourness of his mood dampened the spirits of the rest of them. And things really got gloomy when they arrived in Abu Rodeis after dark to find all of the repair shops closed. It was Thursday night, and Friday was the Moslem Sabbath. Abu Rodeis was a small port city on the Red Sea, the center of the Sinai's oil industry that the Israelis had captured from Egypt in the Six Day War. Nathan finally located a captain he knew in the armed forces stationed there, and was able to get the tire fixed. But by then it was midnight and they were all exhausted. Nathan reluctantly agreed to a four-hour rest, but got them up at dawn to push on.

Shortly after seven he pulled the bus over to the side of the road and consulted his map. "Our only hope is to take a shortcut," he announced. His finger traced a faint line on the map for the others. "This road cuts straight from here over to the Mitla Pass. That will save us almost sixty or seventy miles. It should be about four or five miles ahead of us now."

"That's a road?" Sarah asked dubiously.

"Not much of one," Nathan admitted. "But we used it in '67. It's rarely traveled, but it's passable."

"Are you sure, Nathan?" Miri asked. "It's been six years since the war, and you were in Jeeps and half-tracks then."

"Miri," he said, not too patiently, "we aren't going to make it otherwise."

"We could go right to Tel Aviv," she countered. But it was obvious she was not convinced of that herself.

"Good. That will save us half an hour."

Brad shrugged. "Let's do whatever it takes to get you home in time."

"Good," Nathan said, not waiting for any additional comments. "Miri, you drive. I need to watch the map."

"Let me drive," Ali volunteered. "I'm the only one who hasn't taken a turn."

"Okay," Nathan agreed. "Let's get going."

It was slightly more than three hours later when the Volkswagen came to a lurching halt, throwing Brad sharply against the back of the front seat. He looked up wildly, unable to get his bearings for a moment after being asleep.

"What is going on?" Nathan demanded, half disoriented himself as he came out of a fitful doze.

Ali turned to face them, his face stricken. "I think we're stuck."

Brad glanced quickly around. They were in a low depression, which hid for the moment the interminable vastness of the Sinai wilderness. It was thirty or forty yards across, and the narrow dirt road was visible where it came out of the depression and disappeared again over the small rise. But between there and where they now sat, there was no road, only a smooth expanse of sand, which even now Brad could see was drifting in the substantial breeze that was blowing outside.

"Of all the stupid—!" Nathan exploded.

"Nathan!" Both Miri and Sarah spoke almost as one.

"I'm sorry," Ali said in despair. "The road was really quite good, and I was making good time. I didn't see the sand until it was too late. I came over the rise and was into it."

"I told you to watch for that!" Nathan shouted as he opened the door and jumped out.

Brad heard Nathan groan, and as he got out to join him, he instantly saw why. All four wheels were up to their hubcaps in the soft drifts of sand. Ali had had enough momentum to propel the bus ten or twelve feet into the stuff before it bogged down.

"Of all the stupid fools!" Nathan said in disgust.

Again both Miri and Sarah started to protest, but Brad beat them both. "That's enough, Nathan!" he said, his voice full of anger of its own. "It could have happened to any one of us, and you know it. So lay off Ali."

Nathan bristled. "Lay off? I warned him about this very thing. You heard me do it."

"Look," Ali said, his face flaming red beneath his olive complexion. "I really am terribly sorry, I—"

"No!" Brad exclaimed. "Don't you apologize. It's not your fault."

"Well, there goes Yom Kippur," Nathan muttered, moving around to the back of the bus to get the shovel.

Miri stepped forward and took his arm. "Nathan," she pleaded.

He pushed her hand away. "Don't 'Nathan' me!"

Sick with shame, she turned to Ali. "Don't pay him any attention," she murmured. "He doesn't really mean it. He's just angry now."

"I'm so sorry," Ali said again, his voice stricken. "I didn't see it."

By three o'clock that afternoon it was clear that Nathan was not going to make it home for any part of Yom Kippur. They had dug, sweated, heaved, and coaxed the Volkswagen through all but the last ten yards of the sand when the rear axle gave a final weak whine of protest and burned out. Nathan kicked at it savagely, cursing in Hebrew. Then he grew surprisingly calm.

"Okay, we may as well make ourselves comfortable. We're not going anywhere."

"Just like that?" Brad demanded. "What do we do?"

"Sit and wait. The army patrols this area constantly, and we're out in the open. They'll find us."

"Can't we walk for help?" Brad persisted.

"The nearest well is thirty miles away, and only a pinprick on the map. We have no compass and only general area maps. We will wait here."

"For how long?" Sarah asked.

"Probably two days," Nathan said. "Tomorrow is Yom Kippur. Patrols will be minimal on the holiday. But on Sunday, I think we can expect to be found. Our bus is bright blue and easily seen. We'll build a fire at night. We have enough food and water for several days yet." He shrugged. "We'll make ourselves as comfortable as possible in the meantime. Our parents will be worried, but they know we can take care of ourselves."

Nathan smiled, as close as he would come to an apology. "We will show Brad and Ali how we Jews celebrate Yom Kippur."

Twenty-four

It was Saturday, October 6, 1973—Yom Kippur, the Day of Atonement, the holiest day in the Jewish calendar. The Bible calls it in Hebrew *Shabbat Shabbaton*—the Sabbath of Sabbaths, for on this day of all days work ceases and great solemnity prevails. It is Israel's day to expiate her sins, to receive atonement and forgiveness from God, and to restore her relationship with him. Even nonobserving Jews abstain from food and drink. One confesses his sins to God and also to his fellow men, since forgiveness from God is signified by obtaining forgiveness of one's neighbor.

Except for the Arab towns in Israel, it was as though all life had come to a halt. All Jewish shops and businesses were closed, and traffic virtually ceased except for an occasional emergency vehicle. No public transportation was running; no places of entertainment were open. Even the Israeli Broadcasting Service shut down for the day. And nearly half of the regular Israeli army, like Nathan, were home on holiday leaves.

Thousands flocked to the synagogues for the five-hour morning service of atonement. Suddenly Israeli army messengers began appearing at the services. Young men folded up their prayer shawls and left, their faces grim. Devout worshippers left the synagogues to find the street filled with speeding trucks, buses, and jeeps, and the air filled with the wail of air raid sirens. Israeli Radio came back on the air, and its classical music broadcasts were continuously interrupted by coded messages laced with such incongruous phrases as "meat pie," "sea wolf," "lady of charm," phrases that sent one hundred eighty thousand reservists to predesignated locations.

Friday night, as Yom Kippur was just beginning, Egyptian frogmen swam underwater and stealthily planted explosive charges in the sixty-foot-high embankment of the Suez Canal. Above them was the vaunted Bar Lev line, named after General Haim Bar Lev, whose brain-child it was. Impregnable bunkers, tank traps, gun emplacements, and miles of trenches laced the entire east bank of the Suez Canal. It was Israel's buffer against another Egyptian attack. On that night of October fifth, Israeli soldiers sat in their bunkers quietly, thinking of families and Yom Kippur celebrations, envious of their buddies who were fortunate enough to be back home. They were totally unaware of what was happening in the water just sixty feet below them.

At precisely 2:00 P.M. on Saturday, a massive artillery barrage was unleashed by the Egyptian army across the canal. At the same time, plungers were shoved home, and the dynamite planted the night before blasted massive holes in the steep sides of the canal's banks. Before the smoke had even cleared, a hundred Egyptian commandos picked up their boats, ran down to the water, and sped across. They stormed up the embankment and attacked the bunkers ferociously with grenades and flame throwers.

Within the next half hour three Russian-built tanks were ferried across to join them. One bulldozed its way into the main bunker and opened fire at point-blank range. Of the fifty Israeli defenders in the bunker, seventeen surrendered, a few fled, and the rest were annihilated. The highly touted Bar Lev line crumpled like soda crackers in a rainstorm, and Egyptian armor and men poured into the Sinai—the Sinai they had fled from in shame and panic just six years earlier. Now it was Israeli soldiers who were caught by surprise. Some fled, leaving their shoes behind; many were captives before they had time to comprehend what was happening. Many more died before they could know that the fourth war between Israeli and Arab in twenty-five years had begun with a vengeance.

As the Egyptian army punched across the Suez, Syria opened a second front on the Golan Heights in Northern Israel. A deafening bombardment from long-range artillery hurled tons of high explosives onto Israeli settlements. Six divisions—one hundred thousand men— backed by fourteen hundred tanks, launched a savage attack across the United Nations demilitarized zone. Israeli intelligence had reported frightening buildups along both Arab borders, but the government had not responded. Later they would claim they waited in order to let the world know without question that the Arabs had struck first. But mobilization had not been called for until a scant four hours before the attack was launched. There was little question but what the Israelis had been caught by surprise.

Later questions about that lack of preparedness would eventually topple Golda Meir's government and bring Moshe Dayan, Minister of Defense and adulated war hero of the Six Day War, under severe criticism. But for now, a stunned nation rushed frantically to fill the breach. On the three o'clock news broadcast in Jerusalem, a newscaster nearly screamed into his microphone. "This is war! It is not just border 'incidents.' We are at war!"

* * * * * *

Brad sat quietly on the blanket, leaning up against the bus. Miri had her head in his lap, her eyes closed, though he didn't think she was asleep. He studied her face, caught in the wonder of her. The tan skin drawn smoothly over high cheekbones, the long, finely sculpted nose, the firm chin and full mouth—they all blended together to create a very lovely face.

She half opened her eyes. "Tell me what you are thinking," she said lazily.

"No way," he said, shaking his head.

She opened her eyes wide. "And why not?"

"Because it would give you an inflated ego."

"Mmmm. That's what I need. Tell me."

"I was thinking that you are very lovely."

She smiled and started to get up, but Brad pushed her back down where he could watch her.

"Really?" she asked. "Was that what you were honestly thinking."

"Cross my heart."

"That's nice. Tell me more."

"You can't handle more. Tell me what you were thinking."

"Where's Nathan?" she asked, turning her head to look around.

"He and Sarah are still up on the ridge. Ali's in the back of the bus asleep. Why?"

"I wouldn't want him to hear this or to tell my parents. But I was thinking that this is the nicest Yom Kippur I've ever had. I'm glad the bus is broken."

Brad nodded. It had been delightful. They had eaten a simple meal yesterday afternoon, and then just before sunset, Nathan, embarrassed because he couldn't remember more, had acted as *cantor* and had sung the *kol nidre*, the hymn used by Jews the world over to usher in the Day of Atonement. It supplicated the Lord, asking for forgiveness for any vows, promises, or obligations the individual may have overlooked during the year that would interfere with his obtaining God's forgiveness. Nathan had a rich tenor voice, and the plaintive, haunting melody of the prayer, sung in the vastness of the Sinai, deeply stirred Brad.

Today they had spent in quiet relaxation, Ali and Brad joining the three Jews in their abstention from food. Nathan and Sarah had gone for several walks, giving Brad and Ali ample opportunity to talk Mormonism with Miri. She had not reimposed her previous restrictions on Brad again. In fact, she now seemed to welcome his earnest attempts to sway her. They had read the original requirements for the Day of Atonement as given to Moses and recorded in the Book of Leviticus, Brad pointing out the symbolism of Christ. It had been a slow, lazy, enjoyable day.

He touched her cheek lightly. "I love you," he said happily.

Miri reached up and took his hand, but left it against her cheek. "And I you. I think back to how rude I was to you those first few days, and I get a cold, scary feeling. What if you hadn't stayed?"

Brad smiled with the memory. "We had some real times, didn't we? I used to stay up nights planning how to get back at you."

"And was this part of your plan, to make me fall in love with you, so I would have to be nice to you?"

"Of course. Right from the beginning. Between my irresistible charm and brilliant strategy, you didn't stand a chance."

She stuck out her tongue at him. "It's hard to believe now, but do you know what first attracted me to you?"

"No, what?"

"Your deep sense of humility!"

She squealed as he poked her in the ribs, and started to roll away from him, but he pulled her back.

"Don't go, I'll be nice." She lay back and closed her eyes.

"Brad?" she said after a moment.

"What?"

"If things work out, what are your parents going to say?"

"About us?"

"Yes, about you marrying an Israeli." She paused, her face sober. "About marrying a Jewish girl."

"You mean what *did* they say?"

Her eyes flew open, and she sat up straight. "You've told them?"

He nodded. "More or less."

"Brad, when?"

His gray eyes were teasing. "Oh, here and there."

Miri looked at him and grabbed his arm. "Brad! Tell me!"

"Well, I wrote them about you two or three weeks ago and sent them a picture."

Her eyes narrowed. "Where did you get a picture of me?"

"Promise you won't get mad?"

"Where did you get it?"

"That first morning you took me on tour. Remember when we were on the Mount of Olives, and you were pointing out the significant sites as I took pictures? Well, I used the wide-angle lens on one shot and included you in a picture of the Dome of the Rock."

"Well, aren't you sneaky!"

"Sneaky and humble, that's me."

"So?"

"So what?"

She punched him solidly in the stomach. "Brad Kennison, you tell me what you said, and what they said."

"In the letter or when I talked to them on the phone?"

"Brad!" Miri wailed, coming to her knees and starting to pound on him. "You called them?"

He grabbed her fists and pulled her down next to him. "Okay, okay. I'll tell you."

"I can't believe this. Why didn't you tell me?"

"I almost did, then decided it violated our agreement, that it would be putting pressure on you."

"Well," she said, not sure whether to forgive him or not. "So tell me. When did you talk to them?"

"Last Sunday night. My mother's birthday is September thirtieth. So I called her. By then they had received the second letter I wrote them. That was the day after our little experience in the Galilee. I told them about my feelings for you, about how you are trying to find out if the Church is true, the works."

Brad turned to look at her. "So when I called, they were all primed."

"And?"

"Well, they had several questions," he replied, pushing away the temptation to smooth over some of their concerns. "The fact that you are Jewish is their biggest worry."

"Oh." Miri's shoulders sagged slightly, and she looked away quickly.

"Hey!" he said, gently taking her face in his hands and turning her to him. "That is Jewish as in religion, not Jewish as in race. They have grave concerns about my marrying a Jewish girl, but they have no real concerns about my marrying a *Mormon* Jewish girl."

Her eyes brightened. "Really?"

He nodded. "Really. Their biggest question is what I'll do if you decide not to join the Church. They would be devastated if I married outside of the temple."

Miri dropped her gaze and studied her hands. "Just as my parents will be devastated if I *do* join the Church."

Brad sighed. "I know. It seems as though we are not destined to have things work out very easily no matter what happens."

Miri was silent for almost a full minute. When she spoke her voice was very soft. "What other concerns did they have?"

"Well," Brad said, "they were mostly concerned about me. Whether I finally got my head screwed on straight."

Miri laughed softly at that. "I think your head is very nicely placed."

"Thank you. It is all your fault, you know."

"What is?"

"That I got my head screwed on straight."

She looked puzzled and pleased at the same moment. "Why?"

He took her hand and squeezed it gently. "I came to Israel looking for something. I was filled with this terrible discontent, as if I was smothering in a sea of comfort and security. I was frustrated, bitter, irritable, and dissatisfied. Yet I didn't know why. I was in a computer science program at the University of Utah and suddenly realized I wanted to do more with my life than that—as though there was something I had to do, was *supposed* to do. But I didn't know what."

He shook his head. "It was awful. And I was acting like a spoiled kid. My parents should have booted me out of the house. Dad thought it was because of Viet Nam. That's why he encouraged me to come to Israel. To get away and rest."

"I am so happy he did."

Brad nodded. "Ah, so am I. I not only found you, but I found the answer to my other problems, too."

She looked up in surprise. "What problems?"

"Well," he said, "at first I started to study and read about Israel and the Jews so I could answer your questions intelligently. But suddenly I found myself fascinated, totally engrossed. I loved learning about this land, about its destiny. And I knew I had to be part of that destiny, to help others to feel it and see it as I did."

Brad's voice rose in excitement, and he released her hand so he could emphasize his words with his gestures. "The destiny of the Latter-day Saints and the destiny of the Jews and Arabs are just now starting to unfold. More and more they will become intertwined and interdependent."

He turned to her, his eyes shining with excitement. "And then to find you, someone who feels so deeply about this too. It's more than I could ever have hoped for, to find what I want to do with my life, and someone who can and will share in that goal with me."

Miri smiled at his enthusiasm.

"When I told dad all of that, he was satisfied. He knew this wasn't some whim, that you are not just some passing interest."

"I'm glad," she said, snuggling up against him. "I'm glad I am not just some passing interest. And I'm glad he knows I'm not."

"I don't know exactly what I'll end up doing," he went on. "I'll probably teach college. I figure that I will major in history or maybe in Middle Eastern studies. The U of U has an excellent program."

Miri's head came up sharply. "The U of U?"

"Yes. The University of Utah. I figure it will probably take four or five years to get whatever degrees we need to do what we want. But I'll find a job. I want you to be able to be with the children. I want you to teach them about their Jewish heritage, about Israel . . ."

He stopped when he saw the look on her face, then felt his heart sink. "Miri, what's wrong? Don't you want children?"

"Only yours," she said with a forlorn smile.

"What's the matter then?" And finally the light dawned, or so he thought. "Miri, it's going to work out. I know you're going to get your answers. I know it!"

"And if I do, then what?"

"You are baptized. We get married. We start our life together."

"Where Brad? Where do we make our life together?"

"In America, in . . ." His voice trailed off as he saw her eyes drop.

"You would take me away from my people *and* my land?" She paused. "I think you know that I feel almost as strongly about Israel as you do about Mormonism. Couldn't you go to the Hebrew University? If you feel that your destiny is intertwined with Israel's, then why not stay here and raise our family?" She was pleading, beseeching him for understanding. "Couldn't you do much more good here?"

Brad was silent for a long time, considering that. Finally he put his arms around her and pulled her close. "I have considered that," he said slowly. "I even went up to the Hebrew University and checked out all their programs. I would have to become completely fluent in Hebrew before I could really get what I want."

"I speak excellent Hebrew," Miri said, "I could help you."

"I know, but . . ." He stopped, seeking the words to express himself. "But somehow I feel that what I must do is with my own people at first. The Latter-day Saints need to understand our relationship with Israel, both present and future. We have to build Zion in America so Judah will have one ally when the Battle of Armageddon comes. Maybe later the Lord will have a purpose for us here as well."

Miri pushed slowly away from him, her eyes moist, her lips tight. "Maybe this is the answer."

Brad was shaken. "What do you mean?"

"Yesterday on Sinai we asked the Lord to show us what his will is for us. Maybe this is his answer." Her lower lip trembled, and she bit it angrily. "I don't think I could ever leave Israel to live elsewhere. Maybe it is time we face reality. Maybe your God is saying no to us."

She stumbled to her feet and fled, leaving Brad to stare after her.

*　*　*　*　*　*

Half an hour later Brad still sat where he was, sadly watching the lone figure on the nearest ridge. Ali awakened from his nap and, sensing Brad's moroseness, stayed in the Volkswagen bus reading the scriptures.

214

Three different times Brad started to rise and go out to her, then decided it wasn't yet time. He hadn't found the words. He wasn't even sure but what Miri was right. Maybe this was the Lord's way of answering them.

Suddenly Ali spoke through the open window of the bus. "What's that?"

"What's what?"

"Listen!" he commanded.

Brad cocked his head, feeling it now almost as much as hearing it—a low, rumbling sound coming from far away.

"Artillery?" Ali asked.

"Yes, but a long way off."

Ali leaned back and reopened his book. "Probably another Egyptian-Israeli artillery duel across the Suez."

"I suppose," Brad answered, his thoughts already back on Miri. He glanced at his watch. It was one minute after two in the afternoon of Saturday, October sixth, the day called by the Jews Yom Kippur.

Twenty-five

"Are they Israeli?" Brad asked, closely watching the expression on Nathan's face as he peered through the binoculars.

"Of course," he answered, handing Brad the field glasses. They had climbed this high plateau about half a mile from the car when Nathan had first spotted the column of dust. Brad focused in and could barely make out tanks, jeeps, and half-tracks in the swirling dust. They were moving fast, heading north.

"That's encouraging," Nathan said as they rose and started back. "I would judge that road to be only two or so miles from where we are. We'll build a signal fire as soon as it's dark. If that doesn't bring someone, we'll hike to the road in the morning and see if we can intercept some traffic."

They were nearly back to the car when they heard the distant throbbing of engines. Nathan stopped and waved Ali and Sarah, who were walking out to meet them, into motionless statues. "Helicopters!" he shouted, and sprinted up out of the depression they were camped in. Brad and the others followed close behind. There were six aircraft. They passed about a mile to the east of the stranded group, skimming a thousand feet above the ground. The noise even brought Miri running from where she had been sitting staring at the sunset.

They screamed and whistled and waved and jumped

216

up and down, but in a few moments the helicopters disappeared, the sound of their engines dying away.

"We were in the sun," Brad said, jerking his head in the direction of the orange-red ball of fire hanging low in the western sky. "No way could they have seen us."

"Come on," Nathan said, turning back toward the car. "Let's gather some brush before it gets dark. We want to keep that fire going all night."

"Do you think there will be others?" Sarah asked, falling into step beside him.

Nathan nodded. "The artillery has been pounding up north now for over three hours. That's not typical. Usually they trade a few rounds back and forth, then quit. Maybe Sadat is going to get serious and try to regain a little face. He's been threatening to revenge Egypt's humiliation in the Six Day War for over a year now."

"Do you think there will be war?" Sarah asked anxiously.

Brad stepped up his pace slightly so he could hear Nathan's answer. Miri trailed behind, her mood returning with the disappearance of the helicopters.

"No," Nathan responded to Sarah's question. "It's just that the other Arab countries are laughing at Sadat now, saying Egypt is all bluff and bluster. He'll shell us for a day, maybe stage a quick raid across the Suez Canal or something to get people off his back. But that will work to our advantage. We seem to be moving up some forces as backup just in case. I expect more to pass us tonight, so we'll have a fire going to attract their attention." He smiled at her. "I fully expect to be home by tomorrow afternoon."

"Really?"

"You bet. Later tonight when reception improves, we'll try to get a news broadcast from Tel Aviv and see if they indicate what's going on."

If Nathan was aware of the sadness that lay over Miri and Brad, he gave no sign. They cooked a simple meal once the sun set, ending Yom Kippur and their fast. Then Nathan started piling the brush onto their little campfire, making it into a signal fire. They gathered around, each preoccupied with his or her own thoughts as they watched the leaping flames.

"It probably wouldn't hurt for one of us to get out away from the roar of the fire and listen for any engines," Nathan suggested shortly before eight. "We can't keep the fire going full blast all night, or we'll run out of brush." He turned to Brad. "Do you want to go first, or shall I?"

"Miri and I will go," Brad responded, glad for a chance to be alone with her and talk out their impasse.

She nodded and stood up, putting her sweater on. Ali watched them closely. He looked as though he was going to make some light remark, but finally said, "Good luck, you two," as they passed him and headed for the ridge.

Brad put his arm around Miri, and she slipped her arm around his waist, but they walked in silence, both reluctant to revive the pain. It was another beautiful night in the Sinai, the stars like a generous sprinkling of silver dust on black velvet. The heat of the day was now completely gone, and the chill quickly deepened. By the time they were a hundred yards from camp, the silence was profound and deep, almost oppressive after the crackling of the fire.

Brad found a small patch of relatively flat rock, and they sat down. The moon had not come up yet, and he could barely see her face in the starlight. He touched her cheek gently and she leaned against him, sighing deeply.

"Miri?"

"Yes?"

"Let's not give up yet, okay?"

He felt her face relax under his fingertips. "I don't want to give up."

"Let's work on one problem at a time."

"Brad, I can't leave Israel. I just can't! I've been think-

218

ing about it all evening. How can I leave my people when—"

He put his finger gently over her lips. "I know," he murmured, torn with his own emotions. "But the first problem is to get you an answer to your prayers. We can work something out on the other."

"What?" she cried in anguish.

He smiled at her in the dark, though it cost him a lot of effort. "Well, we could compromise and live in London. That's about half way for each of us."

To his surprise, Miri threw her arms around him and hugged him fiercely. "Oh Brad," she whispered. "I don't want to lose you."

"Remember," he said, "if you try to do that, you've got a fight on your hands. So let's talk about something more cheerful."

She took a deep breath and then nodded. "Okay, like what?"

"Like our children," he said. "I'd better warn you, families are very important to Mormons. We like big ones."

"How about four little boys, just like you?"

"And four little girls with dark eyes and jet black hair just like their mother."

"Eight? You weren't kidding about large families, were you!"

"Nope. I love kids, and I don't think there are many more important things you can do with your life than to raise a good family. How many do you want?"

She was quiet for a long moment, and Brad felt his anxiety start to rise until she spoke. "It's funny, but all of a sudden I want eight, if they are ours. You can have your four little girls if I get my four boys."

"A deal," he said, burying his face in her hair.

"We'll name the first one Brad . . ."

"And the second one Miriam. Little Miri."

"Could we name the next one David?" she asked,

warming to the game. Brad's head shot up, and the frown was instantaneous.

For a moment Miri looked startled, and then she laughed out loud. "Not *that* David, silly. David, my brother." The smile slowly faded. "The one who was killed in 1967."

Brad relaxed, a bit sheepish. "In that case, of course."

"I wish you had known him, Brad. He was so good."

"Was he older than—," Brad started, but suddenly Miri stiffened to attention.

"Listen!" she hissed urgently.

Brad jumped to his feet, and Miri joined him in excitement, straining to hear.

"Helicopters!" Brad cupped his hands and yelled. "Nathan, helicopters coming in from the west!" He grabbed Miri's hand, and they ran quickly back to camp.

"More brush!" Nathan commanded, leaping to the stack of fuel they had collected. The fire shot up to twice its size as they hurled more branches on. The deep pounding sound of jet helicopter engines was now clearly discernible, even over the roar of the fire, as Miri and Brad waited breathlessly.

"If they can't see this," Ali shouted, "they had better have their eyes checked!"

The dancing flames were now brightly illuminating the landscape for thirty or forty yards in every direction.

But the pilots' eyes were fine. There were two helicopters, and they came in low at about three hundred feet. For a moment the stranded party thought they were going to fly over, and once again they began to jump and shout. But the two craft circled immediately.

"Oh, they've seen us! They've seen us!" Sarah cried.

The lead helicopter suddenly turned on a high intensity spotlight, blinding them. The second followed suit. The two aircraft circled slowly, one spotlight frozen on the camp, the other methodically searching the landscape around the camp.

220

"What are they doing?" Miri demanded.

"Just checking things out," Nathan explained. "This could be a typical Arab terrorist setup. They want to be sure no one is waiting out there to hit them when they come down."

Evidently the man in charge was a very nervous type, or else the group on the ground looked particularly suspicious, for they were in no hurry to come down. The one craft hovered directly overhead, keeping them pinned in his beam, while the other swept the desert with his light in ever-widening circles.

"Keep your hands in plain sight," Nathan shouted over the noise of the engines, as the helicopters finally began to descend. "Stay put. Let's let them know we're harmless."

In spite of the blinding sandstorm whipped up by the rotors, Brad and Nathan saw the markings on the side of the helicopter before it even touched the ground. They both stared, unable to believe their eyes. The side door flew open and men spilled out, rifles ready and faces grim.

Ali was the first to find his voice. "They're Egyptians!" he cried in stunned surprise.

Twenty-six

It was late afternoon, and the dark canvas was soaking up the heat of the Sinai, making the inside of the tent sweltering. The four of them sat listlessly, still in a state of shock. Miri and Sarah looked haggard and drawn. Nathan sat in a corner, his head in his hands. Brad was in the best shape of the group, but then what they had seen in the last twenty-one hours did not have the same personal impact for him as it had for the three Israelis.

The Egyptian commando raiding party had swooped them up after a brief but thorough search of the Volkswagen bus, and had dropped them at a small army camp, where they were placed under heavy guard. When the soliders discovered they had Israelis in their captivity, half the camp gathered around to gibe and jeer and to gleefully report the smashing success of their army in the afternoon's attack. Ali, treated with cautious respect and some deference, was allowed to translate to his friends as the Egyptians bragged in great detail about the afternoon's triumph. Nathan and the two women sat tight-lipped and silent, Nathan's only comment a muttered reference to an Arab's penchant for bravado and exaggeration.

But when they were transported north this morning to this larger camp near the Suez, it quickly became apparent that the almost ecstatic jubilation of the Egyptian army was not without cause. The road was strewn with the carnage of war: shattered hulks of tanks; still smoldering, blasted trucks; overturned half-tracks; and everywhere in

222

the sand, bodies scattered in the grotesque, twisted agony of death. Some of the wreckage and many of the dead were Egyptian, but the clear majority were Israeli. The Israeli army had been clobbered and badly mauled. Brad held Miri's hand tightly as the shock and horror in her eyes deepened with each new scene. The fury and frustration inside Nathan seethed with each new evidence of Israel's defeat.

Most depressing of all were the hordes of Israeli prisoners. They lined the roads, filthy, barefoot, in some cases bloodstained, and in every case, stunned, their faces without hope.

The truck arrived at the camp about ten-thirty in the morning. A cluster of about fifty tents was surrounded by rolls of barbed wire. The five prisoners were pushed into a small tent and left under the watchful eye of a guard, a silent dark-skinned Egyptian soldier who stared at his prisoners without expression. At noon cans of American C-rations were brought in. Brad, who had eaten enough of those in Viet Nam to last him a lifetime, picked at his. Nathan ate absently, as though eating was a duty to be taken care of with as little thought as possible. Miri and Sarah left theirs untouched. Ali wrinkled his nose at the smell, but finished his.

At two-twenty, the intelligence officer arrived. He spoke fluent English and halting Hebrew. He began with Ali, then took Brad away next. It was a friendly and cordial interrogation but very thorough. He seemed satisfied with what Brad answered and returned him in the shortest amount of time. Nathan took the longest, Miri and Sarah about equal time. Then Ali was taken out again.

Now Ali, followed by the lieutenant, ducked in under the tent flap. "I'd like to speak to all of you together," the lieutenant said. "But I have something I must attend to now. I'll return in a moment." The flap dropped back into place. The guard watched them in silence.

Ali sighed as he sat down on the cot next to Miri and Brad. "I'm not sure, but I think we've convinced him that we are telling the truth, that we are not some undercover group trying to infiltrate behind the lines."

"Bully!" Nathan muttered.

"Listen, my friend," Ali said, "you happen to be an Israeli officer carrying army ID, dressed in civilian clothes, and in a war zone. If he wanted to get nasty, he could treat you as a spy and make things very difficult for you. But he seems satisfied."

"Do you have any idea how the war is going?" Miri broke in before Nathan could respond.

Ali shook his head. "Obviously he didn't sit down and reveal all their plans, but as near as I can gather from what he did say and from hearing the soldiers talk, the Egyptians hold the entire east bank of the canal. The Syrians have attacked Israel on the Golan Heights, but much to the Egyptians' disgust, they are evidently not doing as well."

"What about the other Arab countries?" Nathan demanded.

"Staying out of it, except for token support."

"What about Jerusalem and Tel Aviv?" Sarah asked.

Suddenly Brad felt ashamed. It had never occurred to him to assume the war had extended into the heartland of Israel. No wonder Miri looked so stricken. On every hand they had seen evidence that the Israeli army was smashed and in retreat. Why shouldn't they assume that their homes and families were under siege too? He took Miri's hand and held it tightly.

"I think the Egyptians had a limited objective," Ali explained. "Get across the canal, grab some land, and dig in until the major powers halt the fighting. They've achieved the first part. There doesn't seem to be any talk of pushing much further."

"That seems like near-sighted strategy," Brad said.

"Not if you understand Arab politics," Ali explained.

"Anwar Sadat is in a shaky position. He's threatened again and again to avenge the humiliation of the Six Day War but has taken no action. He does not have the charisma of Nasser, and his people are restless. He must unite them behind him. That he has unquestionably achieved in this move. He has shown the world that the Arab can stand and fight."

Brad couldn't help but note the pride in Ali's voice.

"Even if he were to be driven back across the canal tomorrow, he has won. He has achieved a stunning defeat of the Israelis. Every Arab can once again hold up his head and be proud."

Nathan leaped to his feet, bringing the guard to alert attention. "The Israeli army is not defeated," he cried. "The Arabs will yet turn their tails and run."

Ali shrugged, obviously a bit angry himself. "Perhaps. But the Arabs I have seen here are not turning their tails. And the myth of the invincible Israeli warrior is shattered once and for all."

Nathan leaped at Ali, unleashing the frustration and rage that had been boiling in him for the last twenty or so hours. His fist caught Ali high on the left cheek, catapulting him backward across the cot. Brad was on his feet in an instant, throwing his shoulder into Nathan's chest and driving him hard against the far wall, but Nathan was on his feet again like a cat, thrusting Brad aside. The muzzle of the guard's rifle stared directly at his head, pulling him up short. The flap of the tent flew open, and two more soldiers darted in, weapons ready.

Brad hurried over to where Miri and Sarah were helping Ali to his feet. The ring Nathan wore had laid open an ugly three-inch gash along Ali's cheek, which was now dripping blood down the side of his face and onto his shirt. He touched it with the back of his hand and stared at it, then into Nathan's eyes, which were still filled with fury.

"You Israelis!" Ali said softly. "You can insult us all

you want. But you are not so good at facing the truth, are you." He stood unflinching as Nathan lunged forward again and was shoved back roughly by the soldiers.

"What is going on here?" The lieutenant burst into the tent, pistol drawn.

The guard who had been in the tent throughout spoke rapidly in Arabic. The lieutenant listened and then stepped forward, tipped Ali's head to the light, and examined the cut. He said something in Arabic, and one of the other soldiers darted out of the tent. He was back in a moment with a first-aid kid.

"What did you say to this brave Israeli to cause this?" the lieutenant asked Ali in English, as he began daubing at the cut with antiseptic.

"He suggested that the myth of the Israeli super-warrior was gone forever," Brad said, still fighting to control his anger against Nathan.

The officer turned and gave Nathan an appraising look. "Ah," he said sadly. "I think the Israelis are very good winners, but not so good as losers."

He finished, taped a large gauze patch over the cut on Ali's face, then stepped back. "You are a foolish man, Colonel Shadmi," he said. "If it were not for Ali Khalidi, I would be dealing with you not as a prisoner of war, but as an undercover agent. It is tempting to follow my original instincts, but we Arabs are not a vindictive people. We honor our commitments. You shall be sent across the Suez in the morning for interrogation."

The lieutenant then turned to Miri and Sarah. "I wish that I could release you ladies, but the Israeli military uses women. I see from your papers that you are both in the reserves. I am afraid you also must be treated as prisoners of war."

Brad started to step forward to protest but caught Ali's quick look and almost imperceptible shake of the head.

"I assure you," the Egyptian continued politely, "you will be treated with the utmost respect and courtesy. We

226

shall take you back to Cairo, so you will have better conditions than here. Supply trucks will be here in the morning, and you may return with them."

Brad suddenly felt sick, but he kept his face impassive as the lieutenant turned to him. "Mr. Kennison. As an American you have no part in this war. I have just checked with a war correspondent from the London *Times* who is here now. He will be returning to Cairo at noon tomorrow to file his reports. He said he would be glad to have you share his jeep. We are sorry that you have been caught in our problems here in the Middle East."

Again Brad caught Ali's eye and the shake of his head. He nodded to the officer. "Thank you. I appreciate these arrangements."

The lieutenant turned to Ali, but before he could speak, Ali stepped forward. "I have a special request, sir." He shot Nathan a look of pure contempt, visible for all to see.

"Oh?"

"I would share in the glory of this hour that Allah has given us."

The lieutenant looked surprised. "In what way?"

"I would like permission to join your command and help redeem the shame of six years ago."

Nathan spat in disgust, and the lieutenant spun around and slapped him across the face with the palm of his hand, a ringing blow that rocked Nathan's head back. "Pig!" he shouted to Nathan. "An Israeli does not spit in an Egyptian's tent." The lieutenant spoke rapidly in Arabic, and the two soldiers grabbed Nathan and prodded him out of the tent.

The Egyptian then turned back to Ali, his eyes angry, his chest rising and falling rapidly.

"I would like to help you teach all Israelis where to spit," Ali said calmly.

"Done!" said the Egyptian. Once again he went to the tent door. He stuck out his head and called sharply.

Three men came in, and the officer rapidly barked out his orders. The first motioned to Ali, who passed Brad with his eyes lowered and left the tent.

"Ladies,"the officer said,"if you will follow these men, they will show you to your new quarters." He stuck out his hand and blocked Brad's movement toward Miri. "I assure you, Mr. Kennison, they will be treated as ladies." He motioned with his hand, and Miri and Sarah followed the remaining two Egyptians out of the tent. The anguish in Miri's eyes drove through Brad like a red hot spear.

"Mr. Khalidi has told me of your feelings for the beautiful young Israeli," the lieutenant said, "not that one could miss that himself. All will be well, and after the war—" He shrugged, stroking his mustache. "We will see to your comfort here until tomorrow, Mr. Kennison." He stepped to the flap. "However, under the circumstances, you will please confine yourself to this tent."

Brad nodded glumly.

"Without exception," he warned sharply.

"I understand."

When the lieutenant had gone, Brad stared at the flap, then sat down heavily on the cot. "Oh, Miri!" he said softly.

Twenty-seven

Brad sat on the edge of his cot, his head in his hands. It was past three in the morning, but his mind was working at top speed. In an hour or two the trucks would come for Miri, Sarah, and Nathan, and there was nothing he could do about it. Once they crossed the Suez and were taken into Egypt, that would be it. The lieutenant had promised Miri and Sarah courteous treatment, and Brad believed he meant it, but once they left here, who would guarantee his promises? At best it would be months before they would be returned to Israel. At worst—Brad shook that off, not willing to face the possibilities.

It seemed hopeless. Brad lay back on the cot in despair, conjuring up one wild scheme after another, discarding them almost instantly. Somewhere around midnight he had heard the guard outside his tent changed, and he had tried to bluff his way past the new man. He had smiled, gestured, pointed, and talked enthusiastically, but the guard had never wavered. His face was as stony as that of the Sphinx, and the point of the rifle was the same. Though Brad's Arabic was limited to less than a dozen words, he clearly understood the man's harsh command and his implacable expression.

Back inside the tent Brad had searched meticulously in the pitch blackness on his hands and knees, for anything to cut through the canvas. But the two cots and a small portable toilet were the only items in the tent. He finally managed to pry off one of the thick wooden legs of one of the cots, but the edges were smooth and round, the wood too thick to break into a jagged edge. For a brief time he had considered trying to sneak outside and take out the guard, but when he peeked out the tent flap, he met the man's gaze, wary as a mongoose watching a cobra, and Brad let the flap drop quickly.

He half hoped Ali would find a way to intervene, but as the hours wore on, his hope waned. And in spite of his deep disappointment, he could not blame his friend. He remembered the bitterness in Ali's eyes that evening they first met, as he told Brad of the shame he had felt during the Six Day War. Who could point the finger of accusation at the young Arab for wanting to be with his people when their hour finally came? Add to that Nathan's hot-tempered stupidity, and Brad was left with few expectations.

For the sixth or seventh time that night, he swung off the cot and knelt beside it, pleading for help. Then once again he resumed his staring into the darkness.

Ten minutes later, when four Israeli jets came rocketing over the camp at less than five hundred feet, the battering ram of sound they hurled along below them brought Brad to his feet in a startled leap. It was like the concussion of an artillery shell exploding beneath one's chair, and he looked wildly around for a moment before he realized what had happened. Outside, the camp exploded in a wild hail of gunfire, but the startled soldiers might just as well have tried to shoot down the moon. At five hundred and fifty miles an hour, in the three or four seconds it took for the troops to react, the jets were half a mile away and unleashing their fury on the emplacements lining the banks of the canal. The wild shooting ended as Brad heard the officers and noncoms screaming at the men to hold their fire.

The second wave of F-4 Phantoms were less than thirty seconds behind the first, and Brad instinctively ducked as the deafening sound rocked the tent again. He understood almost instantly what was happening. Russia had furnished the Egyptian armed forces with the SAM VI, surface-to-air missiles with a deadly accuracy that had stunned the Israeli air force. This was their answer—treetop-level attacks at night using sophisticated ground-searching radar. And just as suddenly as Brad had understanding, he had an answer. Groping quickly around the cot, he found his makeshift club and stepped to the flap of the tent.

Come on, Israel, he urged fiercely, *just one more flight.* He didn't have long to wait for his command to be obeyed. The third wave of fighters blasted overhead and were gone almost before the mind could register consciousness of their passing. The guard pivoted in his tracks as he tried in vain to follow the source of the earsplitting sound. It was his last conscious act for that night, for Brad was out of the tent in a flash, swinging the leg of the cot against the base of his skull. He collapsed with a soft moan. Brad caught him before he hit the ground and dragged him inside the tent. Then he opened the flap, intent on retrieving his club and the guard's rifle, but he jerked up short with a grunt of disgust. In the light of the half moon, the figure of an Egyptian soldier running rapidly toward him was perfectly clear.

Cursing himself for not taking the rifle first, Brad stepped up against the wall near the doorway and held his breath. The footsteps pounded up, then stopped right outside. Brad made a club of his fists and raised his arms high as the flap of the tent pushed open slightly. Just as he tensed for the swing, he heard the urgent whisper.

"Brad!"

He nearly shouted for joy. "Ali!"

Stepping quickly inside, Ali turned on a flashlight and revealed his broad, grinning face, the white bandage a gleaming patch on his cheeks.

"Man! Am I glad to see you."

"I tried to get away a little earlier," his friend said, "but things at the office have really been hectic." He dropped the beam of the flashlight so that it revealed the sprawled figure on the floor. "I see you have been busy too."

"Yes, thanks to the Israeli air force. Do you know where they are holding Miri?"

"Yes, but hold on a minute. The initial surprise is over out there, and all we have now is a very alert camp. We've got to create some diversion of our own." He swung up his other hand, which held a bundle wrapped in a khaki shirt. "They have been watching me like a hawk, so I haven't been able to get much."

As he opened up the makeshift pack, Brad saw two kerosene latterns and a sprawl of matches. "Directly behind us is the ammunition dump. It's under guard." He handed Brad one of the lamps and a handful of matches. "Wait here until I get into the motor pool. Once I get something going, see what you can do with the ammunition dump. I'll meet you back here, and we'll go get the others."

Suddenly overwhelmed at what this meant, Brad touched Ali's arm. "Thanks. I was afraid you really meant it when you said what you did to the lieutenant."

"I did," Ali said sadly, "but the Mormon in me has to take priority for now. Maybe later—" He shrugged. "Let's go. Give me about two minutes."

Two minutes later Brad was out of the tent in a flash, pausing only long enough to grab the guard's rifle before running in a low crouch toward the rear of the camp. He could hear the angry rumble of explosions to the north, and saw the flashes of light that accompanied it.

The ammunition dump was exactly as Ali had described it, and Brad saw the silhouette of the lone, patrolling figure almost immediately. He dropped behind the cover of a small clump of brush and waited for Ali's handiwork. A moment later a pillar of flame shot into the air, as the gas tank of a truck near the perimeter of the camp exploded. With a cry, the guard leaped away, unslinging his rifle.

Brad's lips were tight as he ran to the dump. It wasn't a particularly large cache of ammunition—less than a hundred boxes—but it would be sufficient. He pried the lids off the first three boxes with the bayonet on the rifle, pleased to see that there were mortar rounds packed in a strawlike material. He unscrewed the lid of the kerosene lamp's reservoir and splashed the liquid inside the boxes.

Quickly he moved around the stack and popped open the lids on two different boxes. Hand grenades. On a sudden impulse he snatched three and shoved them into the pockets of his windbreaker. Again he splashed the kerosene. He was so intent on what he was doing that he nearly singed his eyebrows when he struck the match and the kerosene whooshed into flame. He tossed a match into the first boxes he had opened, picked up his bundle, and sprinted back the way he had come. His little blaze was nothing compared to the truck, but it would very soon attract someone's attention.

Ali was waiting at the rear of Brad's tent. He nodded in satisfaction as he saw the flickering light behind Brad. "We do good work, boy!" he said, grinning. "All right, let's go."

Fifty yards away, Ali darted around another tent like the one Brad had been in. "This is where Miri and Sarah are," he whispered. "The guard out front is gone. Be careful. He may be inside."

At that moment the first box of mortars went off with a tremendous roar. The concussion shook the ground.

"That will help!" Brad muttered with satisfaction.

"I'll get Nathan and meet you right here."

Brad smiled. "Think he'll come with *you*?"

Ali patted his rifle. "It will be a pleasure to persuade him." He leaped up. "Hurry now!" He darted off.

Brad slashed the canvas with one savage tear of the bayonet and heard startled movement within. "Miri, it's Brad!" he whispered as he dove through the opening.

The dive saved his life, for he hit the legs of the guard, who, instead of rushing to join the others, had gone in to watch his charges. When Brad slashed the tent, the man swung his weapon at the opening. With a startled yelp, the guard dropped the muzzle of the weapon and pulled the trigger. It went off so close to Brad's face that he felt the burn of the powder on his cheek. The roar nearly blasted out his left eardrum.

Brad lunged at the man's legs and drove forward. They crashed heavily against the wall of the tent, rocking it violently, and the guard's weapon clattered to the ground. As he went for it, Brad brought his knee up with all the force he could muster and caught the man full on the chin. His head snapped back, and he hit the floor like a sack of spoiled potatoes.

Brad was still for a moment, hunched over, gasping for breath, holding his left ear.

"Brad, are you all right?" Miri said, rushing over to him.

He stood up and shook his head violently to ease the pain. "I'll be okay. Hurry, out the back."

Miri's eyes were wide. "But how did you ever—?"

"Ali! He's getting Nathan right now."

Another explosion shook the camp.

"That's our little diversion," he added with a touch of pride in his handiwork.

They saw Nathan and Ali almost immediately coming toward them in a running crouch.

"Oh, Nathan!" Miri cried, giving him a brief hug.

Ali whipped out a length of rope. "All right, wrap this around your wrists so it looks like I've got you tied up. Brad, keep that rifle hidden until we get to the jeep."

234

"Jeep?"

"Yes," Ali said modestly. "I didn't want everything in the motor pool to go up."

"Wait a minute!" Brad said in an urgent whisper. "Who's going to drive the jeep?"

"I am," Ali replied.

"With four dangerous prisoners to guard, *you* drive the jeep?"

Ali suddenly looked ill. "I didn't think about that. I was so glad to find some transportation."

"Inside the tent," Brad commanded. "Quick! Ali, give me the flashlight."

Once inside he flashed the light at the unconscious Egyptian. Ali grunted at the sight. "The Egyptians are going to love you."

Brad ignored that. "Nathan!" he commanded, "you're it. I could never pass as an Arab, not even in the dark." He knelt quickly and started unbottoning the man's uniform.

"I can't either!" Nathan protested.

"We have no choice. Just keep your head down. Come on, man! Get that uniform on. We've got to have two Egyptians to pull this off. Move!" He yanked off the man's pants.

Nathan quickly began making the switch in uniforms.

Sarah stepped up to Brad. "Do you know what it means if Nathan is caught in an Egyptian uniform?"

"Sarah!" Nathan commanded sharply.

She ignored him. "He could be shot as a spy."

"Sarah," he said more softly. "And what about Brad and Ali, and what they are doing?"

She bit her lip and stepped back.

Under any other circumstances it would have caused the other four to double over with laughter. By the time Nathan got the brown uniform buttoned over his clothes, he looked like two quarts of water poured into a pint jar. Brad simply gave him a quick smile and shook his head.

"All right, let's go. When we get to the jeep, Nathan

will drive. Ali, you're in command so you sit in the back and keep the gun on us."

The camp was in an uproar still, men running wildly about, and automatic rifle fire was splitting the night air, though Brad assumed they were blasting away at shadows. The moonlight was now overshadowed by the flickering light from the motor pool area, where three trucks and a half-track were blazing fiercely. The ammunition dump was putting on its own spectacular as explosion after explosion ripped the air.

They made it to the main entrance of the camp, a narrow zigzagged opening left in the rolls of concertina barbed wire, without a single challenge. Nathan and Sarah were in the front of the jeep, Miri and Brad in the back, with Ali perched on the rear platform where he could cover them all. Ali spoke rapidly to the guard, who nodded and walked back quickly into the makeshift guard station where a field telephone was visible. He picked it up and began to speak.

"What did you tell him?" Brad whispered to Ali, aware that twenty men were within fifty feet of the jeep in either direction, dug into foxholes and trenches.

"I told him Lieutenant Fahoud wanted the prisoners taken back across the canal immediately."

"Who is Lieutenant Fahoud?" Miri asked.

Ali grinned. "The officer who interrogated us. He's in charge of all POWs."

"So what's he doing now?" Brad asked, looking at the guard inside the hut.

"Calling Fahoud to check," Ali said calmly.

"Ali!" Brad hissed.

"You think they'll find him in this madhouse? If we get away clear, we are ten times better off."

"Get away where?" Nathan hissed. "We don't even know where we are!"

Ali savored the little surprise he had been saving.

"One mile straight ahead and we come to the road that leads to the Mitla Pass."

"And how many Egyptians between here and there?" Nathan murmured, unimpressed.

"You are on the perimeter of the forward command post," Ali said proudly. "All the Egyptians are now alongside us or behind us. Why do you think Fahoud is so anxious to get you out of here by this morning?"

"Then we've got a chance," Miri said, breathlessly.

"Oh oh!" Brad said between clenched teeth. "Your friend has got someone on the phone. He was waiting for a minute, but now look at him."

The guard listened for a moment, then talked back into the phone, nodding his head vigorously. He glanced out quickly at the jeep, then nodded again.

"I think they're on to us," Brad said quickly. "All right, listen. I've got a grenade." He handed it to Miri, ignoring her startled look. He eased up the rifle he had been hiding on the floor. "Miri, when I say, you lob the grenade next to the hut. Nathan, you punch this baby and move it. Stay down, we've got a dozen automatic weapons at our backs."

Suddenly aware of his pounding heart, Brad took another grenade from his pocket and eased out the pin. "Okay? Now!"

The jeep shot forward as he lobbed the hand grenade toward the closest machine gun emplacement and whipped up the rifle. Ali was nearly hurtled off the back when Nathan popped the clutch. He grabbed wildly and caught Brad's neck.

"Hang on, Ali!" Brad shouted as the two grenades went off almost simultaneously. He threw his arm around his friend and hauled him down as far as he could into the narrow seat on top of him and Miri.

The surprise was total, and it took nearly fifteen seconds for the Egyptians to react. But when they did, the

237

perimeter erupted in a blaze of gunfire. Nathan had his foot to the floor and speed-shifted through the gears without lifting it. The jeep had blackout lights, but Nathan had switched those off at the gate, anticipating this very thing. The light of a half moon was enough to see the thin ribbon of asphalt stretching out in front of them. Nathan didn't bother to zigzag, wanting distance more than movement. He cursed at the jeep in Hebrew, urging it to top performance.

"Stay down!" Brad shouted as he felt Ali suddenly grunt and lunge upward. The young Arab instantly collapsed back on top of Brad and went limp.

"Miri! Ali's been hit!" He wiggled out from under Ali's weight and squatted down on the floor, pulling Ali down onto the back seat. Miri, hunched down as far as possible herself, straightened halfway and tried to pull Ali's head into her lap.

"Miri!" Brad screamed, "get down!" Her scarf whipped off and disappeared, her hair buffeted by the wind.

"No!" she cried, trying to straighten Ali's twisted body around on the seat.

The jeep was now five hundred yards from the camp, and at sixty miles an hour was covering eighty-eight more feet every second. At that distance they were no longer visible, though still within killing range of the weaponry. The Egyptian line was pouring fire in their general direction, but it was blind and spreading out widely across the desert terrain.

A moment later Nathan shouted back at them. "Here's the main road. Hang on!" The tires screeched as he leaned the vehicle into the corner.

For a moment Brad thought they were going to roll, but Nathan knew his job well. The jeep went into half a broadslide, then fishtailed back into line as Nathan opened it up again.

Brad leaned forward. "Ali's been hit," he yelled into the wind.

"How bad?"

"Can't tell. How far to Israeli lines?"

"Who knows?" Nathan shouted back, the wind whipping his voice away. "I would guess five to ten miles. Maybe fifteen."

"Will the Egyptians follow us?"

"Not in anything faster than this," Nathan responded. "And not when we're headed toward the Israeli army."

Brad looked at Miri, who was staring at Ali and gently brushing his face, tracing the outline of the bandage on his cheek.

"Is he—?" Brad yelled, not daring to ask.

"He's still alive," she answered, "but he's hurt bad."

"We've got another problem," Nathan shouted back. "We can't go slamming into Israeli lines at sixty miles an hour in an Egyptian jeep. Once we're sure we're not being pursued, we'd better stop until it gets light, and get off this uniform."

"No!" Miri shouted. "We've got to get Ali help as soon as possible."

Brad reached over and touched her hand. "Nathan's right, Miri. It won't help Ali if an Israeli tank blasts us off the road. Dawn is in half an hour."

"He's going to die," Miri sobbed, tears streaming down her cheeks. "He saved us, and now he's going to die."

Twenty-eight

They sat on empty ammunition boxes, staring at the closed flap of the tent that housed the Israeli field hospital. Brad was oblivious to the heat of the midmorning sun on his back, and incessantly smoothed the sand with the toe of his shoe, jerking up his head whenever someone came to the doorway of the tent, then dropping it again to stare at the ground.

Miri and Sarah sat next to him, their faces drawn, their eyes red and filled with anguish. For the first half hour, they had exchanged occasional comments of encouragement and hope for Ali's recovery. Then gradually they had lapsed into a bleak silence.

The bloody carnage of war paraded before their eyes as helicopters clattered in from the front and disgorged their maimed and wounded cargo to be hastened into the field hospital. The camp was only ten or fifteen miles from where a massive tank battle was raging, and each new set of casualties bore witness that the Israelis were being badly mauled.

Once the Israeli commander had verified the escapees' identities—a task requiring over an hour, since the Egyptian lieutenant had taken their wallets and identification—he strongly urged them to catch a ride eastward where things weren't quite so tenuous. But Brad and Miri both adamantly refused. Nathan finally talked quietly with the officer, and he reluctantly agreed to let them stay. Nathan went off then in an attempt to find transportation to his own unit, which was engaged in a desperate struggle of its own in the Golan Heights of northern Israel. Brad, Sarah, and Miri came to this spot to await word of Ali.

Miri suddenly stood up. "Here comes Nathan."

Somewhere the Israelis had found Nathan a uniform and he carried a Uzi submachine gun on his arm. His eyes were deeply sober, his face almost haggard. Brad and Sarah stood up to join Miri as he approached.

"My helicopter has arrived," he said without preamble, taking Miri's outstretched hands. He pulled her to him and gave her a fierce hug. "Captain Goldman has promised to get word to mother and father and let them know we are all right. As soon as you know about Ali, he'll see that you all get back to Jerusalem."

He pulled away and gave her a quick kiss on the cheek. "It will be okay," he said firmly. "They caught us by surprise, but we're recovering quickly."

Miri forced a smile. "Take care, Nathan," she said.

Brad could feel the anguish and fear that lay beneath that simple farewell and suddenly remembered she had done this once before, sent a brother off to battle with a kiss and a brave smile. No wonder her eyes were glistening.

Nathan turned to Sarah and, to everyone's surprise, including Sarah's, kissed her hard and long. "I'll see you again, when this is over," he said, his voice deep and growly to hide his emotions. "Okay?"

She nodded through her tears.

Nathan gripped Brad's hand in that crushing grip of his, which Brad returned with equal firmness. "Brad," he started, then shook his head. "What can I say? That's twice you've risked your life for my family. We stand forever in your debt."

Brad took a breath and was about to speak, but Nathan went on quickly. "I hope to be able to say this myself . . ."

He glanced quickly at the hospital tent. "But if I can't—if you get a chance to talk with him, will you tell him . . ." Again his voice trailed off, and he looked away.

Finally he went on. "Tell Ali I've known many brave and good men. He was the best. Tell him for me, Brad."

"I will," Brad said. "I will." He put his arm around Miri, who was openly crying now.

"And tell him that I was a fool," Nathan added lamely. "I wanted to tell him that myself, and I will if we both make it through this. I am so sorry."

"I'll tell him. Good luck, Nathan." Brad pulled Miri close as they watched him turn and stride away without looking back.

* * * * * *

It was shortly after noon when an older man in a khaki-colored surgical gown and with a surgical mask draped around his neck stepped out of the tent and blinked at the bright sunlight. The three were on their feet as one, as he arched his back and stretched out the pent-up tension in his body.

"You Kennison?" the doctor asked in heavily accented English.

"Yes."

"He would like to see you, but only for a few moments, please."

"How is he?" Miri asked, beating Brad to the same question.

The doctor shook his head. "Not good. The bullet hit his spine and fragmented. He's been in surgery for over three hours. I'm still not sure we got it all. We're going to give him blood now; then we'll transport him to Tel Aviv, where they are prepared to treat him better." The doctor's eyes were bloodshot, and he rubbed the stubble on his chin wearily. "I don't know. He's in critical condition." He motioned to Brad. "Come with me."

Inside the huge tent there were no partitions, just row after row of beds filled with the battle-shattered refuse of

242

war. The smell of antiseptic mingled with the unmistakable odor of blood, burnt flesh, and imminent death. It was a smell Brad knew only too well. Sinai or Saigon, it didn't really matter much to bodies of vulnerable flesh and sinew. War was oblivious to geography.

The surgeon motioned Brad to a bed. "I shouldn't let you be here," he said, "but he insisted on seeing you the moment he came out of the anesthetic. Only a minute now."

"Thank you," Brad said, and he stepped up to Ali's side.

Ali opened his eyes and managed a wan smile. Brad struggled to keep the shock from his face. The eyes were dull and almost gray, the face so pale it almost matched the new white bandage on his cheek. Brad took his hand and gripped it firmly.

"We did it, didn't we," Ali said weakly.

"*You* did it!" Brad answered. "Not we—*you* did it."

Ali shook his head slightly, too feeble to protest.

"Nathan asked me to—"

"I know, I know," Ali murmured. "Tell him I'm not angry with him." His eyes closed for a moment, and Brad noticed with sinking heart the shallowness and rapidity of his breathing.

"How do you feel?" Brad asked

Ali grinned, a faint shadow of the infectious smile that Brad so loved. "Only my cheek hurts," he said. "How's that for logic?"

"Ali," Brad said, leaning over slightly, "would you like me to administer to you?"

"That's why I asked for you."

Aware of other eyes watching, but not caring, Brad laid his hands on Ali's head for the second time that day. Early that morning, while huddled in the jeep waiting for the dawn, as Ali's head lay cradled in Miri's lap, Brad had laid his hands on him and, filled with inspiration, blessed him with the strength to live until they could get help for him. Now he took a deep breath and began again. He had packed consecrated oil when they left Jerusalem, but it was in a Volkswagen bus stranded somewhere to the south of them.

"Ali Mohammed Gamal Abdel Khalidi," Brad started, remembering with a sudden surge of emotion the image of a young man in a T-shirt and faded jeans hoisting an old bag into the storage bin of an airplane, then sticking out his hand to introduce himself.

He swallowed hard and then continued slowly, waiting, hoping for the promises he so desperately wanted to pronounce. But they didn't come. He rebuked the pain, promising Ali comfort and rest. And then the tears came as, under the direction of the Spirit, Brad told Ali how the Lord felt about him, of the Lord's great pleasure with this son of Abraham, of the special mission he had among the Arab peoples.

Brad finished and stepped back, blinking away the stinging in his eyes.

Thank you, friend," Ali said with a deep sigh. His eyes closed, and he fell silent for a moment. Then his eyes fluttered open again. "Brad," he whispered, "I want you to tell my mother something. And Ahkmud."

"Tell them yourself," Brad said, trying to keep his voice even. "You'll be flying to Tel Aviv by helicopter in just a few minutes."

Ali waved that aside, the effort exhausting him. "Please Brad. I'm not going to Tel Aviv. Try to help them understand."

"Understand what?"

"Why I did it. For Israelis. That will be difficult for them."

Brad felt the tears spring to his eyes again, and he squeezed his friend's hand gently. "I will, Ali. I will."

"Tell Miri . . ." He stopped, mustering strength. "Tell Miri it is true."

244

Brad nodded, unable to speak, anguish tearing at his soul.

For almost a minute Ali lay there quietly, his eyes closed, and Brad thought he had fallen asleep. But then his eyes flickered open again.

"I so much wanted to go on a mission," he murmured. "To my own people."

"You will, dear friend," Brad said, fighting to keep his voice steady. "Think how many Arabs there are waiting for you in the spirit world."

Ali's eyes widened. "That's right," he said. "That's right." He smiled weakly. "You always were better at Mormonism than me."

"Maybe so," Brad said in a hoarse whisper. "But not at being a Christian."

At that moment a nurse walked swiftly up to them. "I'm sorry, sir. You'll have to go now."

Brad nodded and took Ali's hand in both of his, tears brimming in his eyes.

"Farewell, my good friend, " Ali whispered.

Brad squeezed his hand. "I'll see you again. Until then, God be with you."

He turned and followed the nurse blindly out into the brilliant sunshine.

Twenty-nine

Brad was standing with President Marks and the BYU students outside the mosque in Bethlehem when he saw Levi Shadmi's car drive up. Levi and his wife were in the front, Miri and Sarah Millstein in the back. Brad excused himself and went over to meet them.

"Hello, Brad," Levi said solemnly as he came around to open the door for his wife. Brad opened the rear door and helped Miri and Sarah out.

Both were dressed in black, as was Miri's mother. Miri's eyes were sorrowful and her face pale and drawn, which only served to heighten her loveliness and intensify the ache in his heart for her.

President Marks came over, and Brad quietly introduced him to Miri's parents and to Sarah. Miri touched his arm after a moment. "Brad, I know they are almost ready to start the funeral, but may I talk to you for just a moment?"

He nodded, and they moved a short distance away.

"I'm sorry," she said in a low voice. "I know today is hardly the time to bring this up, but—" She stopped, her lower lip trembling.

Brad felt a sudden sinking of his heart. "What?"

"They announced this morning that they are transferring my unit to the Galilee tomorrow."

"Oh no! I thought you said you would stay in Jerusalem."

"That is what they first told us. But we are a logistical support unit, and they need us on the Golan Heights."

"For how long?" he asked, sick at the thought of her being that near to the fighting.

It was now Wednesday, the fifth day of the Yom Kippur War. The Israelis were slowly turning the tide of battle, but even the most optimistic military spokesman had stopped talking about a repeat of the Six Day War. There were not going to be any swift, decisive victories this time.

Miri shook her head. "Even if the war ends soon, they are saying that they will keep our unit on active duty for a time. At least three months, possibly six."

"Oh, Miri! Can't you do anything?"

She bit her lip and shook her head. "Sarah and I had to get special permission to come to Ali's funeral today. We start loading up at six o'clock tomorrow morning."

She looked up into Brad's face, her dark eyes close to overflowing. "Many things have changed in the last four days," she said. "I know you must be with the Khalidis after the funeral. But when you are finished, will you come and see me? I must talk to you before I go."

"Of course."

"No matter how late you are?"

"Yes, I'll come."

She touched his arm and went back to her parents. Brad watched her, a deep sense of foreboding adding its weight to the terrible sorrow that already lay heavy on his heart.

* * * * * *

When it was all over—the funeral, the burial in the Moslem cemetery, the long, poignant talk with the Khalidi family—Brad didn't go to Miri's. He drove the battered old Volkswagen to the crest of the Mount of Olives, parked it, and walked down to the spot where he and Miri had begun their first tour together.

The sun was setting, leaving the western sky a flaming

247

orange and the golden roof of the Dome of the Rock a burnished crimson. He stared out across the Kidron Valley for a long time, barely aware of the settling darkness and the lights that blinked on one after another.

On that first morning the sun had been rising; now it was setting. He shook his head at the thought. Was his experience in Israel now setting too? What if Miri told him she had found her answer? When he had come out of the field hospital, Miri had taken one look at his face and begun to weep. Five minutes later, when the doctor had stepped out and shook his head, Miri had thrown herself into Brad's arms and sobbed bitterly.

When she finally gained control of herself she had suddenly pushed away from him and cried out, "Why? Oh God, if you are God, why won't you hear us?"

She had lapsed into a profound sorrow and had said little for the remainder of that day when they were finally sent back to Jerusalem with Ali's body.

Brad stood up and thrust his hands deep into his pockets. Miri had commented on that first early morning about the irony of the name of this city—Jerusalem, the City of Peace. Now he fully understood the irony. Peace? Everytime he thought of Ali, he felt his insides knot up and twist with pain. Viet Nam should have made it easier, he thought bitterly. There he had learned to steel himself against the screams for the medics, against the still forms lying face down in the mud, against the empty bunks afterwards. But he hadn't had any warning this time. There had been no time to throw up the old defenses again.

And now Miri. On the top of Sinai, his hopes had soared. Outside an army field hospital they had shattered. So what now? Could he set aside his convictions? Rationalize that all she needed was time? That after marriage she would accept the Church?

He shook his head with sudden intensity. No! How could he then face a man who had given his life for his convictions? How could he say, "But Ali, you don't understand how much I loved her!"

The answer was simple and inescapable. He couldn't. If Miri could not accept . . . He let the thought trail off in his mind, still finding too much pain at the end of that sentence. But he knew he would hold firm for his beliefs. He turned and walked slowly back to the car.

* * * * * *

The Shadmis were gone—perhaps at Miri's request—and Brad and Miri sat in the living room alone, almost hesitant to talk.

Finally Miri spoke. "What will happen to Ali's school now?"

"It will go on," Brad answered. "Ahkmud said that Ali had gathered a very competent staff who will carry it on. The Khalidis will continue to fund it as a memorial to Ali."

"I'm so glad," Miri said, a tear in her eye.

"The gift your father and uncle gave will also help a great deal."

"My father?"

Brad was suddenly hesitant. "Maybe that was to be a secret, although the Khalidis didn't say anything about it. They gave—," he paused, deciding to let the Shadmis reveal the details if they wished, "a substantial amount in gratitude for what Ali did for you and Nathan."

"That makes me glad," Miri said, "though nothing ever can fully repay what he did."

Brad nodded.

Miri looked at him closely, took a deep breath, and sighed deeply. "So now it is time to talk about us."

Brad nodded again, not trusting himself to look at her in return. "Yes, it is."

"Have you given up on me?" she asked, so softly that he almost missed it.

Brad looked up in surprise. "No." Had he? He was unquestionably discouraged, but had he given up? He shook his head firmly. "No, Miri. I haven't given up yet."

"You know that we have two major problems."

"Two?"

"Yes. The first is whether I could ever join the Church."

"You work that out," Brad said fervently, "and there are no other obstacles."

She smiled at him, eyes sparkling. "May I take that as a proposal, Mr. Kennison?" She lowered her eyes. "I understand the conditional part. But if I could ever be converted?"

Brad reached over, took her hand, and looked into her deep brown eyes, hardly able to say what he had to say. "If you were to feel right about being baptized—not just for me, but for yourself—then there are no other conditions. But—" He took a deep breath. "But if you can't I . . ." He shook his head sadly. "I can't, Miri. How could I face myself? How could I face Ali?"

She put her finger to his lips and stopped him from saying more. "I understand, Brad," she said, her voice filled with emotion. "But when you say there are no other conditions, does that include not leaving Israel?"

Brad had known they had to face that one too, and he was ready. "There are no other conditions, Miri."

Her eyes widened. "Do you mean . . ."

"I mean that I love you enough to stay in Israel with you. I will enroll at the Hebrew University." He smiled. "But you would have to teach me Hebrew."

Her eyes were suddenly brimming with tears, and she brushed them away impatiently. "You would do that for me?"

Brad nodded. "I understand what Israel means to you, Miri. I've asked you to give up enough already. However, I warn you that I will try to change your concept of Zion until you see that Zion—as we see it in the Church—is the only ultimate hope for Israel. I will try to convince you that the greatest thing you could ever do for your people is to raise sons and daughters who understand and love their Jewishness, but who understand Zion's role in the future of Israel. It is a far greater challenge to raise Zion children than it is to raise Zionist children."

"Could it be possible that you really love me enough to stay here?" she asked, her voice trembling with wonder.

"It is not only possible, but true," Brad said gently, pulling her to him.

"Which brings us back to the first condition," she said, turning away from him.

"Yes."

"Are you still praying for me?" she asked after a long silence.

"Of course, night and morning and every time I think of you, which is constantly."

"Do you believe the Lord will answer your prayers?"

Brad hesitated. "I don't know. He won't force you against your will, no matter how much I want it. And he surely knows how much I want it."

Miri took his hand in hers and interlocked their fingers. "Brad, what would you say if I told you that he has answered them?"

Brad stared at her, unable to speak.

"He has answered your prayers, Brad. And mine."

"Miri, what are you saying?"

The tears spilled over and ran down her cheeks. "I am saying that I know, Brad! I know! I understand! I believe!"

He took her by the shoulders, then gathered her into his arms. "Are you saying what I think you're saying?"

She smiled through the tears at his excitement and nodded.

"But how?" he asked. "How?" He was still unable to believe his ears.

"Ali," she said, her voice breaking again. "It was Ali."

Brad held her close to him as she struggled to get her emotions in hand. Finally she looked up. "On Mount Sinai you said that Jesus had to be a God *and* a man because he needed to be like us, have the same problems, but he had to be free from that situation so he could help us."

Brad suddenly understood. He spoke again the words he'd said that morning on the mount. "How can a man locked in chains help others escape captivity?"

Yes," she replied. "Ali was one of us in that Egyptian camp. But he was free. Yet he loved us so much—even Nathan, who treated him so shamefully—that he was willing to die to help us." She fought for control again, then went on. "If a man, a good man, could love that much and that unselfishly, suddenly I can conceive how a *perfect* man could love enough to give his life for all men. When you told me about Ali's last words in the hospital, I couldn't get over it. Even then, his thoughts were only of others—for his family and their possible bitterness, for the Arab people, and—" Miri stopped. "And for me," she whispered.

Brad nodded, still not daring to believe what he was hearing.

"Because of Ali, I could finally understand. And for the first time I wanted to know if Jesus was really the Messiah. Not just for you, Brad, but for *me*! So I could accept him and believe in someone who could love that perfectly."

She stared down at her hands. "I didn't sleep much the night we got home. I spent half the night reading and praying. Then I fasted all day yesterday. After I finished work at my unit, I remembered what you said about the special feelings you had in the Garden Tomb. It was what I wanted to feel too, so I went there."

Her shoulders rose and fell as she took a deep breath and let it out in a long sigh. "For a while I almost gave up. Nothing happened. It was as though whatever I was seeking was just beyond my reach. If I could touch it, it would dissolve away. Finally, as I sat there, I decided to read the New Testament, the accounts of the crucifixion and resurrection."

The tears brimmed over and ran slowly down her cheeks, but through them her face was radiant. "And suddenly it came. As I read, the most wonderful feeling of peacefulness came over me. And I found myself weeping—for joy! I *knew* that he was real and that he had heard my cries for him."

Brad tenderly brushed a tear from the corner of her eye with his thumb. "You knew last night, and you didn't call me?" he scolded gently.

"Yes, but once I had solved the first problem, I came face to face with our second problem. Could I leave Israel for you?"

"You don't have to," he said. "I'll stay here."

"I have a better idea," she said, her eyes sparkling. "A compromise."

"What?"

"I'll go to the Galilee, and you go back to America."

Brad jerked back and stared at her. "What are you saying? I just got you back. I'm not going to leave you. I told you, I'll stay here."

"And be happy?" she asked him gently.

"If I'm with you," he said, not quite as firmly as he should have, "I'll be happy."

"You big, wonderful liar," she said, kissing him firmly. "Okay, if you don't like that idea, here's another compromise."

Knowing he was being teased, but not sure why, Brad narrowed his eyebrows with suspicion. "All right. Let's hear it."

Her eyes were literally dancing with pleasure. "I'll go to the Galilee tomorrow with my unit, and you come up with President Marks and the rest of the branch on Friday afternoon."

"President Marks?"

"Yes. And you'll have to bring white clothes for both of us. I understand that is the appropriate dress for a baptism."

Again she had him reeling, and she was loving every minute of it. "I met with President Marks this afternoon," she said happily. "It's all set. Except—" she smiled shyly, "I wasn't sure who to get to do the baptizing."

Brad grabbed her and pulled her to him, holding her tight. "Listen, you! There'd better not be any question about that."

Finally she pulled away. "Wait," she commanded, "I haven't told you the rest of my second compromise yet."

"All right," Brad said, completely caught up in the joy of her mood. "Go ahead."

"On Friday we'll have the baptism. On Saturday, we'll go to church. Then I'll return to my unit, and you return to America." She put her hand over his mouth to cut off his protest. "The moment I'm released from active duty, I'll fly to Salt Lake City. And we'll start planning our wedding. Remember, we have to wait a year from this Friday. That will be October 12, 1974. You'll need to get into school as soon as possible, and I'll have to find a job."

Brad stared at her.

"And you promised me I could have a canopy at the reception." She smiled in delight at his expression. "I love you, Brad Kennison," she said softly, and kissed him before he could protest.

"But Miri!" he said finally, pulling away from their embrace. "What about Israel?"

"You must promise to make lots of money to bring me back here often."

"I probably won't make lots of money, but I promise I'll bring you back."

"And the children, too? All eight of them?"

"Absolutely. But what changed your mind?"

Her expression was soft and full of love. "You. And President Marks."

"President Marks?"

"Yes. At my baptismal interview this afternoon, I told him everything. How I felt about you. How I felt about

Israel. In his usual, kind way, he was very blunt." She laughed at a sudden thought. "He would make a good Israeli."

"What did he say?"

"He said if I loved anything, other than the Lord, more than you, I wasn't worthy of you."

"Bless his heart," Brad said, still half in a daze with it all. "And you've been stringing me along all night? You knew it all along."

Miri quickly sobered. "I'm glad now I did, Brad. I expected that you would tell me that I had to leave Israel. I was going to act hurt for a moment, and then tell you I would." Her eyes were misty again. "But instead you said you would stay here with me. I'll never forget that. Never! I want you to know I love you that much too. More than Israel."

Brad kissed her then, putting all the joy and delight that was surging through his soul into it. She gave herself to him without reservation. This time there were no barriers waiting to drop between them.

Then gently he pulled away. "Miri, what are your parents going to think of all this?"

She touched his arm. "They think you are going to be one fine son-in-law."

"Better than David?"

She gave him a long, speculative look. "Except for the Porsche."

Miri yelped as he pinched her ribs.

"And what about your becoming a Mormon?" he asked.

"That is more difficult," she admitted. "But I told them just before you came tonight. I think they knew it was coming."

"And?"

"My father surprised me the most. He listened to it all without a word. Then finally he said, 'If it makes you like Brad and Ali, I suppose there could be worse things happen to you.' They won't come to the baptism, but it could be much, much worse."

"That's wonderful!" Brad said. He took her face in his hands, gently and with great tenderness. "I can't believe it. I just can't believe it."

She snuggled up under his arm. "You had better believe it, Mr. Kennison. You made me a conditional proposal, and I've met your conditions. You're stuck with me now."

"Forever?" he asked, holding her close.

"Forever!" she murmured.

Thirty

The officiator looked around the room at the smiling, eager faces. He had finished his counsel and advice to the couple who sat on his right, and now he stood up. An expectant hush filled the sealing room of the Salt Lake Temple.

Miri was radiant in her wedding gown, her dark eyes glowing with happiness, the white veil in sharp contrast to her black hair. Brad held her hand, his eyes as full of joy as hers. They sat with their backs to the one great mirror on the wall, and facing the other one across the room so that they could see their reflection going on and on into eternity.

The officiator held a white leather Bible in his hands. He let his gaze travel around the room and finally stop at Brad and Miri.

"This is a very special privilege for me," he began. "It is always an honor to seal a worthy young couple for time and eternity. But this has added significance today, for we are witnessing the fulfillment of prophecy."

Brad's mother, who was sitting next to Miri, reached over and squeezed her hand happily.

"May I read with you the words of Ezekiel," the officiator said, opening the Bible to a premarked place. "From Ezekiel, chapter thirty-seven, verses sixteen and seventeen, we read: 'Take thee one stick, and write upon it, For Judah, . . . then take another stick, and write upon it, For Joseph, the stick of Ephraim.'"

He paused and smiled at Miri and Brad, then continued. "'And join them one to another into one stick; and they shall become one in thine hand.'"

Brad took Miri's hand and slipped it through his arm.

"Now, we know that this scripture has reference to the Bible and the Book of Mormon becoming a combined witness of Jesus Christ. But I firmly believe it has a wider meaning as well. Let me read verse twenty-two. 'And I will make them' . . .," the officiator paused, "meaning Ephraim and Judah—'I will make them one nation in the land, . . . and one king shall be king to them all: and they shall be no more two nations, neither shall they be divided into two kingdoms any more at all.'"

He closed the book and motioned to Brad and Miri to stand. "And so, Bradley Scott Kennison, if you will kneel here at the altar as a representative of the tribe of Ephraim—and you, Miriam Esther Shadmi, if you will kneel across the altar from Brad as a representative of the tribe of Judah—we shall proceed to make you one in the hands of the Lord."

PROPERTY OF
L. D. S. BUSINESS COLLEGE
LIBRARY

PROPERTY OF
L. D. S. BUSINESS COLLEGE
LIBRARY